DALKO

DALKO

THE UNTOLD STORY OF
BASEBALL'S FASTEST PITCHER

BY BILL DEMBSKI, ALEX THOMAS,
AND BRIAN VIKANDER

Foreword by
"SUDDEN" SAM MCDOWELL

Influence Publishers
7556 Rolling River Parkway
Nashville, TN 37221

First edition: 2020
10 9 8 7 6 5 4 3 2 1

Printed in the United States of America.
ISBN: 978-1-64542-710-0 (Hardcover)
ISBN: 978-1-64542-711-7 (eBook)
ISBN: 978-1-64542-712-4 (Audiobook)
Cover design by Bruce Gore
Cover photo by Forrest Jackson for *Time* magazine, 1960
Publisher's Cataloging-in-Publication Data
Names: Dembski, William A., author. | Thomas, Alex, author. | Vikander, Brian, author.
| McDowell, Sam, foreword author.
Title: Dalko : the untold story of baseball's fastest pitcher / by Bill Dembski, Alex
Thomas, and Brian Vikander ; foreword by "Sudden" Sam McDowell.
Description: Includes bibliographical references. | Nashville, TN: Influence Publish-
ers, 2020.
Identifiers: ISBN 9781645427100 (Hardcover) | 9781645427117 (ebook)
Subjects: LCSH Dalkowski, Stephen Louis, Jr. | Baseball players—United States—
Biography. | Pitchers (Baseball)—United States—Biography. | BISAC BIOGRAPHY
& AUTOBIOGRAPHY / Sports | SPORTS & RECREATION / Baseball / General.
Classification: LCC GV865.D26 D46 2020 | DDC 796.357092--dc23

In Memoriam

Stephen Louis Dalkowski Jr.

June 3, 1939—April 19, 2020

"Fastest Ever"

Contents

Foreword

by "Sudden" Sam McDowell

A six-time MLB All-Star, Sam McDowell was one of the fastest, if not the very fastest, pitcher in Major League Baseball throughout the 1960s. Three times he led the majors in strikeouts. He retired with a lifetime ERA of 3.17, better than a third of the pitchers in the Baseball Hall of Fame. When opposing hitters described McDowell's fastball, they said it came to the plate "all of a sudden, man, all of a sudden." Thus, he earned his nickname: "Sudden" Sam McDowell.

This is the story of a pitcher who threw an unmatched four-seam fastball and yet remained his entire career in the minor leagues. He became a pitching legend in an era when instant news did not exist. His journey, described in these pages, is both enlightening and tragic, offering remarkable insights into the game of baseball and life in general.

My path first crossed this pitcher in 1961. I was joining the Cleveland Indians for my first spring training, and, initially, I was sent to the big club. For an eighteen-year-old kid with only one season of "D" ball under his belt (the lowest rung on the minor league ladder), this opportunity to rub shoulders with major league players was unusual.

Later that spring, I would be sent to the Indians' minor league spring training facility in Daytona Beach, Florida.

During the final weeks in Daytona Beach, I was selected, along with thirty other ballplayers, to make the trip to Miami and play against another organization's minor league teams. This was uncommon at the time because we typically played only against our own organization's teams. We drove in a dilapidated bus, the one used for transporting "rookies," not stars like Vic Power, Johnny Temple, Jimmy Piersall, Tito Francona, and Mudcat Grant.

As we piled out of our bus and walked to the Orioles' field, we all heard an arrestingly loud "*pop, pop, pop*" resonating throughout the entire complex. It created an unsettled feeling in our stomachs, and we wondered who (or what) was making that sound. This was in the day *before* catchers' gloves could make that sound. Rawlings had not yet invented the HOH-X, known as the "popper," the glove that catchers would wear when warming up their star pitchers in the bullpen. Looking across the field, we located the source of the loud popping. It was a pitcher warming up. Immediately, my teammates began chatting about how they hoped they wouldn't face this guy today or anytime soon.

The guy was throwing effortlessly—no grunting or huffing. We heard only two distinct sounds: the *hissing* as the ball cut through the air traveling toward the catcher, and the *explosion* as the ball hit the catcher's glove. Of course, not every offering would hit the glove, and the wild ones were not lost on my teammates. Then, regaining control, he would pitch strike after strike after strike . . . just plain easy gas!

We all wanted to get a closer look at this pitcher and his heat. The closer we got, the more awesome he became. His fastball was simply unbelievable. It was tremendously difficult to follow the flight of the ball. His speed was beyond anything that any of us had ever seen (or heard) before on the diamond. What made his speed even more astonishing to us was his physical stature (or lack thereof). Nothing stood out about how he looked. He was an *ordinary* guy, perhaps just a little stocky. He wasn't tall or muscular. He wasn't fat or skinny. Just kind of *regular*.

What especially commanded our attention was how effortlessly he threw the ball. He seemed to have the perfect mechanics: the perfect windup and the perfect release. All we could say was "*WOW!* Where did he come from? He must be someone's No. 1 go-to guy, the ace on someone's staff." While we didn't get to see him in a game that day, we just knew that very shortly we'd see him in the American League.

After we finished batting practice, one of our guys found out the name of this flamethrower. The name was, of course, Steve Dalkowski. It was a name that none of us would ever forget from that day to this. While in the clubhouse, getting ready for the afternoon game, the players had only one topic in their thoughts and conversations . . . this guy named Dalkowski.

On the bus ride back to Daytona Beach, most of the talk was about the octane coming out of the left arm of Dalkowski. Postgame conversations were typically about the game just played. But we had just witnessed a once-in-a-lifetime guy throwing a baseball with such speed that we just knew he would land in Baltimore very soon. This guy could really bring it.

In baseball, superhuman feats like this are uncommon. When you see a hitter barrel one up to the tune of five hundred feet or a right fielder with a *cannon* gunning down a fleet-footed runner by three steps as he attempts to go from first to third on a base hit or, as in Dalkowski's case, a guy firing "invisible" bullets . . . well, this just isn't the norm in baseball. Such feats make you stop and reflect on your own mortality, your humanness in the face of the superhuman!

In the years after this encounter, I would hear the many stories that traveled throughout baseball's grapevine about Dalkowski's remarkable feats on and off the diamond. Stories of his blinding speed, of his wildness, of nearly killing a batter when he hit him in the head, of shattering an umpire's mask in six places and knocking him out cold. Stories about him blowing it by "the Splendid Splinter" (Ted Williams), of 283-pitch games, of 18-strikeout and 18-walk games, of hitters leaving the box after two strikes and telling the umpire, "I don't want the next one . . . you can have it!" Stories of Dalko throwing balls through wire fences and wooden walls, and, of course, stories about his legendary drinking.

Many of these stories blossomed and were enhanced over time. The embellishments kept his legend alive, making Steve larger than life. No other player in the game had an inventory of stories about him like Steve. *NO ONE*. Even today, when I attend baseball winter meetings, BAT (Baseball Assistance Team) gatherings, or my team's spring training, the subject of my own fastball and velocity will surface. Then it isn't long before one of the "real ole timers" will refresh our memories with a story about Dalkowski, the guy that many consider the fastest pitcher of all time.

Throughout the history of our game, it's been endlessly debated who could bring the greatest heat from the hill to the hitter. Who had the best fastball? Who was the hardest thrower of all time? Who had the best gas on his fastball? I am proud to have my name mentioned in a very elite group of pitchers, which includes Nolan Ryan, Sandy Koufax, Randy Johnson, and Cy Young, as the hardest throwers in baseball history. Recently, MLB put together a disc that rated the top ten fastballs of all time. I was likewise included in this select group of hurlers.

And yet, I will tell you this about Steve Dalkowski with absolute certainty, after seeing and listening to his fastball, and witnessing some very wild pitches: I truly believe he threw a lot harder than I did! It's likely he delivered the fastest pitch I ever saw!

Unfortunately, I never got to see him pitch in a regulation game. We were always in different leagues during our time in the minors. Even in 1963, when I was sent back to Jacksonville, in the International League, and Steve was with the Rochester Red Wings, he didn't pitch in the three-game series that we played in Rochester. I wish that he had pitched because his legend was alive and well with our entire team. Everyone wanted to see him pitch. Yet I did get to see him doing his sidework, and it was still electric! As always, when Dalko was throwing, everyone, and I mean *EVERYONE*, would gather and speak of his fastball with reverence and fear.

Baseball history is filled with players who have faced mental blocks—both pitchers and position players. Many of the hardest throwers have had control issues because "the goal" is to throw hard first and everything else "be damned." Look at the early careers of Koufax, Ryne Duren, Rex Barney, Ryan, and, of course, myself. We, and many others, had control issues because we couldn't get past the only goal of throwing hard, harder, hardest. When we learned proper focus and concentration, our careers began to flourish. With the appropriate focus, we may have occasionally dropped a touch in velocity, but we also began to spot it up and change speeds. We were then dealin'. We became pitchers and not just throwers.

In my view, Steve Dalkowski had the same problems and mental blocks that all hard throwers have. Clearly, he didn't possess the skill set to "right the ship" on his own. But most of us don't possess that skill set either, requiring proper coaching to give us the help we need. Unfortunately, the coaching around Steve wasn't good enough to help him get through the blocks that he had both mentally and physically.

Please understand that I am not disparaging anyone who was trying to help Steve. Everyone was well intentioned. Managers and coaches of the day simply didn't have the "tool kits" that we have today. How could they? The insights now available to coaches are based on the research and formal education that I pursued in the fields of sports psychology, counseling, and addiction in my postplaying days. I was privileged to apply this new skill set to assisting MLB ballplayers for eighteen years. Each day I reflect with pride on this pursuit.

When I look into myself, I see a thread of Steve Dalkowski in Sam McDowell and in every hard thrower who has ever taken the hill. Yet the benefits of sports psychology are relatively new to the game today, and it was *terra incognita* in the 1950s and 1960s when Steve was pitching. Among the many tragedies Steve suffered, I believe that this was the saddest: the inability at the time to correct what today would be correctible. Today, we know what would need to be strengthened in Steve's outlook and approach.

Through my work as a career enhancement professional, I recognize how alone and helpless Steve must have felt when he couldn't address and remedy his pitching issues. Ever since the game of baseball was invented, self-declared (and well-intentioned) pitching coaches have constantly tinkered with a pitcher's mechanics, no matter what the pitcher's problem. By tinkering with a pitcher's mechanics, coaches refocus a pitcher's attention away from other negatives. Ironically and inadvertently, the control issue might abate briefly, leading the pitching coach to believe that his work on the pitcher's mechanics had solved the problem.

But such a fix tends to be temporary. The real problem is usually mental, not mechanical. Fears cause control problems because the mind is a "powerful weapon" for good and bad. Simply put, most control issues are caused in the mind, not in the mechanics or physics of pitching. Pitchers have many fears when they are on the mound, and if their mind plays on all of the potential negatives, they cannot focus on the location and intent of the next pitch. As a pitcher myself, I can relate to this predicament. Steve most likely experienced the same kinds of issues that I did.

Like many pitchers, Steve needed someone to help him simplify the game so that he could focus on what he could control, and let the rest go. Hitting a baseball at the major league level is difficult . . . *PERIOD.* The sweet spot on the barrel is only 3 inches long and 1.5 inches wide. The ball hit anywhere else on the bat means that you have done your job as a pitcher, which is to say you have prevented 100 percent on-time hitter contact. You have moved from real to effective velocity, and the hitter's ability to hurt you has been minimized.

Instead of trying to strike out every batter, you are now using all of your fielders. Also, by relying on the entire team, you are now playing the game at nine-to-one odds. Understanding this principle can eliminate a lot of the pressure and many negatives associated with being on the bump. Surely, this understanding could have helped Steve. It did me, when I understood it. I finally realized that I didn't have to strike everyone out!

Steve's inability to correct his course was a tragedy for baseball and fans alike. How the national stage would have appreciated Steve's mercurial ability, his work ethic, his desire to succeed, and his superhuman efforts on the field! Baseball fans always respect and appreciate great performances and efforts by a player. Major League Baseball missed out on experiencing the full greatness of Steve "White Lightning" Dalkowski. Yet the game of baseball did get a glimpse of Steve's greatness and was immeasurably enriched by it!

This book is a layered account of what was and what might have been.

ONE

New Britain Phenom

"Baltimore to call up hurler Steve Dalkowski"
—Associated Press, August 31, 1957

Diamond No. 1 at Walnut Hill Park was nothing special to look at: a baseball field atop a broad hill in a city park. Dirt infield, no fence. On an average day, anybody might walk by without giving it a second glance. But this was not an average day. Cars jammed the streets in every direction. Early arrivals were already parked at the curb, on the grass, or wedged bumper guard-to-tailfin along Grand Street going downhill toward the east. Several of the cars had out-of-state plates, though they would have stood out even without them—flashy, expensive Cadillacs, Imperials, and Packards in a blue-collar town defined more by Plymouths, Fords, and Studebakers.

It was the second game of the season and one of the first pleasant days of the year. Warm sun, blue skies, and temperatures in the seventies signaled that the long, snowy New England winter had finally given way to spring. Fans knew they had to arrive two hours before game time

1

to get a seat. The crowd filled the bleachers to overflowing and stood along the baselines. A lot of them were students at the high schools whose teams faced each other on the field. Their families were there too, as were other townspeople. Then there were the out-of-towners with the fancy cars, conspicuous by their quiet, intense concentration on the game, and, on an April day in Connecticut, by their deep suntans.

The crowd came expecting an incredible baseball game, and they were not disappointed. The thrilling show that they witnessed took the form of an unforgettable pitching performance, courtesy of an unassuming high school senior who was on his way to becoming the fastest-throwing pitcher in baseball history. Five hundred people didn't show up for high school sports in the middle of a weekday afternoon unless there was the prospect of something spectacular happening. There was. And it did.

The boys in the home team dugout at diamond 1 had grown up together. They were neighbors in the nearby apartments and housing projects. Their fathers worked side by side in the scores of tool factories that gave New Britain, Connecticut, the nickname "Hardware City"— blue-collar men who made a decent living with their hands in these prosperous years after World War II. Some of their mothers worked in the factories, too, while others stayed home to keep house and look after the children as their own mothers had done.

These boys loved baseball. In 1950s America everybody loved baseball. During the summer they played for one of the industrial leagues in town, where teams such as the Fuller Brush Crew Cuts were sponsored by local businesses. After the school year started, they played for the Golden Hurricanes of New Britain High. And this season the whole town was talking about exactly one player.

He was on the mound for his first start of the season. Steve Dalkowski was a seventeen-year-old senior who at first didn't seem to stand out from the rest of his teammates. He stood five feet, eleven inches, and weighed 170 pounds. He was trim and athletic, with a square-shaped face, deep-set eyes, and medium-brown hair. He looked like any healthy young man from a middle-class Polish family who played baseball in the spring and football in the fall.

The difference—what all those fans were there to see—began when he delivered the ball to home plate. With a smooth, seemingly effortless lower-body motion, he separated his hands and loaded his throwing shoulder toward the shortstop position. As his right hip moved toward the plate, his lead foot began to cut the distance between him and the hitter. As his lead foot hit the ground, his lead hip opened up and released the loaded throwing shoulder. His throwing arm came forward with the speed of a snake striking its prey. The left arm took a short inside route near his left ear, absolutely perpendicular to the ground. Then Steve's arm came straight over the top. He released the ball out over his landing leg, finishing his throw with a distinctive flick of the wrist. His pitching motion was all one fluid, almost invisible blur. The quickness of his delivery deprived the hitter of vital reaction time and of a clear release point. For the hapless opponent at the plate, finding and tracking the approaching baseball was somewhere between difficult and impossible.

Some fans compared Steve's pitching motion to cracking the whip. The sun-weathered major league scouts watching that day called it "short-arming" the ball. One instant the ball was in the pitcher's hand, and the next it was in the catcher's mitt with a loud, sharp *crack* like a gunshot. The only other evidence of its journey was a threatening sound that people close to the plate could hear: the ball *sizzled* as it split the air. One spectator said it *buzzed* like a bee. Another said it sounded like cloth ripping. Whatever it was, the ominous noise made each hitter's trip to the plate even more intimidating. Batters could hear Steve Dalkowski's fastball, but they couldn't see it. And they certainly couldn't hit it.

Biz Mackey, Negro League Hall of Fame catcher who played from the 1920s through the '40s, understood the difference between average and exceptional fastballs: "A lot of pitchers have a fastball but very, very few—Feller, [Lefty] Grove, [Walter] Johnson, a couple of others besides Satchel [Paige]—have had that little bit extra juice that makes the difference between the good and great pitcher. When it's that fast, it will hop a little at the end of the line. Beyond that, it just tends to disappear." It was clear to anyone watching that this young pitcher had the "extra juice" Mackey was talking about.

No one taught Steve to pitch the way he did. It just happened. As major league pitcher Vida Blue would say years later, "It's easy, man. I just take the ball and throw. *Hard!* It's a God-given talent. No one can teach it to you."

Steve's dad first heard the sizzle years earlier when the two of them played catch. By the time young Steve was in the eighth grade, his father, Steve Sr., could catch for only a short while before his hand was too sore to continue. Steve Jr.'s friend and next-door neighbor Andy Baylock, the catcher at New Britain High during Steve's junior year, had to develop a technique for cupping his hand inside the catcher's mitt to cushion the blow of these unbelievably hard throws. He held the glove almost horizontally as he waited for the pitch, then allowed his wrist to hinge up as he caught the ball. Even so, he still had a purple index finger and a sore thumb after every game. Pro catchers would one day trade notes on the "blue darts" they endured on Steve Dalkowski's account.

After Baylock graduated and went on to college, catcher Bob Barrows became the recipient of Steve's unforgiving fastball. In his first start that spring, the opening contest of the 1957 season, Dalkowski pitched a complete-game no-hitter against East Hartford. The headline in the next day's *Hartford Courant* crowed, "Dalkowski Pitches No-Hit Shutout: New Britain Ace Beats Hornets 2–0, Fans 20." It was, the paper said, a "brilliant" victory and a "sensational" display of pitching.

Once again, an enormous crowd had assembled at Walnut Hill Park on this mild April afternoon for Steve's second start of the season.

Could their ace deliver two no-hitters in a row? Few would bet against him. How could anyone hit him? As Walter Johnson put it, "You can't hit what you can't see." While a costly mental error denied him a second straight shutout, Steve led his team to a 10–1 win in a game lasting three hours and fifteen minutes. Dalkowski had hurled back-to-back no-hitters. In his first two games of the year he had notched 39 strikeouts and allowed only one run over 18 innings. Fans left Walnut Hill that afternoon knowing they had seen something very rare in the baseball world.

The wins and praises kept coming. During another game against East Hartford on May 22, Dalkowski again struck out 20, raising his strikeout total against Hornet batters to 40 in 18 innings. Two days later against the district champion New London Whalers, Steve and the 'Canes pulled off a stunning upset as an estimated eight hundred fans crowded into the Walnut Hill grandstands for the show. After walking three batters in the first, Dalkowski settled down to strike out 24—thought at the time to be a state record—giving up only two hits on the way to a 5–0 shutout victory. Later in the month Steve struck out 16 with one hit in six innings against Weaver High before being relieved. He then moved to left field and contributed to the offense, getting a hit and scoring a run. The 'Canes won, 8–5. He ended his senior year with a 7-2 record and 150 strikeouts in 69⅔ innings.

The big league scouts were paying attention. On June 18, 1957, eighteen-year-old Steve Dalkowski graduated from New Britain High. The school yearbook, *The Beehive*, featured a photo of Steve in action with a caption noting that he had "been scouted by the Major Leagues." (His form in that grainy black and white picture might have reminded some scouts of Sandy Koufax, then in his third year with the Brooklyn Dodgers. The two appeared to have strikingly similar pitching motions and recoil.) Three days after accepting his diploma, Steve signed with the Baltimore Orioles, who noted in their press announcement that the young southpaw had been "sought by all 16 clubs in the majors." The men whose job it was to pick a winner heard the sound of a once-in-a-lifetime fastball and recognized a legend in the making. He could simply throw a baseball faster than any of them had ever seen.

The New Britain Phenom would indeed become a legend. But Steve's Dalkowski's story, despite its promising beginnings, is also the story of a once-in-a-generation gift that many believe was squandered. A talent drowned by overindulgence in alcohol, sabotaged by wild nights and bad company. Others insist Steve never had a chance. That with the right coaching on the field and the right counseling off it, he might have risen to be one of the stars in the Baseball Hall of Fame instead of a sports trivia footnote of mythical proportions.

Time and storytelling, myths, and legends have blurred many of the facts in the decades since Dalkowski signed a minor league contract with the Orioles. The big-league call he hoped for would never come. Instead, his career would unfold as a tragedy of near misses, frustration, and years of diligent hard work offset by bad habits and hindrances that would bring him as close as a mortal could get to greatness without ever achieving it. Even so, based on all the available sources and on eyewitness accounts from pros who saw the game's fastest pitchers in action over the years, Dalkowski was faster than any of them. He was the fastest ever. No player who saw him in action would challenge the truth of that claim.

The story of Steve Dalkowski is a powerful, fascinating, infuriating, inspiring, sixty-year odyssey ranging over many miles and through worlds long since vanished. He lived his last years in a sun-dappled room in a retirement home at the edge of Walnut Hill Park, just down the hill from the scene of his early years and legendary pitches and stunning triumphs. Out his window, he could see the same trees that once looked down on a promising young man who seemed destined for baseball immortality. By the time of his eightieth birthday, his body had grown weak and lethargic. It was not always possible to hold a conversation with him. He lived in a dense fog of alcohol-induced dementia.

Like all great odysseys, his journey eventually took him home, back to a quiet place only a few minutes' walk from where it all began. Yet the legend that took the mound on diamond No. 1 as the New Britain Phenom back then still endures today.

It will always endure.

TWO

Ace or Terror?

"Dalkowski posted a 3-2 record last year and, like most southpaws, was extremely wild."

—*The Hartford Courant*, April 20, 1956

There was never a time when Steve Dalkowski didn't throw fast. Some called his ability to throw fast a God-given talent. Others ascribed it to a unique combination of physical skills and innate flexibility. Another compared it to the thunderbolts of Zeus. Whatever its ultimate source or explanation, Steve's ability to throw fast came to him naturally, a one-in-a-million talent possessed by a good-natured, likable, hard-working boy born into a family that loved baseball.

Steve's father, Steve Sr., played shortstop for one of the industrial league teams popular in and around New Britain, Connecticut, in the 1950s. This blue-collar town a few miles southwest of Hartford was famous as Hardware City, "the Detroit of tools." One factory after another turned out thousands of hammers, wrenches, pliers, socket sets, and similar products every day. Many of these companies sponsored

9

community baseball teams. Baseball was the great team sport of the era and, along with boxing, the nation's most popular spectator sport.

Steve Sr. was a buffer at the Stanley Tool plant, polishing burrs and other imperfections from freshly forged tools near the end of the production process. His wife, Adele, worked in a ball bearing factory. Their first child, Stephen Louis Dalkowski Jr., was born June 3, 1939, at the local hospital on Grand Avenue across the street from Walnut Hill Park. A daughter, Pat, followed five years later.

Young Steve showed an interest in baseball from an early age, and his father encouraged him to play. The two of them spent day after day in the park, with Steve shagging fly balls, fielding grounders, and developing his baseball skills. Childhood friend and future teammate Andy Baylock remembers that Steve's dad didn't want him pitching when he was very young. But by the time the Dalkowskis moved into the federally funded Corbin Heights housing project, when Steve was in the sixth grade, the young southpaw had already made a name for himself. His coach at Washington Junior High, Vin Cazzetta, later a college and pro basketball coach, may have been the first to notice the sound Steve's fastball made as it cut through the air. He called it a "buzzing," something neither he nor any other junior high coach had ever heard before. Cazzetta considered Steve a "phenom" from the first time he saw him pitch. Though barely in his teens, this boy already had the speed that made batters dread stepping into the batter's box. None of them wanted any part of him when he was on the hill.

The Dalkowski family were faithful members of Red Sox Nation. Steve Sr. loved taking them to games in Boston's Fenway Park. A special treat for young Stevie and his little sister, Patti, was a trip to Fenway on August 6, 1953, to see Ted Williams play in his first game since being discharged from the Marines after the Korean War. Boston's rivals that day were the hapless St. Louis Browns, who were on their way to a miserable 54-100 season, their last before moving east to become the Baltimore Orioles in 1954. None of the Dalkowskis could have imagined how, in four short years, the visiting team they watched from the right-field bleachers that sunny afternoon would radically change their lives.

Williams was still working to retain his majestic swing after a sixteen-month absence, his hands badly blistered from too much batting practice. With the Red Sox trailing by a run in the ninth, runners at the corners and one out, manager Lou Boudreau told Williams, "Ted, I've got to use you now."

Facing screwballer Martin Stuart, who had come on in relief, Williams took a called strike and a ball before ripping the third pitch down the right-field line, just foul, as the crowd roared and jumped to its feet. On the fourth pitch he popped out to first baseman Dick Kryhoski. "Stuart threw me four screwballs," Williams later explained. "That is a good ball to hit on the ground, but I wanted to get it up in the air, not hit into a double play. But I got under it too much." The Sox tied the game but eventually lost in the tenth on a home run by the Browns' Bobby Young.

Back home in Corbin Heights, Steve finished out the baseball season at school and, like many boys in the neighborhood, rolled straight into the Courant-Jaycee Baseball League. This was a summer league cosponsored by the *Hartford Courant* newspaper and the local junior chamber of commerce. Each team had its own sponsor that paid $85 per season to cover the costs of team T-shirts and other expenses. Steve played for the Caval Tool Bobcats, sponsored by a local company that made turbine parts and other precision components. The Bobcats earned the 1953 Junior Division crown with a record of 14-1. In their last game, a 12–0 win over the American Motor Phils, fourteen-year-old Steve pitched the last three innings while going four-for-four at the plate. (His prowess on the field contrasted with occasional absent-mindedness elsewhere. On team photo day, Steve was the only one who didn't wear his uniform.) The next year, playing in the Senior Division, Steve and the Bobcats were again division champions, with Steve starring both on the mound and at the plate.

Corbin Heights was a new apartment complex of sturdy two-story brick units, with kids playing in the streets and laundry flapping in the breeze. The family of Steve's close neighbor and friend Andy Baylock had moved in about the same time as Steve's. This was when Andy was in the seventh grade, and it was a good move for the Baylocks. The post-war housing shortage had forced the family to split up for three years after the place where they lived was sold. Now all the members of the Baylock household were back together under one roof. As neighbors, Steve and Andy discovered they both loved all kinds of sports. Steve's sister Patti and Andy's sister Cathy also became good friends. When the boys weren't practicing baseball, they were riding bicycles, playing with their friends, and listening to records. Steve's parents regularly took all four children to the beach along Long Island Sound.

Steve also played Little League baseball the first year they lived in Corbin Heights, but Andy, a year older than Steve, was too old. All he could do was look on with envy as Steve climbed aboard the city bus, glove in hand, to go to practice. Later, when the boys' ball games were too far away for them to ride their bikes, Steve's dad was glad to drive them and then stay to watch them play. To Andy, Steve Sr. and Adele Dalkowski were "nice, kind people."

Andy was already an experienced varsity catcher when his friend joined the high school team as a sophomore in the spring of 1955 (New Britain was a three-year high school). Watching Steve pitch at Washington Junior High, high school coach Bill Huber told his catcher to go out and buy the best glove he could find. He was going to need it. During his first year at New Britain High, Steve played left field while also posting a 3-2 record on the mound. The *Hartford Courant* reported that "like most southpaws," Steve was "extremely wild" that season. "He still has plenty of control trouble."

Sitting in the bleachers one afternoon before a game, Patti for the first time apparently heard the distinctive hiss of Steve's fastball that opposing batters already knew and dreaded. At first she didn't realize what it was, this loud whistling sound that she later described as "Whoosh! Whoosh! Whoosh!" Then her dad looked around and said, "I think that's your brother warming up."

On his second start for the varsity as a sophomore, Steve struck out 18 and walked 18 in an 11–3 win over the Hartford Owls. He pitched the complete game, averaging two strikeouts and two walks per inning while throwing an incredible 178 pitches. By all accounts, though, he was throwing as hard in the ninth inning as he was in the first. It was a look into the future of Dalkowski's all-or-nothing approach to throwing (which under today's typical pitching guidelines would be 70 to 80 pitches over the limit). Was his arm bulletproof, or were these high pitch counts setting the stage for problems later on?

For Steve's junior year season in 1956, he and senior right-handers Joe Willis and Jim Fucini formed the core of the pitching rotation. Dalkowski and Willis also took turns in left field on days when they didn't pitch. Baylock and Len Pare, both seniors, were the team's top catchers. Pare, the team captain, had been the starting catcher for two years. At the beginning of this season he moved to third base, and Baylock took over as the regular starter behind the plate. This was when he developed his unusual technique for handling the Dalkowski fastball: keeping his wrist and elbow loose as pivot points, starting out before each pitch with his mitt almost parallel to the ground, then rotating it up to intercept the ball while cupping his hand inside to form an air pocket.

Years later Andy explained that he thought Steve's incredible speed was thanks to a combination of big hands, an unusually flexible shoulder joint that could rotate more than 180 degrees, and a coordinated motion that propelled the ball in a smooth, fluid manner. Andy described it as "segmented acceleration, almost like a chain reaction," or what today's pro pitching coaches call "cracking the whip"—the kinematic sequencing of the critical elements for throwing a baseball. Essentially, as a pitcher moves toward the target, his hips pass the energy to the shoulders; the shoulders move the energy to the elbow/forearm; and the elbow/forearm transfer the energy to the hand and baseball for release.

Steve was the consummate natural athlete: fast, coordinated, and instinctive. Bill Huber, beginning his fourth year as coach of the New Britain High Golden Hurricanes, thought Dalkowski's long arms also helped him. He explained that Steve "had a fluid delivery" that was very fast, and his pitching motion had "that whipping action you want." According to Huber, Steve's arm came down so far on the follow-through that his left elbow hit his right knee after every release.

Although Steve was throwing smoke from the beginning, the young pitcher felt that his velocity was increasing every year. He believed the secret might be in his powerful wrists and the flicking motion he used when he released the ball. He had been able to throw harder than anybody in town by the time he was fifteen. By age seventeen his devastating fastball was off the charts, but he was still nowhere near the strike zone much of the time. The biggest problem was the way the ball appeared to rise uncontrollably on its way to the plate.

Lenny Pare, Steve's catcher his sophomore season, tried everything he could think of to get Steve to keep the ball down. He made countless visits to the mound to remind Steve to throw at the batter's shoes. "Throw low! Throw low!" Steve would manage to keep the ball down in the strike zone for a few pitches; then it would start creeping up out of the strike zone again, forcing Pare to jump high in an effort to glove the errant offerings. "He'd let go and it would just rise and rise," Pare later recalled, forcing him to make yet another trip to the mound to remind him what to do. "He had a short attention span," Pare said. Fortunately, Pare added, Dalkowski would regain his focus once he had loaded the bases with walks and find a way to get the last out of an inning when he needed it most.

Steve was so intent on bringing the heat with every pitch that he very rarely threw anything but his four-seam fastball, even though

Coach Huber thought he had a very good curve. Explaining his reasoning later, Steve said, "My off-speed stuff was terrible. They hit it. But they didn't hit the fastball. So why throw the other stuff?" As any great pitcher will tell you, don't speed up the bat if they can't touch the express. Steve's fastball cultivated the dangerous side of pitching, and when he was around the strike zone he was effective. In fact, Steve and Len didn't even have signals for different kinds of pitches. The only signal Pare gave meant "Okay, ready."

Like Baylock and Coach Huber, Pare noticed Steve's spare pitching motion and his whiplike delivery. He also learned to predict a strike. Pare said that when Steve brought his arm straight over the top instead of slotting it at one o'clock as he usually did, it was always an inside strike. When the arm came over at one o'clock the ball might go anywhere. A quality pitching coach today would recognize that the difference in Steve's arm slot had to do with his timing from first forward movement to foot-strike. When Steve was at the right place at the right time, he was coming out of his natural twelve o'clock slot. But Steve and his coaches didn't recognize this—not then, not ever. If a pitcher's timing changes on each delivery, the manner in which he generates power will change, and that means his mechanical components will differ on each pitch. No repeatability, no consistency.

Batters were justifiably wary of this unpredictable southpaw. Steve never had to worry about brushing back batters because they never dug in. As Sandy Koufax stated, "Pitching is the art of instilling fear." Steve had that part down well. Pare was afraid that if Dalkowski ever hit a high school player in the head, it would kill him. Fortunately, he never did, though Steve himself worried about the prospect of hitting a batter. About once a game he would throw a pitch behind the batter's head, bringing a look of stark terror to the hitter's face. Then the next three offerings would be way outside because Steve didn't want to hit anybody. Typically, the batter would swing at anything by that time in order to end the target practice and get out of the box. As Baylock later observed, "High school kids aren't going to stand up there and wait for the perfect pitch. They'll swing at anything." Especially if they think the next pitch might put them on the seat of their pants, or worse.

An over-the-top pitch was usually the straightest, fastest pitch Steve could throw. Len broke his wrist trying to catch one during summer American Legion ball. It was, he said, "a vicious pitch." Pare eventually had to have wrist surgery. Another teammate who dreaded seeing Dalkowski take the mound was Grove Steele, New Britain's first baseman. Just like his pitches, Steve's pickoff throws to first came screaming in like rockets.

While he never injured a high school player with a pitch, Steve did bring down a catcher once. His father was warming him up, crouching in front of a brick wall that served as a backstop. One of Steve's pitches tore through the web of Steve Sr.'s glove, ricocheted off the wall behind him, hit him in the back of the head, and knocked him unconscious. Momentarily terrified that he had killed his father, Steve was relieved to see his dad wasn't badly hurt.

On April 25, 1956, Steve played the first game of his junior season, a highly anticipated pitching duel with Hartford High School senior Pete Sala, "ace left-hander" of the Owls. Sala had been the district's top pitcher the year before, with 110 strikeouts and 44 walks over 67 innings and an ERA of 0.79. Steve got off to a shaky start at Walnut Hill Park, loading the bases in the first inning with two walks and a hit batsman. But Dalkowski then struck out the side and gave up only three more walks the rest of the way, mixing fastballs and a sharp curve (despite Steve's saying he threw only fastballs). It was the pitching duel the fans had hoped for. Sala allowed six hits, walked five and struck out 14, while Dalkowski gave up four hits, walked five and struck out 17, leading the 'Canes to a 3–2 victory.

Steve couldn't find the strike zone or his focus a few days later in his next start, this time against the last-place New London Whalers. After Steve struck out six and issued eight walks in two-plus innings,

Coach Huber yanked his star pitcher and sent him to play right field. The Hurricanes lost 9–4.

May 8 brought the two best pitchers in the state together for a rematch, this time for undisputed first place in the Capital District Conference. Hartford sportswriter Jimmy Cunavelis called it "as great a pitching duel as the most demanding fan would ever ask." Steve mixed speed and wildness in a thrilling display, striking out 20 batters against eight walks and three wild pitches over 10 innings, while Sala fanned 17 and gave up only one base on balls.

Through nine innings, the two southpaws, each throwing mostly four-seam fastballs, were locked in a scoreless tie. The Hurricanes' Bob Barrows had the only hit off Sala that day, a slow roller down the third-base line that should have been handled for an out to keep his no-hitter alive. Then with two outs in the tenth, a tiring Dalkowski gave up a bloop single (one of only two hits he allowed) and wild-pitched the runner to second. Steve then walked the next three batters, giving the Owls the only run needed in their 1–0 victory. Local commentators bemoaned that only a small crowd had seen such a great game, blaming it on the 3:30 start time and wondering why high school games couldn't be scheduled later in the afternoon. Within a year, sparse crowds would not be a problem whenever Dalkowski was on the mound.

Steve balanced his hard-fought loss to Sala with an extra-inning win on May 15, again striking out 20 in a 5–4 win over the East Hartford Hornets. Later in the week he played left field and scored a run in a 5–3 loss to Bulkeley High.

After the end of the school year, Steve once again played in the American Legion tournament in addition to his Courant-Jaycee League team, now with the oldest boys in the Graduate Division. Between July 19 and August 9 that summer, he threw four shutout victories for the Caval Tool Bobcats, three of them no-hitters, in an incredible display of pitching dominance. During the first of those four games, against the previously undefeated Veeder-Root Indians, "fire-balling

Dalkowski" struck out 10 and walked three with no hits given up in a 6–0 win called after five innings because of darkness. In his next start, this time against the Newington Fenns, he pitched a second no-hitter. On July 31 Steve barely missed his third no-hitter in a row, giving up a single in the sixth on the way to an 8–0 shutout win over St. Anthony's. He pitched another no-hit shutout on August 9 against the Sage Allen Phils, a 2–0 victory in which he struck out 14 and walked five. The stats indicate that Steve displayed more focus and control during summer league play than during high school games. This contrast is consistent with later periods during his career when Steve did some of his best pitching in a relatively relaxed environment when the pressure was off.

As the high school baseball season began for Dalkowski's senior year in April 1957, he was by all accounts the brightest star on the team. Both Baylock and Pare had left for college as did Steve's Hartford rival Pete Sala, who went on to play a season at the University of Connecticut and four years in the Pittsburgh Pirates organization. Word was that major league scouts already had Dalkowski in their sights. His sister, Patti, heard of spectators driving hundreds of miles that year to see her brother pitch at Walnut Hill Park.

Steve was a young master on the mound whose almost supernatural pitching skills were starting to attract nationwide attention. Yet for all the accolades, Steve had developed into a relatively quiet, shy teenager. Though an indifferent student, he was well behaved and obedient. He had plenty of friends, and all his peers liked and admired him. Coach Huber was pleased to see that Steve's success hadn't gone to his head. He ran diligently to keep in shape and was in top condition for games. No workout was too strenuous or too much trouble. He followed Huber's instructions without complaining. Steve joined a social club at school called the Royal Knights, known as the "jock club" because its members were athletes. He came to club meetings but didn't say much. He was a leader on the playing field but more a follower the rest of the time, content to go with the flow.

As Steve began his last year at New Britain High, the most important factors shaping his future career were firmly in place. He could throw a baseball faster than anybody had ever seen. When he was accurate, he was a phenomenon—a "phenom" in the parlance of baseball; when he was wild—which was often—he was a terror. Even he seemed not to know where his pitching talent came from or how to harness it. When he was throwing strikes, nobody could touch him. When his control was off, he didn't know what to do to get it back. Still, he never gave up, always worked hard, and was always eager to please. Off the mound he was friendly, generous, and respectful to adults. He was also easily influenced by friends, always eager to fit in and be one of the gang.

Beginning with the first mention in the local press of Steve Dalkowski's pitching skills as a junior high standout, stories of his speed were always tempered with stories of his wildness. But before he was a pitching sensation for New Britain, Steve was a star on the football team. The field of battle where his success was most complete and unalloyed during those years was not the diamond but the gridiron.

THREE

Gridiron All-Star

"One of the finest halfbacks around, young Steve was nothing less than a sensation."

—*The Hartford Courant*, June 22, 1957

The New Britain football team got a new head coach in the fall of 1954. John Toner, a former star player at Boston University, took the helm of a so-so squad known more for effort than results. It was also the year Steve Dalkowski and his friend Bob Barrows, both sophomores, joined the squad in the backfield. Steve was not a starter at the beginning of the season, but was the first off the bench if a backfield starter was injured.

By Steve's junior season, Toner had taken the measure of his team and focused on versatility and speed to improve their prospects for 1955. Dalkowski, who had lettered on defense as a sophomore, would be the team's key left-handed passer while Barrows, who played short-stop on the baseball team with Steve, threw with his right. These were two outstanding players on a team sorely lacking in depth. While the

21

linemen of the Golden Hurricanes weighed an average of 195 pounds, Steve tipped the scale at only 155 and Barrows at 150. No doubt their mothers were relieved when local dentists joined forces to make custom plastic mouthpieces for each team member free of charge.

With Dalkowski and Barrows alternating at quarterback, the Hurricanes won their 1955 season opener against Mt. Pleasant Providence, 25–10. Even better, they also won their second game, beating rival Stamford for the first time in ten years, 19–6. By the time they won their third game in a row, against Weaver High, the two junior quarterbacks had cemented their reputations throughout the league as a dangerous duo against opposing defenders.

Another win, 36–6 over Norwich, gave Steve and the Hurricanes their fourth consecutive victory as Dalkowski and Barrows took turns at quarterback throughout the game. New Britain scored on their second drive, with Dalkowski running for a touchdown from seven yards out. He also earned star reviews for his ball handling.

"Undefeated New Britain High Whacks East Hartford 33–6" boasted the headline in the *Hartford Courant* after a fifth consecutive victory put the Golden Hurricanes in sole possession of first place in the league. A homecoming crowd estimated at thirty-five hundred saw their boys in maroon and gold rack up a fifth consecutive victory for the first time in fifteen years. Dalkowski ran two yards for the 'Canes' first score, capping a long series that began after they recovered a fumble on the visitors' 13-yard line. On the extra point attempt after the third touchdown, Steve and the team rushed the ball over twice only to be called back both times on penalties. Unruffled, Dalkowski reset his line, took the snap, and completed a 12-yard pass to Joe Willis in the end zone. As always, the young QB seemed to stay cool under pressure and get the job done.

New Britain's next game, a 39–6 blowout of New London on October 29, showcased Steve's superb passing skills and agile running ability. Fans noted his knack for scoring points at key moments and a leader's gift for assessing the situation and acting fast. He completed a 50-yard pass to set up the Hurricanes' third touchdown. Early in the second quarter Steve intercepted an errant Whaler ball and returned it 39 yards.

By the end of the regular season, New Britain had posted a stunning 9-0 record. No opponent had scored more than one touchdown against them. In only two seasons, Toner, with help from Dalkowski, Barrows, and a fleet-footed receiver named Steve "Zig-Zag" Zisk, had taken his team from also-rans to an undefeated season against state rivals. But the biggest excitement of the season was yet to come.

Each year in December the Kiwanis Club of Miami, Florida, sponsored a benefit exhibition football game for underprivileged children. For 1955 they invited the New Britain Hurricanes to play the Miami High Stingarees in the Orange Bowl. The invitation was front-page news in the *New Britain Herald* as editors mirrored the excitement of a New England industrial town whose team had been invited to play in one of the most famous sports venues in the country.

The Miami Kiwanis Club offered New Britain $3,500 toward the cost of the trip. That left $9,500 (more than $80,000 in current dollars) to be raised by a working-class student body of about sixteen hundred. But to the citizens of New Britain and the surrounding region, it wasn't just the high school being honored, it was the entire community. Hartford radio station WHAY and TV station WKNB spread news of the invitation and the fund drive, as did Hartford and New Britain newspapers. WHAY announced plans to broadcast the game live from Miami. TV stations in Hartford and New Haven would send film crews to shoot highlights for later broadcast.

The whole town rallied to the cause. Factories, unions, civic groups, and even out-of-town businesses delivered bags full of money to the school at the rate of thousands of dollars a day. Municipal workers gave $446, school employees donated $311, and New Britain students themselves collected $141 to help send their team on its way.

Within a week the school took in more than $15,000, prompting the fundraising chairman, Judge Frank J. DiLoreto, to plead with donors to stop giving. "No, absolutely no more donations should be made," he said to the local press in a front-page statement, explaining that "we have more than enough money, and we do not wish to oversubscribe too much."

The school's chartered Pan American DC-6B Super Clipper left the airport at Windsor Locks, Connecticut, at 9:30 a.m. on December 6 for a four-and-a-half-hour flight. On board were the football squad, trainers, coaches, and chaperones, plus a handful of school board members and fans who paid their own way. Most of the boys had never flown before. Though motion sickness pills were distributed to all the players, no one needed them during the trip. New Britain High Principal Vincent Sala offered players' parents the option to send their children by train, but all granted permission for the flight. Principal Sala was moved by the level of support for the team and assured everyone that the experience would include educational components—visits to an aquarium, botanical garden, and a biological laboratory.

Once in Miami, the team took time for swimming and sightseeing, but they focused dutifully on preparing for the game. On Wednesday, December 7, they practiced after dark at a local field to get a feel for running their patterns under the lights. It was the first time the team had ever played at night. There was another night practice the next evening, following a day of chalk talks, light scrimmages on the hotel pool deck, and watching film of the Stingarees in action. Steve and his friends spent their spare time shopping, sightseeing, and giving autographs to local girls. A photo in the *Hartford Courant* showed Dalkowski and Barrows, along with team captain Don Welch, signing autographs while surrounded by smiling Miami High coeds.

By the time of the 8:15 p.m. kickoff on Friday, December 9, the temperature at the Orange Bowl had dropped from the low eighties to the high fifties—chilly for the home team but a balmy winter's night for the Hurricanes. It snowed three inches in New Britain that evening. Coach Toner had dreaded the prospect of playing on a hot, humid field and was no doubt happy with the conditions. While both teams were undefeated for the season, Miami was the favorite. This was no surprise since they had the home-field advantage, weighed an average of ten pounds more per player, and, at twenty-eight hundred students, had a much larger pool of player prospects.

The long odds did nothing to dampen the visitors' enthusiasm. A crowd of more than fifteen thousand, including as many as one thousand from New Britain, watched the two teams play to a 6–6 tie with three minutes left in the first half. (One of the fans taking in the action was 14-year-old John Powell who, later known as "Boog," would play his own part in the story of Steve Dalkowski and in the history of baseball.) Taking the snap at the New Britain 37, Dalkowski completed a pass for 27 yards. Another Dalkowski pass advanced the Hurricanes to the Miami 17. A third pass from Steve hit his receiver at the six and he ran in for the score, giving New Britain a 12–6 lead as the teams headed to the locker room. This was already a victory of sorts. Miami's defense had allowed only an average of three points per game all year. No opponent had scored more than one touchdown.

But that was the high watermark for New Britain. Outweighed and hampered by the Stingarees' seven-man line, the 'Canes offense began to tire and made it past midfield only twice during the second half. A third-quarter punt by Miami quarterback Joe Caldwell rolled out of bounds two inches from the New Britain goal line. Unable to advance, the Hurricanes punted 36 yards, which set up a scoring drive for Miami. The Stingarees capped their performance with another touchdown in the fourth, coming from behind to win, 20–12.

The loss scarcely mattered to the New Englanders. 'Canes fans in the stands and at home were rightly proud of their team. Though it was the Hurricanes' only loss of the season, the boys had given it their all and made an impressive showing. Coach Toner graciously conceded to the Miami press that Miami had the better team. All the same, he took the opportunity to slam officials for what he considered bad pass interference calls. In summary, Toner said, "The officiating stunk."

Neither the loss nor questionable calls diminished the boys' enjoyment of the rest of their Miami adventure. After the game Friday night, the team was treated to dinner at a Miami Beach restaurant courtesy of Stanley, the tool company where Steve's father worked. On Saturday the Kiwanis Club provided a fleet of cars to take the boys to the newly opened Seaquarium in nearby Key Biscayne. After church and a swim at the hotel on Sunday, the team took a sightseeing cruise. Monday they toured Miami by bus, then enjoyed a fishing trip on a chartered boat.

Regardless of the final score, the New Britain Golden Hurricanes returned home on December 13 in triumph. After breakfast in Miami Beach, the team lifted off in their chartered airliner a little after 11 a.m. One of the fans on board, the owner of a New Britain sandwich shop popular with team players, helped flight stewardesses serve the passengers their lunch of filet mignon.

Escorted from the airport to New Britain by state police, the team was greeted by "a roaring welcome from thousands of townspeople." A parade of Twirlettes, cheerleaders, the drill team, and the school band led the way to the high school campus, where another fifteen hundred well-wishers waited impatiently. The mayor, Principal Sala (who later referred to Steve's pitching rival Pete Sala as his nephew, though he was not), the chairman of the school board, Coach Toner, and others heaped congratulations and praise upon "the city's goodwill ambassadors."

The boys were happy to be home. Many of them carried souvenirs of their trip. Dalkowski, wearing a cap he bought in Miami, admitted to a reporter that as glad as he was to be back, the fact was "we were just getting acquainted with the place."

For the 1956 season, Coach John Toner moved Dalkowski, now a senior, to right halfback and installed Barrows at quarterback. Steve, listed that year at 168 pounds and described as one of the state's finest halfbacks and "a crack southpaw passer," said he liked the switch. The team's opening game was against Mt. Pleasant High of Providence, Rhode Island, rated No. 1 in their state. Toner was worried that inexperience in his offensive line would be a liability. He was right. In spite of Barrows's passing and Dalkowski's ability to "carry the mail," New Britain lost, 19–13.

From that point on, however, Steve's running and passing skills helped carry the Hurricanes to win after win. By November, New Britain boasted two consecutive seasons of unbroken in-state victories and were preparing to play archrival Hartford High in the sixtieth annual face-off between the two schools. On the bitter cold afternoon of November 9, the Hurricanes shellacked Hartford, 42–0, with "a near-perfect blend of speed and deception," according to the local press. Steve was the key to three touchdowns, with scoring runs of 42 yards and one yard on "superb" ball carrying and a pass of 38 yards for another six points. The *Hartford Courant* ran a photo of Steve barreling into the Hartford line. Partway through the third quarter, with 42 points already on the board, Coach Toner sent his reserves onto the field and played them for the rest of the game.

The traditional Thanksgiving Day football game between New Britain and Bulkeley High was always one of the highlights of the season. Now that New Britain had pulled off back-to-back undefeated seasons against state opponents and garnered the previous year's invitation to the Orange Bowl, the anticipation that November was even higher than usual. A paid attendance of 11,500 fans crowded the football bleachers at Willow Brook Park on a wet, chilly afternoon as they watched the home team play a masterful offensive game. Against a strong defense, the 'Canes scored seven touchdowns on their way to a 45–13 win. "Peerless" Steve Dalkowski scored three touchdowns on the ground for the 'Canes—a fleet 41-yard sprint and short runs of five yards and one yard—again showcasing his strength and agility.

To no one's surprise, Dalkowski was the winner of the James M. Conley Memorial Award as the outstanding football player of 1956. He received a $100 scholarship and an engraved football. There was speculation that he could go to Seattle University in Washington, where he might have a chance to make the football team despite his undersized build compared to the average college football player. His prowess in the backfield demonstrated not only great athleticism but also his ability to think on his feet and to throw the football where he wanted it to go. His success as a football player was complete and unqualified. He was also an honorable-mention high school All-American.

Steve never applied to college, ending whatever chance he might have had to develop his impressive natural football ability, even though according to one account he was offered a scholarship to Notre Dame as a quarterback. Since college teams are essentially the "minor leagues" of pro football, he ruled out the one practical path to a gridiron career.

It's fair to say that Dalkowski was an athlete with the power, coordination, desire, and stamina to excel in any sport that interested him. He played football, was a decent point guard on his high school basketball team, swung a golf club from time to time, and pitched baseball from April until September every year in three leagues—school, American Legion, and Courant-Jaycee. In the end, he chose to follow baseball. That meant tackling the challenge he faced even after so many years and so much success during his schoolboy career: he still seemed to have no idea where the five-ounce horsehide was going once it left his hand.

One question that arises—and a reason for taking a detailed look at Dalkowski's little-known football career—is that his record-setting football performance casts his future struggles as a pitcher in a new light. In the backfield Dalkowski was a leader, a strategist with a confident command of the situation. He was famously accurate as a passer, consistently delivering the goods. It was a far cry from his maddening unpredictability on the mound and a sense that neither he nor anyone else could do anything about it.

Steve carried the same intellect and athleticism that made him a football hero onto the pitcher's mound. According to Orioles scout Walter Youse, Frank McGowan had secretly watched Dalkowski on the football field. He wanted to learn more about the young prospect without drawing attention to him lest another agent sign him first. Part of his interest in Steve came from observing his outstanding left-handed passing ability. The difference in outcome for Steve in playing the two sports might have been on account of something every pitcher knows all too well.

Quarterbacks, leaders that they are, are still surrounded by their team. They're close physically on the line and during the play. Each player knows how the play should unfold, recognizes the role of every member on the team, and reviews those roles as the play develops. They're thinking and moving together like a well-oiled machine.

In stark contrast, a baseball pitcher is absolutely alone on the hill. He is the center of attention and focus by both teams. In all of team sports, a baseball pitcher alone can almost win a game by himself if he comes close to a perfect performance. No other team sport offers such opportunity. Or such pressure.

While the pitcher has the support of eight teammates, each with a crucial responsibility, power pitchers such as Dalkowski rarely consider using their nine-to-one odds; they simply bring the heat. Pitchers routinely face lonely pressure. But when lonely pressure morphs into forbidding isolation, a pitcher can lose his focus and concentration. He might then start ruminating about the last pitch he threw or how the next one might cost him the game. He can't control or affect those scenarios. He can only control the pitch leaving his hand at the moment. A case of nerves can be his downfall. If he gets distracted by past results or future possibilities, if he lets self-doubt creep in, if he stops concentrating on the process of focusing on *this* pitch, he'll soon be in trouble and on his way to an early shower.

Steve Dalkowski's football career demonstrates that he was a consummate athlete. Baseball history tells us there's far more to the story—more than a budding phenom whose potential remained stubbornly untapped. The major league scouts who secretly watched Steve play football and who hovered around diamond 1 at Walnut Hill Park in the spring of 1957 saw an athlete of rare promise—a jaw-dropping flamethrower. They saw the wild man, too, but surely somebody could figure out how to tame him.

FOUR

Worth the Gamble

"Harry Brecheen said Dalkowski had the best arm he ever saw."
—Frank "Beauty" McGowan, Orioles scout

With the start of the high school baseball season in April 1957, all eyes were on the fireballing southpaw from Corbin Heights. Steve Dalkowski was the talk of the town, with fans and sportswriters already speculating over his chances at making the big leagues. But as Gerald Crean wrote in the *New Britain Herald* the day before the season's first game, Steve still hadn't figured out how to control his fastball. "His big weakness, wildness, is causing grave doubts," Crean wrote. "Steve, who once struck out 18 men in a game and walked the same number, reportedly has had batsmen biting the dust fairly regularly to avoid his erratic tosses in practice games." It's a fate that would stay with Dalkowski throughout his career: an incredible number of strikeouts equaled by an incredible number of walks.

Steve had already been contacted by a number of major league teams. Coach Bill Huber fielded calls from at least nine. Huber could tell them that Steve's work ethic was second to none. He was quick to respond to instructions and always eager to do what he was told. He had a humble attitude, without a hint of cockiness or bragging, and was friendly and popular among his teammates. He was mild-mannered and quiet—except when he was on the mound with a baseball in his hand. Then this self-effacing choirboy transformed into a human rocket launcher, relentless and invincible when he was on his game.

Huber could also tell inquiring scouts that yes, his star performer was wild and had always been wild. Anyone who could harness that power would have a gold mine on their hands.

Several Hurricanes, including Dalkowski, came down with colds in the days before the opening game of the season against East Hartford on April 18. Though he was not feeling up to par, Steve was still the starter. Team captain Bob Barrows had moved to catcher from his spot at shortstop the year before. Steve and Bob had been a powerful combination as quarterback and halfback on the school's championship football team. Now with Andy Baylock and Len Pare both away at college, Bob donned the catcher's mask to partner with his friend on the baseball diamond. Besides, he was the only player who could handle Steve's pitches.

Hundreds of spectators showed up for the game at Walnut Hill Park—a big crowd for a high school contest at 3:30 on a Thursday afternoon. Steve threw one pitch ten feet over Barrows's head and hit a batter with another. Except for those misfires, he was in top form that day, runny nose or not. The game was scoreless until the seventh, when Hurricane right fielder Mike Halloran singled, stole second, then scored as the catcher's wild throw to second went into center field and rolled all the way to the fence. New Britain scored again in the eighth to win their first game of the year, 2–0.

Dalkowski had opened his senior year season by pitching a no-hitter with 20 strikeouts and six walks. Observers familiar with Steve's pitching style noticed that he didn't seem to be trying to blow every hitter away with what Baylock had called the "gas." He looked more settled, his game more deliberate and refined. Writing in the *Hartford Courant*, Jimmy Cunavelis concluded that Dalkowski "could hardly have improved on the sensational mound display today" on the way to a "brilliant" victory.

Steve's next start on April 24 against Weaver High drew more than five hundred fans, the largest crowd at a New Britain high school baseball game in years. Locals who'd shown scant interest in baseball before had come to see Dalkowski's first win of the season. Now they were back for more excitement, and they brought their friends with them. Baseball was suddenly the rage. No one expected to see a second consecutive no-hitter, but no one was willing to rule it out, either.

The first couple of innings went well before Dalkowski hit a rough patch. Seemingly out of nowhere, the old wildness bugaboo threatened to swamp Steve in the third after he had struck out the first two hitters on seven pitches. It was like flipping a switch. His control simply evaporated. Third baseman Vaughn Sargasian walked, then stole second and third. Second baseman Dave Murray drew another walk, putting runners at the corners. Shortstop Bobby Fago stepped into the batter's box representing the go-ahead run, with the 'Canes up, 2–0. As Steve pondered his next pitch, Murray bolted for second. Dalkowski turned and threw to shortstop Joe Cody covering second for what seemed an easy tag, but Murray stopped short back in the basepath as Sargasian then sped for home. A classic "sucker play." Cody hesitated. His throw to the plate was late and wild, allowing an unearned run and ending Steve's streak of scoreless innings at eleven.

Steve hit a batter, threw a wild pitch, and walked 11 in the course of an exhausting three-hour-and-fifteen-minute game. On the other hand, he regained his focus well enough to strike out three batters in the third and fifth, on his way to fanning a total of 19, and so gave the record crowd the show they'd come to see. Spectators seemed eager to overlook Steve's crazy moments, relishing every menacing fastball, and counting strikeouts more than walks.

Weaver's center fielder, Stan Goodman, gave Steve his only real challenges in the batter's box. In the fourth he laid down a perfect bunt along the third-base line, which Steve fielded then fired to first just in time to get Goodman. Leading off in the eighth, Goodman squared up a Dalkowski fastball, driving it into the left-center-field gap. 'Canes center fielder Jim Havlick made a sensational running catch to preserve the no-hitter. The final score was 10–1, in New Britain's favor.

Steve Dalkowski had done it: back-to-back no-hitters. The whole town was abuzz with news of their sports star's latest triumph. No one could remember a high school pitcher ever doing what he'd just done. The next day, local sportswriters proudly compared the "fireballing southpaw" with New Britain native Johnny Vander Meer, the Cincinnati Reds left hander who pitched consecutive no-hitters in 1938, the only major leaguer in history to do so.

Steve's performance also riveted the attention of major league scouts who were coming to Connecticut to watch him play, contributing to the massive crowds at Walnut Hill Park and the snarl of cars that choked surrounding streets for every game. Scouts were easy to pick out in the sea of pale New England faces. They were older gray- or white-headed men, noted New Britain sportswriter John Wentworth, "conspicuous by the deep tans they wore and the 'crow feet' around the eyes which come from watching a lot of baseball games. They . . . were here to watch this boy Dalkowski."

According to former Yankees scout Roy Carter, top prospects would have stood out immediately on the field even before the game began. "A great player sticks out like a sore thumb," Carter explained. "If you look at players on the field and you don't see one or two that stand out head and shoulders above the rest, you don't have a major league prospect."

If pressed, coaches and scouts will agree that a pitcher's sole responsibility is to get outs and get them with the fewest number of pitches possible. Even so, baseball has always been obsessed by hard-throwing pitchers such as "Bullet" Bob Feller, Rex Barney, Bob Turley, Herb Score, Ryne "the Flame" Duren, "Sudden" Sam McDowell, and Sandy Koufax. So when scouts saw someone who could throw a baseball as hard as Steve Dalkowski, any other guidelines for assessing a pitcher's potential would be promptly discarded. Dalkowski could bring it, throw gas, deliver the heat, serve the high-rising cheddar—any and all metaphors were applicable. What Casey Stengel said of Ryne "the Flame" Duren would hold equally true for Steve: "Whenever he came into the game, people would stop eating their popcorn."

Coach Huber fielded calls from representatives of the Yankees, Red Sox, Braves, Dodgers, and Giants, among others, wanting to know when Dalkowski would be pitching. By most accounts, every team in the majors courted Steve; a few sources reported that the Cleveland Indians were the lone club to take a pass. In the days before the baseball draft began in 1965, scouts often worked like detectives, following leads on a promising player and scouting him in secret, keeping news of a young prospect to themselves in hopes of signing him before word got around to the competition. Dalkowski was such a phenomenon and his reputation grew so fast that scouts arriving in New Britain found their peers already perched in the grandstands beside them.

During the blowout victory over Weaver High, one of the scouts chatted up sportswriter John Wentworth about Dalkowski's reputation. That afternoon Steve was on his way to 39 strikeouts in 18 innings for the season to date. Just then a ball sailed past Bob Barrows's glove and careened into the fence, ricocheting almost to the visiting scout's feet. "Looks to me as though the boy needs to be tamed down just a might," the man wryly observed. "He's got a live pitch, though, hasn't he?"

Any batter who ever faced Dalkowski would heartily agree that he had "a live pitch," including the batter whose bat broke without him swinging it. Ducking reflexively to avoid a Dalkowski heater headed straight for him, this batter held the bat level in front of his body in hopes of deflecting the ball. The pitch hit the stationary bat just below the trademark, shattering it.

With New Britain leading Weaver, 10–1, through six innings, many of the spectators at Walnut Hill had started to drift away, though not the tanned contingent squinting through the late-afternoon sun at the Hurricanes pitcher going through his spare, short-arm motion on the mound. They stayed for the last out, watching, analyzing, jotting down an occasional note. What they'd been hearing was true. This Dalkowski kid had a fastball that was a once-in-a-lifetime discovery, meteoric in its velocity, splitting the air with a noise that sounded like ripping cloth. But Steve had to figure out how to keep the ball down and consistently get it over the seventeen-inch-wide plate. Although coaches, catchers, passers-by, and others had been telling him that for years, none of them ever could advise him how to do it. Consequently, without a plan or direction in place, a solution to the throwing strikes problem continued to elude Steve. Yet everyone knew that he worked hard every day to find the answer, never complaining, never giving up.

John Wentworth summed up the thoughts of many local fans in his column for the *New Britain Herald* the day after the Weaver game. "It's a long haul to the majors; a lot of obstacles must be overcome. But the more one watches the gritty young man, the more one is inclined to feel that the old Hardware City is due to have a pitching representative one day. He's a great competitor, as all those who have watched him run, block, and tackle as a high school halfback will agree. He'll never scare. And very important, he works hard at the business of pitching. . . . You just can't sell this youngster short."

It might have been around this time that Steve gave a pitching exhibition at a fair in nearby Berlin, Connecticut, along with two other local high school pitchers: Gary Waslewski, who later pitched six seasons in the majors including a start for Boston in the 1967 World

Series, and Henry Mora. When his turn came, Steve threw a rocket that went over the catcher's head, over the backstop, and disappeared into the distance.

A few minutes later a surprised and upset man walked into the nurse's station at the fairground. He explained that he had briefly stepped into the woods to take care of some personal business and suddenly felt a sharp blow in his back. He'd heard no one, and nobody seemed to be around. Then he saw a baseball roll to a stop beside his feet. To prove his story, he held up the offending ball and lifted his shirt to show a big welt on his back. He wasn't seriously hurt. Evidently neither he nor the nurse ever pieced together—or could have imagined—the whole scenario.

As scouts checked their notes and reflected on what they'd seen, they raved about a phenomenally live arm belonging to a kid a few weeks shy of his eighteenth birthday. His fastball was a lightning bolt. His control was a disaster. He was soft-spoken, shy but friendly, and a tireless worker. And while no one could teach a pitcher to throw as fast as this young hurler did, surely somebody could teach him how to control his missiles.

The one piece of the puzzle they didn't have, couldn't imagine, and which none of them would have for a while yet, was that Steve Dalkowski was already on his way to becoming an alcoholic. Like so many threads of the Dalkowski narrative, stories about his early drinking are numerous and sometimes mutually exclusive. His sister, Pat, repeatedly said over the years that their father was a heavy drinker and that drunkenness was a common state of affairs in blue-collar Polish households, once describing it as "almost a way of life." The family's friends and neighbors lived the same way, headed by hard-working, hard-drinking men who spent long weeks in the factories, then relaxed and blew off steam in the neighborhood taverns over the weekends. Their father, Pat said, might be drunk from Friday night until Sunday afternoon, but he knew he had to sober up for work on Monday morning.

It's not known exactly when or how Steve started experimenting with alcohol. During one interview later in life, Steve said he started drinking when he was twelve or thirteen by sneaking into a neighbor's wine cellar with friends. Another time he said he never drank wine until after his baseball career was over and that he started out drinking beer in the ninth grade. In another version of the story, he started drinking at sixteen. Early in his career he told a teammate he drank a lot in high school and was arrested for breaking into a liquor store.

Years later his friend and teammate Ken Cullum recalled that Steve would drink after workouts at the park. "Someone always knew him in these shot-and-beer bars and bought him drinks. When the bar closed, they would get a bottle and go someplace else."

There are stories of Steve and his father hitting bars together and Steve driving home because his father was too impaired. Some accounts say his early drink of choice was vodka, which is a favorite of alcoholics because it doesn't have much taste or smell and is relatively easy to conceal. Steve's friend and neighbor Andy Baylock later said he didn't remember Steve drinking when they were growing up. He understood that Steve started turning to alcohol as a senior, after Andy had gone off to college.

Coach Huber had no idea that his star pitcher was drinking on the sly. His teammates knew, however. Cullum remembered Steve hanging out with older boys who "went in that direction." Ever friendly and always eager to please, Steve likely went along with the older crowd, happy to be accepted, participating in shenanigans beyond his years and experience to their amusement and his detriment.

There is no evidence that Steve's drinking affected his playing of sports in high school. It's possible that in the same way his father could get plastered over the weekend yet recover to take on his responsibility as the family breadwinner on Monday, Steve could drink to excess and still bounce back to fulfill his duties on the mound. Whatever drinking he did at the time was kept hidden.

Dalkowski's back-to-back no-hitters to open the 1957 season produced a lot of chatter in the diners and coffee shops around town about whether he could make it three in a row. Not only did he and the Hurricanes lose their next game, they lost big, an 18–5 steamrolling by New London on April 30 that lasted a grueling three hours and twenty-two minutes. New Britain pitchers walked 17 during that contest with Steve accounting for most of them. His next start, on May 7 against Hartford High, was even worse. In the second inning he walked six batters, yielding three unearned runs, and he walked three more batters in the sixth to give New London two insurance runs. In seven innings on the mound, Dalkowski gave up only two hits, but balanced his 13 strikeouts with 13 walks. The Hartford Owls won, 5–0, without scoring a single earned run. Owls hurler Mike Heneghan pitched a complete game giving up two hits to go with his 10 strikeouts and two walks, retiring the final 14 hitters in a row. The mysterious Dalkowski control switch had switched off again.

Steve bunched up his walks once more in his next start to ruinous effect, yet this time managed to pull out a win. With New Britain ahead going into the fifth, Dalkowski hit one batsman and walked six which, along with an error, gave Bulkeley High four runs. By the end of the sixth, New Britain had evened the score at 4–4. In the ninth, Dalkowski, batting, dumped a Texas Leaguer into right and was driven home by his catcher Bob Barrows's long single over the left fielder's head for the 5–4 victory. Steve tallied 18 strikeouts and 14 walks in that game, throwing a one-hitter.

Dalkowski's next game as a starter was a 13–4 victory over the East Hartford Hornets on May 22. It was New Britain's fourth win in nine games, and Steve had been on the hill for all four of them. In this game he struggled as usual with wildness, and that, along with an error, let to all four East Hartford runs. He countered the 13 bases on balls with an extraordinary 20 strikeouts.

An afternoon contest several days later was one of those moments when all the stars aligned and the Dalkowski magic was on full display.

Compared with a previous outing against New London, a three-hours-plus marathon with 17 walks, this game was a comeback masterpiece: four walks, two hits, and 24 strikeouts in a breezy one hour and fifty-five minutes in front of a standing-room-only crowd of more than eight hundred. The strikeout total, remarkable at any level of baseball, was heralded as a state record. Only once in the history of professional baseball has any pitcher ever struck out 24 or more hitters: Ron Necciai struck out 27 for Class D Bristol of the Appalachian League in 1952. (Five years after his record-setting performance for New Britain, Dalkowski would be pitching for Kingsport in the same league, though Bristol would no longer field a team.)

As his high school career moved into its final days, Steve was on the mound to start an away game against Weaver High on May 29. He got into trouble early, allowing a run to score on a wild pitch with the bases loaded in the first. After that he calmed down, relatively speaking. He settled into a typical Dalkowski outing, giving up nine walks but tallying 16 whiffs and allowing just one cheap infield hit. He was relieved after six innings with his club ahead, 6–1, and the Hurricanes went on to win, 8–5.

The scorekeeper for Weaver High that day, Henry Berman, provides some amusing insights about scoring a game when Dalkowski was on the hill. While Steve "threw remarkably fast he was also remarkably wild." Because a Dalkowski inning was rarely routine, Henry's scorecard was "chock full of scribbled symbols that showed balls, strikes, walks, Ks, HBP, errors, players advancing on wild pitches, and an occasional hit," making it hard for even the scorekeeper to know by the close of the game exactly what had occurred inning by inning. However, the most vivid memory that Berman holds to this day is "Dalkowski on the mound letting it all hang out and batters wishing they were somewhere else."

With the 8–5 victory over Weaver, the Dalkowski high school era came to a close. His senior year record of 7-2 with 150 strikeouts over 69⅔ innings gave him a stunning ratio of two-plus strikeouts per inning. His walks per inning were almost as high.

On June 3, five days after the victory over Weaver, Steve Dalkowski celebrated his eighteenth birthday. On June 18 he received his high school diploma. Clearly, the boy had a future in sports. If he'd wanted to try his hand at college football, reporters thought he might have a shot at Seattle University, where there was a connection with former New Britain resident John Castelli, who'd started coaching basketball the year before. Steve could of course play baseball there, too. Sportswriters and others keeping an eye on Dalkowski's prospects speculated that if he didn't get a pro contract to play baseball that he might enroll at Seattle.

But Seattle never had a chance. By the time Steve graduated, he, Coach Bill Huber, and the Dalkowski family had already been approached by a swarm of big-league scouts interested in acquiring Steve's services. Years later Steve's sister, Pat, remembered the row of flashy Cadillacs lined up along the curb in front of their Corbin Heights apartment as the baseball bigwigs took turns coming to the front door, introducing themselves, and making their case. "They were wonderful fellows," Steve's mother, Adele, told sportswriter Pat Jordan years later. She remembered the "big, beautiful cars" parked up and down Governor Street. One scout had a chauffeur. "I couldn't even concentrate," she said. "And oh, how they were dressed! Rubies and diamonds! They were big shots."

While the Red Sox may have had an inside track because they were Steve Sr.'s favorite team, or the Yankees might have had an edge because of the winning dynasty they had forged in the 1950s (and because they sent a former New Britain resident to plead their case), the winning offer came from a team with a shaky past and an uncertain future.

There had been a minor league baseball team in Baltimore, Maryland, since 1903. In 1954, the Triple-A Orioles were succeeded by the former St. Louis Browns, who moved to Baltimore and adopted the

Orioles name and mascot. Their last years in St. Louis had been difficult, with a miserable performance on the field (they went 54-100 in 1953) and a budget so squeezed that they had to scrounge used baseballs to play their final few home games. In 1957 the team was still adjusting to life in a new city, and they were on the lookout for promising young talent. The Orioles' top brass believed Dalkowski was one of the best of the crop.

To negotiate with this New Britain boy and his father, the Orioles sent Frank "Beauty" McGowan, a top scout known and nicknamed for his graceful moves in the outfield during his playing years. McGowan bounced back and forth between the majors and the minors for twenty seasons, playing his last major league game for the short-lived (1936– 40) Boston Bees at age thirty-five. After retiring as a player in 1939, he joined the Orioles organization.

A Connecticut native, McGowan was convinced that Steve Dalkowski had the makings of a major leaguer. He'd seen the boy's leadership and athleticism on the gridiron as well as on the baseball diamond. Yes, he was wild and completely unpredictable every time he walked to the mound, but McGowan believed that someone within the Orioles organization could harness that unfocused energy and transform Dalkowski into a pitching sensation. McGowan might well have also noticed the huge crowds Steve attracted playing high school ball. Fans everywhere loved anyone who could throw hard cheese almost as much as they loved the guy who can go yard. Here was a pitching sensation that supporters of the fledgling Orioles would pay to see in action.

On top of that, Orioles pitching coach Harry Brecheen advised the Baltimore organization that Dalkowski was worth the gamble. A generation younger than McGowan, Brecheen in 1946 became the first left-handed pitcher ever to win three games in a single World Series. He was nicknamed "the Cat" because of his ability to spring off the mound to cover bunts. As McGowan later recalled, "Harry Brecheen said Dalkowski had the best arm he ever saw."

Beauty McGowan and the other scouts jockeying to get Steve Dalkowski's signature on a contract were hamstrung because of the so-called "bonus rule." This rule was enacted by Major League Baseball in 1947 in response to complaints that the wealthiest teams could sign up all the promising new talent in a year even if they didn't have room on their major league roster for them. This kept the best young players off competing teams while they were being trained and seasoned in the winning bidder's farm system. The bonus rule stated that if a player received a signing bonus of more than $4,000, that player had to go immediately to the team's major league roster for two seasons. This kept the most prosperous teams from stockpiling good young players. It also kept the cost of these players low since it served as a *de facto* bidding cap.

Like most players at the beginning of their professional careers, Steve Dalkowski was not ready to play in the majors despite his natural gifts as a pitcher. That meant that the most the Orioles or anybody else could offer him as a signing bonus was the $4,000 maximum allowed under the bonus rule. The Orioles paid higher bonuses on occasion when they believed it was worth the risk to bring a prospect straight into the majors.

Players who got this treatment were called "bonus babies." (The same year McGowan was considering Dalkowski, the Orioles signed right-hander Jerry Walker to a big bonus of $20,000 and, as required, immediately put him on the major league roster. Two years later at age twenty, Walker became the youngest pitcher ever to start an All-Star Game, chalking up a 5–3 American League win. Arguably the most successful bonus baby of all time was the Brooklyn Dodgers' Sandy Koufax, who signed for $24,000 in 1955.)

Several versions of the offer Steve Dalkowski accepted from the Orioles have been passed down through the years. The most consistent components of the various accounts are an under-the-table payment of $12,000 and a new blue Pontiac, which would have cost between $2,500 and $3,000 for the most popular model that year. It isn't known whether the often-quoted $12,000 figure included the original $4,000 or was on top of the legal bonus. Some accounts say Steve's father was also offered money. Late in life Dalkowski said he took the Baltimore deal because it was the most money and included a car. There is no record of the offers from other teams. (McGowan had plenty of company in evading the limits of the bonus he could offer. After increasingly frequent accusations of sidestepping the regulation and under-the-table incentives, the bonus rule was rescinded in 1958, retroactive to players signed in 1957. The change made no difference in Dalkowski's contract since he wasn't officially a bonus baby.)

To celebrate the occasion of his signing, Steve Sr. took his son to his favorite local watering hole.

On June 21, 1957, three days after Steve's graduation at New Britain High, the Baltimore Orioles issued a press release announcing, "Orioles Acquire Steve Dalkowski, New Britain Ace." Steve was "sought by all 16 clubs in the majors," the release continued, adding that "the 5-11, 170-pound lefty was signed to a Vancouver, B.C., contract and optioned to Kingsport, Tenn., in the new all-rookie Class D Appalachian League." The team added that their new recruit was "one of the finest halfbacks around last fall. Switched from quarterback to halfback in his senior year last autumn, young Steve was nothing less than a sensation." Underscoring the connection was the accompanying headshot of Steve wearing his football jersey and shoulder pads.

The fact that Steve was signed to a contract with the Vancouver Mounties, though he never played for them, remains a mystery. One possible explanation is that although Steve's current skills were suited for a rookie league team such as Kingsport, his limitless potential made him a player worth protecting for the future. Vancouver in 1957 was part of a short-lived experiment beginning in 1952 that reclassified the Pacific Coast League as an Open League, a sort of super-minor league level higher than Triple-A but still below the majors. At the time, there was no major league franchise west of St. Louis; the Open League was set up because of the possibility that the PCL might become a third, western-based major league organization. Among other special rules, existing major league teams were limited in their right to draft Open League players. This helped Open League teams hold onto their best players in anticipation of the upcoming conversion to major league status. Signing Dalkowski to Vancouver likely shielded him from being poached by another major league franchise. But in 1958, major league baseball arrived in California, leading to the demise of the Open League.

The Kingsport club where Steve actually began his career, twenty-five hundred miles from Vancouver, was new to the Orioles organization. Formerly the Kingsport Cherokees in the Mountain States League, the team had been dormant for two years after the league folded until Baltimore brought baseball back to the town in 1957.

Whatever Steve did in the way of preparing for the start of his career and a dramatic new chapter in his life—planning, packing, saying goodbye to family and friends in the town where he was born and had lived all his life—he did it quickly. The Orioles press announcement was published in newspapers on June 22. Exactly one week later, Steve was on the mound in Kingsport delivering his to-be-reckoned-with heat and writing the first page in the legend of the fastest ever.

FIVE

Beware the Radio Pitch

"Dalkowski's first professional start turned out to be something of a nightmare."

—*Kingsport Times-News*, June 30, 1957

Kingsport, Tennessee, was a world apart from the bustle and business of New Britain and its nearby state capital of Hartford. Kingsport was a city of twenty-five thousand near the North Carolina border in the Appalachian foothills, far from any metropolitan center. Its isolation was one reason Eastman Kodak chose it as the site for one of the biggest explosives factories in the country. Eastman Chemical was the area's largest business and largest employer, producing chemicals for its Kodak film and explosives for the US government.

The Kingsport Orioles revived professional baseball in Kingsport after a two-year break. Though promoters hoped to sell five hundred season tickets to eager sports fans ready to support the new home team, they topped out at only 175. The Orioles organization expected to lose about $21,000 in Kingsport by the end of the season. Class D teams were shoestring operations that had to keep expenses to a minimum. Players traveled in rattletrap cars, stayed in cheap hotels, and made do with meager meal money. Their small salaries were usually paid twice a month and only during the spring and summer months that they played. Even standout minor leaguers worked in the off-season if they wanted more than a subsistence lifestyle. What mattered to the players, though, was that they were the chosen few who got paid for playing the game they loved. And they had a chance of moving up to fame and fortune in the major leagues.

The Kingsport team's first public appearance was an intersquad game on June 22, giving locals a chance to see the new club in action and allowing the rookie players a taste of playing under the lights. By the time Steve Dalkowski made his first start a week later, the Kingsport Orioles had lost their first three games. Steve's inauspicious beginning would make it four in a row. He took the mound against the Bluefield Dodgers, who would go on to win the Appalachian League crown in 1957 even though their lineup was not a powerhouse of potential big-league talent. Only one player from the Bluefield roster, pitcher Jim Duckworth, would make it to the major leagues, and briefly at that.

"Left-hander Steve Dalkowski's first professional start turned out to be something of a nightmare," reported the *Kingsport News*. "The fastballing eighteen-year-old walked four batters and uncorked two wild pitches to set up the Dodgers' big first frame. He didn't get a man out." The sudden change of scenery, the long train ride from Connecticut through unfamiliar territory, homesickness, and opening-day jitters surely had a part to play in Dalkowski's rough debut and the team's 18–8 defeat. At the same time, the performance was comparable to Steve's wildest outings all the way back to his sophomore year in high school. He was completely unable to locate the strike zone.

The next day Steve pitched in a game that produced one of the most enduring of all Dalkowski legends. On Sunday, June 30, 1957, he came to the mound in the sixth inning in relief against the Bluefield

Dodgers at Bluefield on the way to winning a 16–14 slugfest. (The twin cities of Bluefield, Virginia, and Bluefield, West Virginia, shared the team, though the playing field itself was on the Virginia side of a city park straddling the state line.) Dalkowski's leadoff batter was first baseman Bob Beavers, an eighteen-year-old rookie left-hander who joined the Brooklyn organization straight out of high school in Manassas, Virginia. Beavers had doubled his first time up. Like the rest of his Bluefield teammates, he had heard stories about the unpredictable newcomer on the mound and was grateful to be facing him during a day game. In theory at least, the ball would be easier to see than at night.

On the way to Bluefield's victory the day before, Dalkowski walked Beavers on four straight pitches. When Bluefield manager Jimmy Bragan saw Dalkowski emerge from the dugout this afternoon, he told his batters to take a strike, not simply the first pitch, because Steve was so wild. Sixty years later Bob Beavers remembered the moment vividly. Dalkowski's first pitch sailed over everybody's head at the plate and hit the backstop. Bluefield players in the dugout grinned; the batter in the box did not. Beavers felt his stomach churn. The second pitch was a called strike. It was, Bob recalls, the fastest pitch he had ever seen.

The intensity of it set his mind wandering from preparing to swing to the prospect of getting hit. He knew he could get his head out of the way even if he got dotted up somewhere else. The third pitch was high and inside. "I never saw it," Bob said, "but I may have been moving back to get out of the way." There are times when batters who are about to be hit freeze in place, almost an out-of-body experience. The mind sees the action in slow motion in preparation for what is about to happen. The next thing he knew, Bob Beavers was on the ground.

Beavers was wearing the folding head protector inside his cap that was standard equipment for the time, but it was no help. Dalkowski's missile hit him on the top half of his ear, crushing the upper ear—helix, scapha, fossa, antihelical fold, and antihelix—then ricocheted almost to second base. The scene was eerily similar to an infamous game a generation earlier at the Polo Grounds in New York. On August 17, 1920, Cleveland Indians star shortstop Ray Chapman was hit in the head by a rising fastball from Yankee submariner Carl Mays and died the next day. It remains the only fatality in Major League Baseball history.

The impact of Dalkowski's fastball, Bob remembered, made "a bloody mess at home plate." Though the ear was smashed and bloodied it was not torn off. According to Beavers himself, it was not torn at all. Whatever shape Bob's ear was in, the batter in the on-deck circle, Gary Melvin, did not want to follow his injured teammate to the plate. Once Beavers was carried off the field, it took all the self-persuasion Melvin could muster to step into the batter's box.

Beavers remembers being taken to the hospital in Kingsport, Tennessee, where he stayed overnight for observation. Steve came to visit him but the hospital wouldn't allow him in. It was routine in those days to have strict limits on visiting hours, especially for nonfamily members. The next day's *Bluefield Daily Telegraph* noted that Beavers "was reported in 'fair' condition at a Kingsport hospital."

The incident gave rise to the tale of Dalkowski's tearing a batter's ear off. Certainly if Bob Beavers's ear had been torn off, the hometown newspaper would have reported such an unusual and grisly event. It wasn't reported because it didn't happen. Only years later would the torn ear become part of the Dalkowski legend. Ten years after Beavers's injury, Dalkowski told his girlfriend (and later wife) Linda Moore that he had indeed torn an ear off with a baseball, but that it wasn't a batter who was hit. The unfortunate target was a man sitting in the stands behind home plate. A fastball ripped through the backstop and tore off the spectator's ear. If Dalkowski's account is true, two separate events became combined over the years in the retelling, although there is no record anywhere of a fan's ear being torn off by a Dalkowski pitch.

Beavers and Dalkowski never saw each other again. Bob traveled with the Bluefield team but didn't play for three or four weeks as required by the team's injury protocol. By then the season was almost over. He pinch hit once against the Salem Rebels ("I think it was the Rebels," he says) before the end of the year, struck out, and that was the end of his baseball career. The choice had nothing to do with his head injury. He had no long-term ill effects and believes he could have continued playing. But he got married, had a child, and had to earn a living wage. "I got a job with A&P [grocery stores] and life continued without baseball," he explained. (Approaching eighty years of age at the time of his interview, Bob Beavers was healthy, happy, and the owner and operator of commercial orange groves in Florida that he bought from former major league catcher Milt May.)

On July 4, pitching great Hal Newhouser took a seat in the stands at Kingsport to see this new pitching sensation for himself. Newhouser, who won back-to-back American League MVP awards in 1944 and 1945 (a heart murmur kept him out of World War II), was working for the Orioles after spending most of his seventeen-year major league career with the Detroit Tigers. Dalkowski struck out 15 batters that Independence Day while allowing only three hits. But 12 walks and 21 stolen bases sent Kingsport down in defeat.

During the Orioles' next road trip to Bluefield, Dalkowski reprised his debut performance by being pulled in the first inning with no one out. He walked the first three batters in succession by throwing 13 balls in 14 pitches, filling the bases. The 17–4 drubbing was Steve's second loss without getting a man out. That didn't stop his coaches and the press from believing he had the best chance of any player on the team of breaking into the major leagues. His fastball was unbelievable. The fans loved it, concentrating (as New Britain crowds had done) far more on his amazing strikeout record than his equally amazing number of bases on balls.

Dalkowski's remarkable firepower had convinced the Baltimore brass that he was worth whatever extra time and training it took to get him under control. As would be the case throughout Steve's career, coaches who had followed and trained young players by the hundreds believed his was a one-of-a-kind talent that could eventually be tamed and shaped into a pitcher of legendary stature. All he needed was a little more time. To that end, Orioles pitching coach Harry Brecheen, who had seen Steve pitch in New Britain and encouraged the team to sign him, and Orioles general manager Paul Richards summoned Dalkowski to Baltimore for intensive one-on-one pitching work. (Richards was both manager and general manager of the Orioles through the 1958 season.)

Certainly, Brecheen had Richards's ear when it came to Dalkowski. He recognized Steve's remarkable gift, and together the two of them sought a more direct and expeditious way to help the promising lefty contribute to the woeful Orioles, a team that could see fifth place in the American League only on the clearest of days. There was even speculation that Steve might pitch in a Baltimore uniform if he made substantial progress in locating the strike zone. But it didn't happen. On August 2 Dalkowski was back on the mound in Kingsport.

Something Brecheen did in Baltimore evidently helped the young player. Pitching in Salem, Virginia, on his return, Steve struck out 19, walked seven, and gave up only two infield hits, although Kingsport errors led to a 5–4 loss. Relying exclusively on his fastball, he had a no-hitter going into the sixth inning and was charged with only one Salem run. Kingsport faded in the ninth when a fielding error broke a 4–4 tie. As sportswriter Frank Creasy wrote the next day, "Steve Dalkowski will be excused if he is seen today muttering, 'Whadda ya have to do to win?'"

As the season progressed, Steve kept up his exciting but erratic performance. On August 22 he started the second game of a double-header against Johnson City, producing 15 strikeouts and 18 walks in 5⅓ innings on the way to a 15–5 loss. The next night he walked 21 batters in 7⅓ innings, besting the major league record of 16 walks in a game shared by four players, the most recent of whom was Bruno

Haas pitching for Philadelphia in 1915. On August 27 Dalkowski surpassed the major league record for wild pitches of 30 in a season set by Leon Ames of New York in 1905. Pitching in relief, he allowed four runs on four walks and three wild pitches during the eighth inning in a 9–0 loss.

Another night in Wilson, North Carolina, with Cal Ripken (later known as Cal Ripken Sr., father of legendary Orioles shortstop and Hall of Famer Cal Jr.,) behind the plate, Steve unloaded a wild pitch that sailed over the catcher's head and through the steel mesh of the backstop. (Seventeen years later, while visiting Wilson as a scout for the Orioles, Ripken went to see if the hole was still there. It was.)

Pitching on the road in Pulaski, Virginia, the last week of August 1957, Steve scored his first professional victory. Manager Walter Youse, on temporary assignment with Kingsport, later remembered hearing what he called a buzzing, "a noise like you never heard," of the Dalkowski fastball as he sat in the dugout. Encouraging him to try his off-speed stuff, Youse told Steve, "Don't throw your curveball so hard. Let up a bit. Throw like maybe a half-speed curveball and try to get it over a little bit." The third hitter for the Pulaski Cubs was Kenneth Fisher, a cocky twenty-one-year-old whose .322 batting average was leading the league.

As Youse recalled the moment, "Well, Dalkowski throws one of these easy-up curveballs and Fisher hits the hell out of it for a double. And he's out there on second base, and you can hear him shouting, 'Dalkowski, you ain't so hot!' and all that. The next time up, Jesus, Dalkowski throws three fastballs like bullets and you could sit in the dugout and hear them buzzing to the plate. The poor guy never had a chance. Our catcher dropped the third one and the guy had to run to first, and you could hear the manager screaming, 'That ought to teach you, you big-mouthed son of a bitch!'"

At the end of the month, the strikeout switch flipped back on again with historic consequences. On Saturday night, August 31, Steve struck out 24 batters, equaling his record-setting high school performance earlier in the year, this time against professional bats. It was also a new record in the Appalachian League for left-handed pitchers, besting the 21 strikeouts by Salem southpaw Mike Sinclair set earlier in the season. When Steve got in trouble in the eighth, loading the bases with two outs, manager Walter Youse moved him to right field and brought in a right-hander to get the out. Dalkowski then returned to the mound in the ninth and got his last three strikeouts. Steve walked 18 during the game and beat Bluefield, 7–5. The Kingsport team's next stop was Salem, Virginia. Youse overheard Felix Pizarro, then the only Latin player on the team, ask his manager, "Hey, Skip, Lefty gonna pitch tonight? If he pitch, *I no play!*"

Dalkowski's final record for his first season as a pro was 1-8 with 115 strikeouts and 129 walks in 63 innings. He established two Appalachian League pitching records in 1957 with 39 wild pitches and 129 walks. Both remain records to this day. "Although he had one of the poorest records in the league," the local press predicted, "left-handed pitcher Steve Dalkowski probably has a better chance of becoming a major leaguer than any other player on the Kingsport squad. Dalkowski has a fastball equal to any in the big leagues, but hasn't been properly introduced to the strike zone yet."

The day before the final Bluefield game, Steve called his parents in New Britain with exciting news. Then as now, the minor league season ended several weeks ahead of the major league wrap-up and the World Series. During this time major league teams are allowed to expand their rosters with promising minor league players to give them a taste of the Show (and a month of major league salary). On the phone, he told his parents he'd heard two weeks earlier that he might get his ticket to Baltimore but waited to tell them until it was a sure thing.

Steve took the train to Baltimore that week, but he didn't pitch in the big leagues. He went for a second intensive coaching session with pitching coach Harry Brecheen and manager Paul Richards. "He's not expected to be given a game assignment this year," reported the *Kingsport Times-News*, "though he may." But he didn't. Bringing a Class D player straight to Baltimore would have been an uncommon move. Records show that no player from Kingsport was called up to the majors that season. However, it raises the question that if Dalkowski was so extraordinary, what would they have had to lose? The Orioles finished fifth in the American League in 1957, 21 games behind the first-place Yankees. The fireballing rookie could scarcely have made things worse. In fact, thirty-five-year Oriole scout Jim Russo later admitted just that. "We should have called him up, say, for an inning or two against one of those Yankee teams that we chased," he said. "Everyone would have paid their way into the park to see those guys stepping in against him!"

What did Steve Dalkowski learn from his first season in professional baseball? What sort of progress had he made as a pitcher as opposed to simply a thrower? Who around him understood that throwing strikes begins in the head, not in the arm? The answers: nothing, none, and nobody. Steve had confirmed that he could throw very hard, that fans and players alike knew of his reputation, and that the strike zone remained lost in some nebulous haze sixty feet, six inches away. He must have at least subconsciously sensed that no one understood the process required to convert him into a pitcher. He must have begun to realize that, no matter how well intentioned those around him might be, he was on his own.

Back in Connecticut that Christmas, Hartford sports editor Frank Cline spoke for Steve's many hometown fans when in his Christmas Day column he wished Steve—along with his old rival Pete Sala and a few other local baseball standouts who had been signed to play in the pros—the gift of a spot on a major league baseball roster in the year ahead.

The Orioles invited Dalkowski to their 1958 major league spring training camp in Scottsdale, Arizona. Whatever hazard he presented on the mound, he had also struck out 24 batters in a single game in Kingsport. He had a raw talent worth developing. Steve left the cold and snow of New England for the Baltimore camp at the end of February and stayed there until mid-April. He had a lot of work to do on his control before he could begin his career in the majors. One of the men watching from the sidelines was Bill Lee, sports editor of the *Hartford Courant*.

By Lee's reckoning, Dalkowski was already ahead of half the pitchers in the major leagues thanks to his blazing fastballs that flew toward batters "with such overpowering swiftness that they look like little white bullets." The best batters respect speed, he wrote, and Steve "has his big league speed right now." Lee continued, "Most of the time the young Connecticut hopeful doesn't know whether the ball is going toward home plate or even over the catcher's head, but when he learns to control his speed, Dalkowski is going to be a very good pitcher indeed."

Lee and other experienced observers thought the young pitcher had an even better chance of making the Baltimore roster than another local boy on the team who had done well—Billy Gardner, who had become one of the top second basemen in the American League. Members of the press also compared notes between Dalkowski and another young Oriole, Dave Nicholson, who landed a $100,000 signing bonus but so far had not delivered the goods. Though they were both struggling on their way up the ladder, Dalkowski seemed to offer the club a lot more promise for a lot less money.

Yet another prospect in the Orioles camp that spring was outfielder Fred Valentine, who went on to a seven-year career in the majors. He would be Dalkowski's teammate in Wilson, North Carolina (1958) and Elmira, New York (1963). Valentine retained a lasting impression of Steve in action with the Orioles squad:

"I guess that everyone in baseball had heard about how hard Steve could throw, and players from all teams came over any time Steve was throwing, even just on the sidelines. Everyone was anxious to see him throw and when he did, no one could believe how hard he threw—*no one!* We all kind of chuckled when it came time to take batting practice against Steve, but no one was very interested in standing in against him because no one could think about hitting. We only thought about how hard he was throwing and ultimately being hit and killed! Whenever Steve pitched, the groundskeepers added another layer of chicken wire to the fence behind home plate because Steve's wild ones had broken through the wire fencing. Today those of us who saw Steve throw consider ourselves lucky. He was the hardest thrower anyone had ever seen. We joked that it took three guys to see his fastball. We saw the fastest ever."

Steve's teammates subjected him to some good-natured teasing about his reputation for wildness that spring in Arizona. Connie Johnson came to the plate for batting practice wearing a complete catcher's getup—mask, chest protector, and shin guards. Coach Eddie Robinson, a former major league player who had faced legendary fastballer Bob Feller, stepped into the batting cage one day to take a few swings. "I've batted against the fastest from Feller on down," he later told a reporter. "I believe this boy is faster. I didn't overpower those fastballers but I did get a pop fly or two. I can't even get the ball out of the batting cage against Steve."

Robinson was signed as a player/coach by the Orioles following his release from the Cleveland Indians the year before. He'd enjoyed a solid career including four All-Star appearances and two World Series (1948 and 1955). His friend Ted Williams called him the most underrated clutch hitter in the American League. Like the rest of the Orioles in Scottsdale that spring, Robinson had heard in advance about the young southpaw wild man from New Britain.

In late 2017, just shy of his ninety-seventh birthday, Eddie Robinson still clearly remembered that season and his impressions of Dalkowski both from a coaching perspective and as a batter facing him at the plate. He didn't recall making the statement quoted by the reporter above, but as a member of the small and shrinking list of living pros who played with Steve, his eyewitness accounts are priceless additions to the historical record.

One of Robinson's key observations is that on the sidelines Dalkowski's control was consistently solid. When there was no pressure, he threw strike after strike. During games however, out there alone on the mound, he got nervous and that's when the wildness took over. Steve's usual pitch was a four-seam fastball, thrown as fast as possible. As Eddie described it, "He had just one pitch, the fastball, and just one approach, throw hard or harder. He'd just rear back and fire."

Robinson estimated he took fifty pitches or so from Steve in practices that season and got several solid hits. He wasn't afraid to face Dalkowski, he said, because Steve never threw inside to him. His wild pitches were way high or way low, not in or out. In one particular spring training game, Robinson remembers Steve coming to the mound in relief. His first pitch hit the dirt five or ten feet in front of the plate, then the second pitch hit the screen twenty feet in the air.

Orioles first baseman Bob Boyd told reporters, "I've never seen anyone throw harder. If only he had control." Overhearing the comment, Steve replied, "Don't worry, I'll get it. I'll work until I do."

Echoing the Hartford sportswriters' pre-season enthusiasm for Dalkowski and his prospects for the majors, encouraging reports from Scottsdale appeared in other papers back East. Writing for the *Baltimore News-Post,* Hugh Trader declared that "the No. 1 pitching prospect in the entire Orioles' chain is a wild lefty named Steve Dalkowski."

A glowing assessment from manager Paul Richards said in part, "[Dalkowski] is another Billy Pierce in potential. [Pierce went on to a distinguished career with seven All-Star appearances and 1,999 strikeouts.] He has as much speed as Billy, maybe more, and he's stronger. He's still wild but he has improved greatly since being in camp with us. . . . He has the inherent ability to be great and eventually make us a pennant contender. Once he has his speed under harness for major control, he wins 20 games each season. . . . They can't hit Dalkowski even now in batting practice when he gets the ball over."

Steve "has the batters moaning," sportswriter Trader continued. "When Richards instructed him to throw the change of pace [change-up] the manager has taught him, it still buzzed in and Joe Ginsberg, the batter, inquired, 'That's a change of pace? Well, don't throw your fastball, kid.'" Here is a rare specific instance of Steve being taught and encouraged to use another pitch. To Ginsberg at least, it didn't seem to slow him down any.

Trader concluded, "Never an overboard optimist, Richards is going to carry the kid [to] the limit. He has fallen in baseball love with him. The skipper actually drools." Richards, always eager to promote from within the system, believed he had a prime candidate for major league stardom in Steve Dalkowski.

That potential was on display later in the spring. After traveling with the team from Scottsdale to Baltimore by rail, Steve got the call to pitch during an exhibition game against Cincinnati in Baltimore's Memorial Stadium on April 13. Taking the mound in the ninth inning, Dalkowski threw his first warmup pitch over the head of catcher Joe Ginsberg. Fans laughed at the sight, but batters waiting to face this young rocket launcher wore solemn expressions. "The most effective pitch the southpaw speedster threw," wrote *Baltimore News-Post* sports editor John F. Steadman, "was the preliminary one which slammed into the screen behind home plate. The Redlegs aren't blind, you know." Batters had their helmets on, but the flimsy protective headgear of the time "would have collapsed like tinfoil if a Dalkowski missile had hit any of them." Had they known Bob Beavers, they could've asked him about that.

When Cincinnati coach Birdie Tebbetts spied Dalkowski heading for the mound, he told his hitters not to stand too close to the plate and threatened to fine any player one hundred dollars who did. With the start of the season just around the corner, he didn't want to risk injury. This was also evidently the day Tebbetts christened Steve's fastball the "radio pitch"—you could hear it, but you couldn't see it.

Dalkowski's first three batters in Memorial Stadium were Alex Grammas, Dee Fondy, and Don Hoak. After seeing Steve warm up, all of them stood with "one foot in the batter's box and the other in the dugout." Steadman noted that the hitters stayed loose, "eager to take leave of home plate and Mr. Dalkowski's unhospitable pitching."

It was three up, three down for the "Connecticut Comet," including a bunt foul from Fondy that sailed into a television booth on the mezzanine, prompting the *Baltimore Sun* to joke that it must have set the record for bunting distance. After two fouls and a miss Grammas said, "I've been playing ball for ten years, and nobody can throw a baseball harder than that." Steve struck out the side on twelve pitches. The exhibition crowd of 7,868 gave him a standing ovation. The last batter, third baseman Hoak, declared, "That kid doesn't throw as hard as Herb Score—he throws harder."

It would be the only time Steve Dalkowski ever pitched in a major league ballpark.

Impressed as everyone was, sports editor Steadman knew that fame was an elusive goal. "Twelve pitches and three strikeouts don't make a career," he wrote the day after Steve's sterling performance in Baltimore. "He still needs work. His delivery and follow-through are awkward. But, actually, when you can blow the ball as hard as he can, the finesse is unimportant." He went on to compare Steve with another promising minor league hurler years before in the Washington Senators system. Joe Krakauskas, who spent seven years with the big club and is best known for giving up the final hit in Joe DiMaggio's fifty-six-game hitting streak, never realized his potential on the mound. He turned completely from baseball to making a living by installing television antennas in Detroit. A cautionary tale to be sure, but no doubt a highly unlikely comparison in the eyes of Paul Richards, a trio of chastened Cincinnati batters, and thousands of adoring Baltimore fans.

SIX

"Make Way for Dalkowski!"

"I have no doubt Dalkowski will be a real star in the big leagues, IF he ever masters control."

—Sportswriter Frank Cline, May 11, 1958

The Kingsport Orioles only survived one year. The team folded before the 1958 season after struggling to fill eight-thousand-seat J. Fred Johnson Park while attracting an average paid attendance in the low hundreds. One of the few reasons the locals had for attending games was to see what sort of antics Steve Dalkowski was up to that night. In the end, even that wasn't enough to keep the team afloat.

Despite Steve's impressive turn on the mound in Baltimore, the Orioles didn't promote Dalkowski to the parent team after Kingsport disbanded. Eddie Robinson believes there were two reasons for that decision. First, Steve couldn't get outs when the pressure was on. To win the game, you have to get outs. Second, in order to add Steve to the Orioles roster, the team had to send someone else down to the minors; there was no one Paul Richards was willing to give up.

For the '58 season Dalkowski found himself on another Tennessee team, the Knoxville Smokies of the South Atlantic League, south of Kingsport along the foothills of the Great Smoky Mountains. He was one of only three players on the previous year's Kingsport team that the Orioles kept on their payroll. The other two, both assigned to Dublin, Georgia, were right-hander Frank Mankovitch and center fielder Ron Zander.

On May 10, Dalkowski struck out 14 and walked 11 in six innings, leading the Smokies to an 8–6 win over Macon. By the end of the month, his record at Knoxville was 1-2. Awe in the face of his fastball and hope that he would eventually make the Show were undiminished. "He's only 18," sportswriter Frank Cline noted, "and if he becomes a Baltimore regular anytime within the next five years the work with him will be well spent. I have no doubt Dalkowski will be a real star in the big leagues, IF he ever masters control."

Manager George Staller set up a wooden target with an open space seven balls wide and eleven balls high, the equivalent of the 1950s strike zone or "Ted Williams strike zone." Staller hoped it would help Dalkowski improve his accuracy and find the plate with greater regularity. Steve demolished the target in less than an hour.

Staller's idea of the target was truly creative. The problem was that it not only failed to address the real problem of Dalkowski's inability to find the strike zone, but it also added to the problem of Steve feeling alone and isolated. Since Staller didn't explain the purpose of the target, Steve approached it the same way he did hitters—throw the ball as hard as possible—with destructive results. Steve needed to relax, previsualize, and sharpen his focus. Throwing hard was easy for him. Throwing the ball over the plate was not. Steve needed a process that he could understand and follow: Throw strikes. Throw balls to a part of the strike zone. Simply prevent 100 percent on-time contact and allow the team to help you. Sandy Koufax pegged the secret to successful pitching when he said, "I became a pitcher when I stopped trying to make them miss the ball and started trying to make them hit it."

Throwing strikes is a two-part process, and the physical piece is number *two*. Of course a pitcher needs a repeatable delivery, but step one occurs in the pitcher's head before he throws. He must decide what pitch to throw, where to throw it, then have the conviction to throw it there. When all of this happens, the odds of throwing a strike are greatly increased. It takes belief and trust to achieve the necessary result: conviction plus execution. Dalkowski probably never thought about any of this. He simply threw every pitch as hard as possible.

After Steve's third start of the season, Staller called Orioles manager Paul Richards to say Dalkowski was doing a good job using his off-speed stuff to set up his fastball. "Man, how I'd love to peel the cellophane off that guy in Baltimore next year!" Richards told reporters.

Early in 1958, middle infielder Frank Kostro was playing for the Augusta (Detroit) Tigers in the South Atlantic League. Kostro, who went on to a seven-year career in the majors, provided a firsthand account of facing Steve Dalkowski:

"Everyone in the league knew about the hardest throwers, and hitters kept track of them. But Dalkowski had a reputation that made him stand alone. There were hard throwers, and then there was Dalkowski. Dalkowski wasn't just fast; he was dangerous when you consider his lack of control. We were leading the league when we played the Knoxville Smokies. Dalkowski was doing what he was known for, throwing the ball hard—harder than I had ever seen a baseball thrown. My at-bat started with a fastball over the catcher and umpire hitting fifteen feet up on the screen, followed by a forty-five-foot fastball in the dirt raising a cloud of dust in front of home plate as it whistled in. That is the last thing I remember, as Dalkowski had shifted my focus from that of a hitter to that of a survivor. The next thing I remember was hearing the umpire call, 'Ball four!' and I was on my way to first base. Dalkowski was throwing well over one hundred mph, period! Everyone who ever faced Steve was thankful he was wild up and down rather than in and out. If he had been wild in and out there would have been dead guys everywhere."

It was during Steve's brief six-week career in Knoxville that the Orioles decided to try and answer the question of how fast his fastball really was. In the days before radar guns, there was no accurate way to measure the speed of a pitch. Walter Johnson and Bob Feller had each pitched alongside a speeding motorcycle, with the speeds of their throws calculated from the cycle's speedometer reading. Based on those tests, Baseball's National Pastime Museum estimates Johnson's pitch would be equivalent to 97 mph and Feller's to 104 mph using today's best technology.

On August 20, 1946, Feller tested his pitch again at Griffith Stadium in Washington, DC, before a game against the Senators, this time by throwing a pitch into a frame holding a pair of photoelectric cells. By measuring the time it took the ball to travel between cells, engineers could calculate the pitch speed. According to the machine, Feller's pitch was 98.6 mph at home plate. Since today's pitch speeds are measured ten feet from the mound, that converts to about 103 mph, consistent with Feller's pitch alongside a speeding motorcycle, which had been timed in the summer of 1940.

Paul Richards and Harry Brecheen wanted to know how fast their promising young southpaw was throwing the horsehide. How did he compare with these two historic hurlers? To find out, they arranged an experiment at the Aberdeen Proving Ground, a military testing facility in Maryland. The army had a range of equipment there to measure the performance of weapons they were developing. The idea was that these devices could be used to measure the speed of Dalkowski's fastball.

Later accounts of the pitching test consistently claim that Dalkowski pitched from flat ground, probably in street shoes, that he took thirty or forty-five minutes to hit the required target, and that his speed was either 93.5 or 98.6 mph depending on the source. All of these statements are incorrect, more examples of the fantasies that have worked their way into the Dalkowski legend.

The test at the Aberdeen Proving Ground took place on Thursday, June 5, 1958, two days after Steve's nineteenth birthday. The Associated Press account was published in the *Hartford Courant* on June 7 with the headline, "Steve Dalkowski Throws Pitches at 85.8 M.P.H." Despite this disappointing number (Steve was widely supposed to be above 100 mph), the article read enthusiastically:

"Steve Dalkowski, young Knoxville pitcher, has positive proof he has a fastball. He's got the U.S. Army to back him up. Thursday the nineteen-year-old hurler took the mound at this Army post's ball field and began tossing warm-up pitches to Joe Ginsberg, Baltimore Orioles catcher. In front of home plate, some Army technicians set up two timing gadgets and checked them out.

"After Dalkowski's arm was warm, he began throwing the fastball that has had Sally [South Atlantic] League batters talking to themselves. The ball was timed at 130 feet per second—or 85.8 m.p.h.—as it zipped across home plate. . . .

"'Steve's got a real live arm,' Ginsberg said later, rubbing his reddened glove hand. 'His ball really moves and always has something on it.'

"Harry Brecheen, the Orioles' pitching coach who went along to watch, just grinned a chessie-cat grin."

In his 2008 book *Beating About the Bushes: Minor League Baseball in the '60s,* former minor league player Tim Sommer gives Dalkowski credit for an expanded version of the story. In this account, Steve said that manager Earl Weaver met a retired army general at the American Legion in York, Pennsylvania, who arranged for the test the next morning using newly developed laser technology and ordered technicians at the base to put together a timing device. Dalkowski was staying in York and was rousted from his hotel bed—still hung over from carousing the previous night after pitching a game—to come to the lobby for a trip to Maryland. According to Sommer, Steve said the army had made a small target out of pine for him to pitch at. After pitching for thirty minutes in his street shoes (no one thought to bring spikes) he failed to find the target and had badly splintered the wood.

Whether Earl Weaver arranged the test with help from a retired general remains a mystery. But we do know the details about the test itself from an article by Frank Cashen with photos by James Kelmartin published June 6, the day after the test, in the *Baltimore News-Post*.

According to Cashen's report, Dalkowski, Orioles catcher Joe Ginsberg, and pitching coach Harry Brecheen arrived for the test at the baseball diamond on the base's athletic field. Steve and Joe were both in full uniform including cleats. As Steve warmed up, Brecheen repeatedly warned him "not to work so fast." The trio met John Bedwell, the engineer who conducted the test, and Frank Hutchins, chief of the Velocity Measurements Section at Aberdeen.

An army panel truck was parked off to the first-base side of the infield between home plate and the mound. The truck housed the electronic brains of a machine called a sky screen, designed to measure the velocity of artillery shells. Two remote sensors were connected to the truck by cables. Each sensor was a cube eighteen inches or so on a side, and they were placed on the ground a few feet from each other between the mound and the plate. The sensors "read" natural skylight through openings in their tops. An object—baseball or artillery shell— registered with each sensor as it passed overhead. Knowing the distance separating the sensors and measuring the time lapse between the object being over one sensor and then the other, the sky screen could calculate the speed of the object.

There was no target other than Ginsberg's glove. Dalkowski pitched from a mound like always. All he had to do was throw the baseball over the sensors. The machine calculated Steve's pitch speed at 130 feet per second, or 85.8 miles per hour. Yet Joe Ginsberg, starting his tenth season in the major leagues, got a red hand from those pitches, raising the question of how accurate the reading was. As Cashen reported, the catcher "took time out to rest his hand which was feeling the sting of Dalkowski's fastballs." It seems unlikely that an 85 mph fastball would give a pro catcher a sore hand.

Years later Dalkowski told his wife that the army didn't actually know how fast his pitch was. This seems right. The two army technicians that day admitted their reading could be wrong because "bright sunlight often affects the machine" and "the trial could be more advantageously staged early in the morning or late in the evening when the sun was not as intense." Cleveland's Bob Feller and Atley Donald of the Yankees had both registered faster times with the sky screen, but, Cashen noted, "that was when both were in their major league primes. And both of those experiments took place in major league parks. Feller holds the all-time record, one of his pitches having been caught at 98.6 miles per hour."

The perplexing truth is that no reliable measurement of Dalkowski's pitching speed is known to exist. This is true of the Aberdeen Proving Ground measurement, which is the only direct measurement of his pitching speed that was ever even attempted and that seems certain to have vastly underestimated Dalkowski's pitching speed. But the absence of indirect measurement through film or video is even more stark. None is known to exist.

Though military tests at the Aberdeen Proving Ground were routinely filmed, no film of Dalko's pitching has surfaced. Major League teams regularly filmed their outstanding prospects during spring training. The Orioles took movies of a host of young pitchers during the twentieth century, but evidently not of Dalkowski. Minor league fans in the stands and on the sidelines shot home movies, and local television stations produced features on up-and-coming players in the minors, but whatever record existed of Dalkowski's pitching motion other than occasional press photos has not survived.

How the greatest arm in history could have escaped being captured in motion seems inexplicable. Yet the effacing effects of time have worked their magic in scrubbing any video of Dalkowski. In some cases, such as the Elmira, New York, flood of 1972, natural disasters later wiped out an entire historical record. As videotape replaced film in the 1970s and '80s, small market TV stations threw out film by the truckload. It's likely that any surviving footage of Dalkowski on the mound has ended up in an attic or basement where nobody will ever recognize its significance and from which it will end up in a landfill.

In any case, the low—and presumably incorrect—pitching speed recorded in Maryland at the Aberdeen Proving Ground did nothing to dispel the Dalkowski mystique in the spring of 1958. As the Baltimore paper gushed, "Move over Sputnik and Vanguard and make way for Dalkowski!" Sputnik and Vanguard were satellites that had recently been rocketed into space. Now there was a new rocket launcher on the scene.

Following the test in Maryland, Dalkowski stayed on in Baltimore for two weeks of one-on-one coaching with Harry Brecheen, similar to the treatment he received the summer before. Yet whatever Brecheen and his colleagues saw during those sessions convinced them to transfer, and thereby demote, Steve from Knoxville, an A-Class team, down to the Wilson (North Carolina) Tobacconists in the Class B Carolina League.

With a population of about twenty-five thousand residents, Wilson was roughly the same size as Knoxville, east of the Appalachians in the heart of America's tobacco country. To make room for the new pitcher on the roster, the Orioles sent southpaw Ted Denney to their Class C team in Aberdeen, South Dakota, and released right-hander Kedy Curl. In announcing Steve's arrival, the *Wilson Daily Times* reported, "Baltimore officials . . . have been giving Dalkowski special training for the past two weeks."

Encouraged by accounts of Steve's fireballing speed and eager to show off his newest acquisition, "Tobs" manager Bob Hooper started Dalkowski the same day he arrived in town on June 16. His debut in a

4–3 win over the Durham Bulls was "highly impressive" according to the local press despite his being relieved in the fourth inning. He struck out six batters in the first three innings but walked the first three he faced in the fourth, then walked in a run later in the inning.

Steve's pitching amazed the fans. They arrived eager for more fastball fireworks in his second start on June 20. The game began with Dalkowski in complete control. Then in the second inning he walked the bases full, allowed a run on a wild pitch, walked the next batter to fill the bases again, and was duly relieved.

Pitching in relief the next night, Steve showed more promise in hanging on to his control. In 2⅓ innings against Raleigh he struck out two, walked one, hit a batter, and didn't allow a hit. The improvement was short-lived. On June 24 Steve recorded his first loss with the Tobs, 6–2, against the Danville (Virginia) Leafs. After a respectable first inning, he walked four to force in a run in the second, then gave up a bases-loaded double that scored two more. The next night he walked in three runs in an 8–4 loss. On June 30 he struck out seven batters in 2⅔ innings but was sent to the showers because of his five walks.

Jack Fisher, signed by the Orioles the year before along with Dalkowski, played with Steve in Knoxville and Wilson during the 1958 season and roomed with him and two other players when they both pitched for the Tobs. He noticed the same thing about Steve that Eddie Robinson saw during spring training. Warming up before a game or in the bullpen, Steve fired one strike after another. There were no lights in the bullpen, which made it hard to see the blazing fastballs that Jack was convinced flew at more than 100 mph. But when Steve got in a game, "all bets were off." Steve's fastball "definitely rose," Fisher added, sometimes sailing over the catcher's head. Fisher believed, as Robinson had, that Steve's problem was nerves. Following an inevitably impressive warmup, he seemed to get "anxious, overexcited, and nervous" on the mound and then his control disappeared. Jack saw that Steve had a "very good 2–7 curveball but never used it. He wanted to throw hard."

The two young pitchers became friends. They talked about home and family, though Jack noticed Steve never mentioned his father. Steve bragged about drinking in high school and breaking into a liquor store in New Britain. Yet Jack said later that he never saw Steve take a drink the whole time they played together. Even though Steve was always broke, Jack didn't think he spent his money on alcohol. "Maybe he snuck it," Fisher acknowledged, "but it would be hard to believe he could keep it completely hidden from his roommates." (The next year, Fisher moved up to Baltimore, where he began a solid eleven-year career in the majors.)

The Carolina League announced its 1958 All-Star Game lineup on July 3. The two lefties chosen for the Tobs' divisional squad were Steve Hamilton and Bill Short. Managers considered Dalkowski but passed him over because of his unpredictable control. An All-Star appearance would either be a triumph or a disaster. No one had any idea which.

On July 15, one day short of a month after Dalkowski arrived in Wilson, the team announced that he and rookie infielder Jim Dunlap were headed to Aberdeen, North Dakota, a further demotion to the Class C Northern League, to make room on the Tobs roster for outfielder Bob Nelson and shortstop Rudy Figueros. Aberdeen was a radical change from Steve's previous assignments in the Southeast. It was bleak and barren compared to the Carolina Piedmont and flat as a table, with temperatures even in July dipping into the fifties.

His first day on the practice field in Aberdeen, Steve was assigned by manager Billy DeMars to pitch batting practice. Steve took the mound and DeMars himself stepped into the batting cage. "He threw a couple right on past me," DeMars recalled, "and I got the hell out of there. I had already played for fifteen years—there was no sense getting killed."

Again Steve had little time to adjust to his new surroundings. On July 18, three days after his move was announced, he took to the mound for the Aberdeen Pheasants. Again his reputation preceded him, both among the fans and with the players. The "new fire-balling left-hander" and "outstanding young hurler" made his debut in the fourth inning of the second game of a doubleheader against the St. Cloud (Minnesota) Rox. The *Aberdeen American-News* reported that Steve had not pitched in two weeks. (His stats did not reflect a mound appearance in a forfeited game on July 11. The Tobs lost that game by forfeit when manager Bob Hooper told umpire Hank Feimster he had run out of pitchers. Later the ump admitted he had made the wrong call and should have allowed Wilson to let a player re-enter the lineup.) Regardless of any cobwebs, Dalkowski pitched three-plus innings of the 9–3 loss on July 18, with nine strikeouts and two hits. True to form, he walked eight.

The game that night gave fans a rare sight—a batter batting out of order in a professional game. Dalkowski worked through the batting order a second time to St. Cloud's catcher, Gene Belcher. But instead of Belcher, Larry Stubing stepped into the batter's box. The crowd yelled that the wrong batter was up even though the mistake would favor the home team. If Stubing completed his at-bat out of order, Aberdeen could appeal and Belcher would automatically be out. Any play resulting from Stubing's plate appearance would be nullified. But the umpire couldn't act until Stubing's turn at bat was over. Aberdeen manager Billy DeMars held his fire.

Both Belcher and Stubing had faced Dalkowski's ferocious fastball once already. Belcher refused to face it again. Stubing wanted another shot, so he batted in Belcher's place. He struck out.

Watching him in his first appearance for Aberdeen, DeMars was amazed at Dalkowski's spare, no-windup windup. To him it looked like Steve never took his foot off the pitching rubber. "Essentially, he had no follow-through," he later recalled. "It was unbelievable when you think about it. He was throwing 100 mph with his arm alone." He told the young hurler he was going to yell at him from the bench to "let it go" every time he failed to follow through. DeMars kept working with him, kept building his confidence. The coach noticed that when they played catch, Dalkowski threw one perfect pitch after another "because his foot was coming off the rubber. So I told him, 'Next time you pitch, just think about having your back foot come over the top and down.'"

According to DeMars, in Steve's next start (though this might have actually been a later game) he walked only five batters and struck out 20. With a whoop of joy, the young pitcher threw his glove "seventy-five feet in the air." Dalkowski and DeMars had their picture taken together for the local paper, with DeMars quoted as saying, probably for the first time anywhere in print, that Dalkowski was the fastest pitcher he'd ever seen.

DeMars's comment that Dalkowski "had no follow-through" is echoed by others. This meant that Steve did not deliver the potential energy from his backside and bring the left leg forward. At the moment that he released the ball, his left foot should have come off the ground and come forward. At the same time, there are photos of him showing that, after releasing the ball, his left hand was almost on the ground. Dalkowski said that he hit his right knee with his left arm so often he put a pad in his uniform to soften the blow. Getting an accurate description of his pitching mechanics is another elusive mystery in the Dalkowski legend.

DeMars's coaching is a perfect example of the process Steve went through again and again both as a pitcher and as a person. With every passing season, even every passing game, Steve wanted the solution to his control problem and hoped that someone would finally lead him to it. In this case, DeMars identified a factor he believed would solve Dalkowski's wildness. Steve bought in and did it for one game. Perhaps because he had something to focus on, which in turn silenced his negative self-talk, his performance improved. But because the real issues of a repeatable delivery and a positive mental process were not addressed and put in harmony, the demons and wildness reappeared immediately, leaving Steve even more adrift.

Certainly DeMars, Brecheen, Richards, and others meant well. But as mental skills trainers and pitching coaches, they simply didn't have the tools or understanding to help Steve in dealing with the obstacles that confronted him. In today's game, no expense would be spared to find specialists that could help Dalko realize his incredible potential.

Steve continued his erratic performances, laboring inning after inning, racking up the strikeouts and bases on balls in almost equal numbers. On July 22, over five-plus innings, he struck out 12 and walked 17. On July 27 he struck out the first 10 batters he faced, but gave up 12 walks and nine runs in 6⅓ innings for a loss. His first win of the year came on July 31 in another cliffhanger. In the top of the first he walked three in a row, then struck out the next three. He struck out 17 and walked 14, throwing enough pitches for a doubleheader in a 6–3 win over the Duluth-Superior Twin Sox.

Dalkowski's start on August 5 was one of his shakiest. The St. Cloud opponents batted around in the first inning, including two walks followed by a three-run homer and a hit batsman. Steve then gave up two more walks and two runs in the third, followed by a solo home run in the fourth. Harry Guckert took over the mound in the fifth. By mid-August Dalkowski had pitched only 32 innings, the fewest of any pitcher on the team, tallying 68 walks, 68 strikeouts, and 15 hits allowed to go with a 1–2 record.

Steve's wildness remained not so much in and out as up and down, especially up. Yet even when under control, his fastball seemed to rise. Though a baseball rising in flight would defy the laws of physics, batters, catchers, and umpires almost universally claimed that Steve's ball rose as it traveled toward the plate. No less an authority than Hall of Fame manager Walter Alston insisted that "the good rising fastball is the best pitch in baseball."

(Then and now, physics experts insist that a baseball cannot rise no matter how many players claim otherwise. In *The Physics of Baseball*, Dr. Robert K. Adair, Sterling Professor Emeritus at Yale and a member of the National Academy of Sciences, notes that a 90-mph fastball "must fall almost three feet on its way to the plate if there is no hop" so that the effect of any backspin "must be such as to 'curve' the ball upward about three feet if the ball is to rise. . . . But who has ever seen a fastball curve three feet?" In conclusion he states, "Therefore, overhand fastballs certainly do not rise, and our calculations are not likely to be wildly wrong.")

DeMars in Aberdeen, along with Paul Richards and Harry Brecheen in Baltimore, had tried for nearly two years to unlock the secret of Steve Dalkowski's control. Even three individual coaching sessions in Baltimore with Brecheen and two months of spring training in Arizona had failed to solve the problem. Maybe he was so nervous that when his confidence wavered, his mechanics fell apart. Maybe it was something about his unorthodox form—sometimes described as whipping motion with little leg kick or the usual body motion—that kept him from throwing the ball where he wanted it to go.

Or maybe he just couldn't see.

On Wednesday, August 20, 1958, Steve pitched for the first time wearing glasses, correcting vision that was 20/60 in one eye and 20/80 in the other. (Eventually, he would have three pairs: one for sun, a yellow-tinted pair for cloudy conditions, and a third for playing under the lights.) The result was phenomenal: an eleven-inning complete game and a 2–1 win. He struck out 20 batters, one short of the league record, giving up only five walks and three hits. For more than six innings in the middle of the game he didn't walk anybody. It was a triumph. Four days later, more than a thousand fans came out to see him pitch a three-hit victory over the Winnipeg Goldeneyes. He struck out 17 to great applause and walked 13 to no great concern. Contrary to the all-too-familiar pattern of starting out strong and coming apart in later innings, Steve started strong and finished stronger, pitching no-hit baseball after the fourth inning.

The last game of the season showed a hint of Steve's old wildness. In the second inning, he walked five batters and hit another. He was overshadowed in that contest against St. Cloud by pitcher Gaylord Perry (a $90,000 bonus baby that year, future 300-game winner, and two-time Cy Young recipient), who took the mound for the Rox with two on and no outs in the eighth and retired six batters in a row for a 3–1 victory.

Maybe Steve's wildness wasn't completely tamed. The good news was that the old unhappy trend seemed to have reversed itself. The graph line was now headed in the right direction. Twenty strikeouts with five walks had given the Orioles management hope that their investment in Steve Dalkowski was about to turn the corner. As far as the Aberdeen Pheasants were concerned, the gamble had already paid off. When Steve had arrived in town in July, the Orioles also sent cash to cover the team's payroll. In the history of the club they had never broken even. Young Steve couldn't be confirmed as the only reason for their newfound success, but he was without a doubt a key component: in 1958, for the first time in franchise history, the Pheasants earned a profit.

SEVEN

Strikeout Sensation

"He has the best fastball of any pitcher I've ever had."
—George Staller, Baltimore farm system manager, spring training 1959

With a name like Dalkowski and a fastball like a bullet, it was inevitable that Steve would pick up nicknames. "Dal," "Ski," and "Dalko" were some of the handles his teammates and the sports press gave him. Dalko had already covered a lot of ground in his short career. In his first year as a pro, he went straight to his inaugural assignment days after graduation from high school. In his second year he was invited to the Orioles major league training camp in Arizona, where coaches and managers decided he needed more seasoning. Despite his continued wildness, in their eyes he improved enough to move all the way up from Class D Kingsport to the Class A Knoxville Smokies. As the season played out, however, he was sent back down to the Class B Wilson Tobacconists and ended the year with the Class C Aberdeen Pheasants.

As the 1959 season got under way, Orioles manager Paul Richards, farm system manager George Staller, and the rest of the Orioles brain trust again invited Dalko to spring training, this time at the team's new complex in Miami. After a workout and drills with the team on February 28, Richards took Dalkowski aside for some one-on-one instruction. As Richards explained, "Steve's falling so far forward now before he lets the ball loose that he's all tangled up and has no idea where his pitches are going." The manager's cure was to condition Dalkowski to let his arm "pull his body into a natural follow-through." Again this didn't match other descriptions or photos of his "short arm" delivery. Even the experts seemed to see different things when they watched Dalko in action.

At nineteen years of age, Steve had already been a pitching star for at least six years, starting when he was a Junior All-Star in his New Britain industrial league as an eighth grader in 1953. For all those years everyone kept saying, "Get the ball down! Get the ball down!" The laws of physics notwithstanding, one eyewitness after another described a ball with such incredible speed and backspin that it rose after it left Steve's hand. Future teammate (and future Baseball Hall of Fame MLB general manager) Pat Gillick would say the ball rose like a rocket as it neared the plate, adding, "If you told him to aim the ball at home plate, that ball would cross the plate at the batter's shoulders. That was because of the tremendous backspin he could put on the ball." Another future teammate, Frank Zupo, would observe, "Steve was very lucky he was wild up and down, and not in and out. If he was in and out, he would have needed a license to kill. He hit Carl Warwick one night in Macon, Georgia, and broke his arm."

Here we have another example of the Dalkowski legend spinning out of hand to Paul Bunyan proportions. In a 2018 interview, Carl Warwick emphatically stated that Dalkowski did not hit him or anyone else on the Macon Dodger squad that season. "And," he added, "I will tell you he certainly did not break my arm, though he had our team's complete attention!"

Dalkowski's fastball might go anywhere. One day in Miami, Dalkowski threw a pitch that missed the backstop entirely and hit a fan in the stands in line to buy a hot dog. The fan had Dalko autograph the ball.

Steve's arm strength was incredible. Teammate Jack Fisher saw him throw wild pitches through a double chicken wire backstop numerous times. Once he watched Dalko hurl a ball from the mound "over the center field fence with plenty of room to spare." Determined to calm him down, manager Paul Richards had Steve "throw all out every day for seven or eight days." It made no difference. Dalkowski "still entered the game with a fresh arm throwing gas."

To Steve's credit, he never got tired of coaches trying different techniques to improve his control. He was eager to please, eager to do well, always ready to learn. He kept himself in top shape pitching, working out, running wind sprints. His professional record so far was an unimpressive 4-15. The previous season he had walked 121 batters in 62 innings. None of it seemed to dim Steve's love of the game or his determination to master his control troubles. If only someone could have gotten Steve to follow Bob Gibson's lead. "My philosophy is simple," Gibson explained. "I believe in getting the ball over the plate and not walking a lot of men." Dalkowski would have done well to heed what Orioles coach Ray Miller preached to all pitchers: "The first thing we tell our new pitchers is that now they have eight guys on their side. If they will make the other team hit the ball, we'll catch it for them. Avoid walks, avoid home runs, and let the fielders do the work."

Steve must have had a haunting realization that he might fall far short of his own dream. There was no shortage of frustrating circumstances: his inconsistency on the mound, his two-walks-per-inning average, his listening to coaches whose efforts didn't produce results everyone hoped for, his peers getting their chance to pitch with the big club, his special treatment that sometimes made him feel more like a freak than a valued teammate. Whether Steve consciously recognized it or not—and he probably did not—he was suffering alone. There was no one he could count on, no one he could turn to. Players who suffer alone can too often attempt to replace that loneliness with substances or with people who lead them in the wrong direction.

Sportswriter Luther Evans spoke for many when he took the measure of Dalkowski's future promise: "If Dalkowski could learn to get his tremendous fastball across the plate, he'd probably soon have his pick of Thunderbirds or Jaguars or Ferraris [a reference to the recent gift of a new T-bird from the Orioles to nineteen-year-old pitcher Milt Pappas, who'd won 10 games his first year in the majors]. George Staller, who manages in Baltimore's farm system, says unequivocally: 'He has the best fastball of any pitcher I've ever had. No one hits him when he throws strikes.'"

Orioles road secretary John Lancaster gave the *Hartford Courant*'s Bill Lee a similar comment, adding that, after three weeks in Florida, Dalkowski looked much improved over the same time last spring. "Some baseball men think he is the fastest pitcher they have ever seen," Lancaster said. At the end of March Steve pitched two innings against the Athletics in a 10-inning, 4–3 exhibition victory. He walked three and struck out one.

Based on what they saw in spring training, the Orioles decided to send Steve back to the Class C Aberdeen Pheasants. At least for the time being, his slide down the minor league ladder was halted. In what would turn out to be a major career milestone for Dalko, manager Billy DeMars was transferred to Stockton, California, to manage the Ports of the California League. His replacement was Earl Weaver. Signed at age seventeen by the St. Louis Cardinals, Weaver labored as a player for nine years in the minor leagues before starting his managing career in 1956. He joined the Orioles organization a year later as a player/manager and managed two minor league clubs in Georgia ahead of his move to Aberdeen.

Weaver saw a lot of himself in Dalkowski. They both loved the game as schoolboys. Weaver's father ran a laundry in St. Louis that cleaned uniforms for the major league Browns and the minor league Cardinals. Earl started hanging around the ballpark at the age of six. Both Steve and Earl were signed at an early age. They both loved the game as pros and poured themselves into it. They both came up short of major league standards time and again in spite of their dedication. By the time the two found themselves on the same team in the spring of 1959, Weaver's dream of a career as a player in the major leagues had faded, yet was still recent enough that the memory of it was fresh. He knew how Dalkowski felt about struggling year after year without quite making the grade. He knew how hard Steve worked and how eager he was to please. Like everybody else, Weaver could see the monumental potential in Dalko's famous fastball. Weaver's special attention to the young player, along with his exemplary ability as a teacher, would coax Dalkowski toward greatness where others had failed.

Steve and Earl began an association, perhaps even a friendship, that would endure through the remainder of Dalkowski's career. Weaver would be his manager, mentor, and coach in 1959, 1962, 1963, and 1964. If ever a guy needed someone he could trust and have confidence in, it was Steve. Weaver might have slipped into that role better than anyone else in Steve's life ever had. Steve had trusted his dad, who took him to bars. He trusted his older friends in high school, who encouraged him to drink. He trusted coaches and other well-wishers to have answers and know what they were doing. Now he was trusting pro baseball to help solve the problems that plagued him both on and off the field (though there was little or no effective help for players with off-the-field issues during the 1950s and 60—in particular, enforcement for such violations as breaking curfews, drinking, and carousing was often lax). Yet coaches always seemed to have him doing something freakish on the sidelines that only heightened his insecurity. Ultimately, even though some of these men had the best of intentions, Steve's trust was misplaced time and again, year after year. No one really knew how to help. No one had his back.

Though Steve and others later credited Weaver as Steve's best pitching coach bar none, Weaver himself knew little about pitching, "and what he did know was mostly wrong," according to the great Jim Palmer, six-time All-Star and Hall of Fame right-hander who later played under Weaver at the MLB level, adding, "Earl couldn't coach pitchers, but he could find them." Weaver himself said recognizing ability was his strong suit. In young Dalkowski, he had found a pitcher with rare ability that he was convinced he could nurture and develop.

Heralded as the "strikeout sensation of the 1958 Northern League baseball season," Steve played his first preseason game of the new year at the Orioles' Thomasville, Georgia, minor league camp to promising reviews. He seemed to pitch as fast as ever, but his control was generally improved. He threw the first four innings of a 6–0 win, giving up one hit and five walks with seven strikeouts. Weaver commented wryly to the press, "I think his control is getting better. He never hit the backstop once."

In two more appearances he pitched a total of seventeen consecutive scoreless innings before the Pensacola Dons ended the streak with a 7–4 win on April 20. By April 26, Steve had finished out the spring preseason schedule and arrived in Aberdeen. He made his 1959 season debut on May 4 with an impressive victory over the Duluth-Superior Twinsox. After walking the first three batters, he found his rhythm, striking out 10 in the first four innings. Fans thought he might set a new league strikeout record, but the pace slowed after he started to tire later in the game. He struck out 15 in all and walked 14 with only two hits through seven innings, backed with superb offensive play that ran the score to 15–2 by the time he left the mound, including three homers that netted a total of nine runs. Reliever Gene Walker gave up five runs to the Twinsox.

By the middle of May the Pheasants had won 11 league games in a row. Attendance was up sharply over the year before. For the game against the Grand Forks (North Dakota) Chiefs on Sunday night,

May 17, almost sixteen hundred fans paid to watch Steve Dalkowski in action. Win or lose, he would definitely put on a show worth the price of a ticket.

Dalko got off to an unpromising start. He walked the first batter, who took second courtesy of a wild pitch. He also walked the second batter. Both runners advanced on a sacrifice fly. Then with one out and runners on second and third, he struck out two in a row. In the second inning, after the leadoff batter reached first base on a fielding error, Steve struck out three in a row. Two more Chiefs struck out in the third, one walked, and one flew out to center. Dalko fanned three in a row in the fourth and one in the top of the fifth, followed by a walk, a pop out, and a ground out.

Chiefs pitcher John Pregenzer, who wasn't in the lineup that night, had heard all the stories about Dalko. Everyone on the team stopped to watch him warm up before the game. Now everybody stood in the dugout with their eyes riveted on the mound. "It was amazing to watch," Pregenzer said, adding that it was the hardest he'd ever seen anybody throw in his life. "He could f----ing bring it!" Pregenzer exclaimed. He moved to the first-base coaching box to get a better look. Dalkowski threw an incredible rising fastball, a four-seamer straight over the top. Batters came back to the dugout muttering about "the ugly noise the ball made going by."

Two other Grand Forks pitchers on the sidelines that night were equally impressed. Jim Dickson remembered that the night before, Aberdeen manager Earl Weaver had Dalko throw batting practice to the whole team and then pitch in the bullpen for six innings in hopes of tiring him out (and maybe settling him down). "He sort of short-armed the ball," Dickson said.

Jim also recounted a story from a year earlier when Steve pitched to Donn Clendenon, a future twelve-year major league veteran who was a member of the 1969 "Miracle Mets." Dalkowski fired two lethal fastballs right by an amazed Clendenon for strikes. Then Clendenon muttered, "What the f--- was that?!" Dalkowski yelled in to a terrified Clendenon, "Hang in there. I got a curve ball for you." Dalkowski reared back and threw an 0-2 knee buckler at Clendenon for strike three. Clendenon quickly and eagerly retreated to the dugout. As Jim concluded, "God, he could throw hard."

The other pitcher watching in amazement from the sidelines in Grand Forks was Steve's old high school crosstown rival Pete Sala, also on the Chiefs roster. It was Sala who'd spread the word to his teammates about Dalkowski's legendary speed and wildness. After he told his Dalko tales in the clubhouse before the game, there was some joking and guffaws, but it got awfully quiet a little later when they saw Steve firing one bullet after another toward the plate.

In the sixth inning Steve gave up a walk and a groundout to shortstop, and struck out two others. As the Pheasants batted in the sixth, catcher Jim Caldwell was hit on the elbow by a pitch, causing a serious bruise that took him out of the game. Danny Bishop replaced Caldwell behind the plate at the top of the seventh. The change made no difference to Dalkowski, who worked equally well with both catchers.

In the meantime, the Pheasants had scored four runs in the third, including homers by first baseman Bill Rozich and third baseman Jim Burton. Steve realized that not only did he have a comfortable lead at the top of the seventh inning, he had a no-hitter going as well. He had only thrown one curveball so far, to Chiefs pitcher Jim Little, and had almost hit him. He didn't throw another one that game. It's likely that Steve, mindful of the power of his pitches and remembering the young batter he had hit in the head two years before, shied away from curves and other off-speed deliveries because he was afraid of hurting someone again.

Gene "Stick" Michael was also in the lineup that night. Michael would go on spend ten years in the big leagues as a player before managing the New York Yankees, eventually to become Yankees GM. Recalling the game, he said, "Steve was really on that night and was lighting up the strike zone exclusively with four-seam fastballs. He was merciless on me and gave me an uncomfortable 0-4 on just twelve pitches. I swung at about half of them but never got the bat on the ball. Each time the ball hit the catcher's glove, it sounded like thunder. This was my first year in pro ball, and I had never seen anyone throw this hard. In the rest of my career I never saw anyone throw harder."

The realization that he had a no-hitter in the works made Steve a little shaky, he said later, but it didn't show in his performance. In the seventh, he walked two and struck out three. The first batter in the eighth, left fielder Ray Murawski, had played with Dalkowski the year before. With two strikes against him, he connected solidly with the next pitch and sent it into short right field. Aberdeen's right fielder, Dave Nicholson, sprinted toward the infield, made a diving catch, and came up with the ball. The next two batters struck out. The Pheasants added a run in the seventh and another in the eighth.

Aberdeen led 6–0 going into the top of the ninth. The fans were electrified with excitement at the thought of seeing their own "strikeout sensation" pull off a no-hitter. The first Twinsox batter stepped into the box. Dalko struck him out. Second batter, strikeout number two. As 1,590 fans held their breaths, the third batter took his place at the plate. Strikeout number three.

The stands exploded with cheers and applause. No one who was there that night would ever forget it. Steve Dalkowski had just pitched the first Northern League no-hitter ever played in Aberdeen. He also tied the all-time league strikeout record of 21, last seen exactly twenty years earlier, on May 17, 1939.

It was the first no-hitter of Steve's professional career and Earl Weaver's first no-hit victory as a manager. Weaver called it a great performance. Next day's Aberdeen *American-News* splashed its sports section headline across eight columns: "Dalkowski Whiffs 21 In No-Hit Triumph." He had struck out every opposing player except leadoff batter Felix Pizzaro, who walked three times. He struck out two batters four times each, walked eight, and in contrast to some of his games that stretched into four-hour marathons, had wrapped this one up in a reasonable two hours and forty-five minutes. Aberdeen sports editor Larry Desautels called the performance "the best of Dalkowski's career."

Branch Rickey, Jr., vice president and farm system director for the Pittsburgh Pirates organization, was in the crowd that night and came into the clubhouse to talk to the Grand Forks Chiefs after the game. "Boys," he declared, "the way he was throwing tonight, he would have no-hit the Big Club. Remember, we have Groat, Big Klu, Maz, Smokey, and Bobby. So, don't worry." He reached into his wallet, pulled out a wad of cash, and gave it to manager James Adlam to buy the team a couple of cases of beer.

EIGHT

Drinks and Debts

"Steve's there, and he says, 'Hey guys, come over and look at this beautiful sight'—twenty-four scotch and waters lined up in front of him. And he was pitching the next day."
    —Steve Barber, Dalkowski teammate and future Orioles pitching star

Earl Weaver must have thought all the patience and individual coaching he and the Orioles had invested in Dalkowski were finally starting to pay off. At last the young lefty was settling down and getting the ball over. Weaver's hopes were reinforced the next week when on May 28, Dalkowski had another shutout going against the Fargo-Moorehead Twins with one out in the ninth inning. Though he gave up two runs he still delivered an exciting, impressive 12–2 win with 14 strikeouts and 12 well-spaced walks that left 15 Twins runners stranded.

June was a mixed bag. On the third of the month Steve headed into the ninth inning with a 6–3 lead then lost his control, yielding a home run, two walks, and a three-run triple. On June 9 he retired the first six batters in a row before giving up a run on two doubles. June 14, after winning four games without a loss, Steve was relieved in the fifth inning during the second game of a doubleheader after giving up six runs in the inning. The Pheasants lost both games that day to Grand Forks, 8–6, and Dalkowski's 11–1 defeat.

One possible explanation for Dalko's poor performance that night is that Earl Weaver was not there to calm him down. Playing second base in the afternoon game, Weaver was ejected in the sixth inning after an extended argument with the officials, then escorted off the field by a policeman.

Another explanation is that, as former Baltimore pitching coach Ray Miller points out, "Baseball is richer in 'situations' than any other sport. What's the score? What's the count? Who's on base? How many outs? For every baseball situation, a player must have a conditioned reflex for every play that can happen. Those conditioned reflexes—those basic situations and the plays that grow out of them—are the fundamentals. This is a game of relaxation, conditioned reflex, and mental alertness." Dalkowski could not follow this logic because his game only consisted of throwing the ball as hard as possible on every pitch.

Steve's next game was his second loss in a row and an even worse showing. He was pulled in the third inning after allowing five runs on "a shower of seven walks and four scratch hits" with seven strikeouts. A complete disaster unfolded on June 30. Pitching in relief, Steve issued free passes to 10 batters in less than two innings, walking in four runs in the top of the ninth for a 15–7 loss. In six weeks he had fallen from record-setting, history-making sensation to pitching basket case.

His steep decline was the last straw for Aberdeen and the Orioles management in Baltimore. On July 3, 1959, Steve Dalkowski was optioned to the Pensacola Dons in exchange for right-handed pitcher Rudy Riska. Dalko left for Florida the same night. Joining the Dons roster brought him back to Class D baseball, where he had started with the rookie league Kingsport team two seasons before. It was as low as he could go. The Dons responded to Steve's arrival by losing 13 games in a row.

In Pensacola he became friends with another young southpaw whose career was also having its ups and downs. As different as their lives and playing histories turned out to be, the two had a surprising number of things in common. Robert "Bo" Belinsky grew up in New Jersey, showed early promise as a pitcher, and was signed by the Orioles at age nineteen in 1956. Now in his fourth minor-league season, Belinsky started the year with the Pheasants, as had Dalkowski, going from there to the Class AA Amarillo Gold Sox before sliding down to the Class C Stockton Ports and then back to Aberdeen.

Writer Pat Jordan credits Dalkowski with observations about Belinsky's wild night life and "them funny cigarettes," and a claim that the two of them drove together from Aberdeen to Baltimore before reporting to Pensacola. (Belinsky, Steve said, was sent down for fielding a bunt and flipping it to first base behind his back.) It took them five days to get to Baltimore. "We stopped in Chicago and went to all the strip joints," Steve explained. "Somebody stole Bo's clothes out of his car, and we spent the night going to every whorehouse looking for his clothes. I never seen Bo so mad. We never did find his clothes."

Belinsky had posted the best pitching record in the Northern League the year before and began his stint in Pensacola with two victories including a 3–0 shutout, striking out 12. In Dalkowski's first game for the Dons, he was pulled in the fifth inning after walking 12 batters. In his second game he walked 10 before exiting in the fourth.

This was the game when a Dalkowski pitch hit the umpire and knocked him out. According to catcher Cal Ripken Sr.'s version of the story, the count was 0-2 on a right-handed batter. Cal rarely called for a curve, but did so in this case. Because of Steve's poor eyesight, Cal's signal for a fastball was a hand on the outside of the right leg. A signal for a curve was a hand below the stomach. Cal signaled for a curve but Dalko didn't see the sign and threw a fastball instead. Always fighting to keep the ball down, Cal had his glove in the dirt. Before he could react, the ball flew over his right shoulder without him touching it and hit umpire John Lupini square in the face mask. The blow knocked Lupini down, broke his mask into three pieces, and sent him to the hospital with a concussion.

While Steve had been trying diligently to tame the wildness that had pestered him all through his career, he was also facing another challenge: his love for and growing addiction to alcohol. Up until this point in Dalkowski's life, his alleged love affair with the bottle is hard to document conclusively. He might have gained a reputation in the clubhouse as a boozer early on, though details are blurred by the passing years and conflicting accounts. It is during Steve's time with the Pensacola Dons in the second half of the 1959 season that an accurate picture of his drinking habits comes into sharp focus.

Steve and Bo Belinsky were roommates in Pensacola. Belinsky already had something of the playboy image that he cultivated in his public persona and that would eventually overshadow his skills as a ballplayer. The two young hurlers first met on a train, Belinsky with his sharp tailoring and cocky self-confidence and Dalkowski with his thick glasses, nondescript clothes, and a cardboard suitcase held together with rope. Bo was the dark, exotically handsome one; Steve had a round, boyish face that earned him the nickname Moon Mullins, after a popular comic strip character.

As future teammate Lloyd "The King of New Orleans" Fourroux noted in a recent interview, "Steve's hero was Bo Belinsky. His weaknesses were magnified because of Bo. He wanted to be like Bo in every way. Steve could have pitched in a higher league if not for Bo."

Steve was awed by his classy roommate and mimicked his behavior. His Pensacola teammates, seeing that Steve was easily led and eager to fit in, egged him on, amused at the sight of Dalko drinking beyond his limit. A night on the town after a game was another form of sport to them, and Steve was part of the entertainment. All athletes need a positive distraction. Baseball players have a lot of free time, especially when they're on the road. They need something that allows them to feel good about themselves that is unrelated to the game or the game results. Steve had no interests to speak of and lacked a positive distraction. Unfortunately, he had developed one very large negative distraction in alcohol.

The trouble came when others had the experience or self-discipline to stop drinking and call it a night while Steve did not. Whether it was because he was already addicted to alcohol, predisposed to it because of his father's drinking habits, or he just wanted to be one of the gang, Steve gained a reputation as a drinker who got hammered almost every night. Isolated on the mound during a game, he morphed into the class clown after hours, desperate to do whatever it took to fit in. According to fellow pitcher Herm Starrette, Steve said he and his father drank a lot together in the off-season, and Steve knew he was good enough on the mound that he could drink and still perform.

Belinsky had an even bigger reputation as a partier, but he managed to get a full night's sleep and pull himself together the next day. Steve just kept on drinking. As Steve's wife Linda said many years later, "I think it was a bad thing for Steve that he got hooked up with Bo Belinsky." One pitching coach later suggested that Belinsky had a million-dollar arm tied to a nickel brain. After Pensacola manager Lou Fitzgerald suffered a heart attack during the season, colleagues suspected the combination of Belinsky, Dalkowski, and fellow teammate Steve Barber was one of the prime contributing factors.

Barber was yet another young lefty pitching for Pensacola in 1959. The following year he would move to Baltimore to begin a fifteen-year career in the majors, including two years as an All-Star. He became the first 20-game winner in modern Orioles history with an arsenal of pitches that included a 95-mph fastball as measured by a high-speed movie camera. In a 2001 interview, Barber pulled back the historical curtain to reveal a glimpse of Dalkowski's after-hours pursuits during the 1959 season in Florida:

"One night Bo and I were together, and we went into this place, and Steve's there, and he says, 'Hey guys, come over and look at this beautiful sight'—twenty-four scotch and waters lined up in front of him. And he was pitching the next day. Then he stopped on the way home and bought a gallon of wine and killed that, too. The next day they just carried him off the mound in the fourth inning."

Whether he was embellishing the story or not, Barber, who died in 2007, was in a position to know the facts. In the same interview he recalled Steve's poor personal hygiene and how his clothes stank. He said he once threatened to cut Steve's clothes up if he didn't wash them. A young single guy who was on the road much of the season would not be likely to have a pristine locker under the best circumstances. If Dalko spent his off hours in bars or passed out, it's no wonder his sweatshirts were smelly. Another part of the explanation is that Steve's nerves and his lack of confidence left him prone to superstition. If he had pitched well wearing a certain pair of socks or a certain T-shirt, he would wear the same item for days in a row, either oblivious to the odor or convinced it was worth the inconvenience.

Steve's move to Pensacola brought him back to a state where another mystery lurks in his legend. The facts are elusive, yielding more in the way of inference and possibility rather than hard evidence. Some of the pieces fit together; others do not. The two sources relied on here are Tim Sommer, who played with Dalkowski during Dalko's last year in professional baseball, and Steve's former wife, Linda Moore. Both got the story from Dalkowski himself in the 1960s.

Merging their accounts, the story is that Steve's father was a gambler who loved the horses and bet heavily at the racetrack. His losses took enough of his paycheck as a toolmaker so that the family was sometimes barely scraping by. As a schoolboy, Steve played baseball in school during the spring, then all summer in community leagues. After high school football in the fall, the rotation started all over again. He played sports year round, mostly baseball. When he played in these community leagues, also called industrial leagues or factory teams, he made money. It isn't clear who paid him or what the criteria were for earning these payments. Steve didn't keep the money, but instead turned it over to his father to help cover his gambling losses.

In Linda Moore's words, Steve's dad "set him up with factory teams all up and down the East Coast, which he would get money for. But his dad had a bad gambling habit, so he always had to give his dad the money for his gambling debts."

Early in his professional career Steve was befriended by other financial benefactors. A couple of fans chatted him up in a hotel lobby in Miami and invited him out to drink. As quoted by Tim Sommer, Steve said that his newfound friends "knew everybody no matter where we went, and I never had to worry about paying."

Dalkowski talked to Sommer about being broke in terms of spending away his signing bonus from Baltimore and struggling to make it to the start of the season on a few dollars a day. However, Steve was not in Miami any time soon after receiving his signing bonus. The bonus was paid in 1957, and the Orioles didn't hold spring training in Miami until 1959 (before that it was in Scottsdale, Arizona). How he could be in Miami in 1959, worried about making ends meet after spending his 1957 bonus money, is a part of the mystery.

Continuing his story, Dalkowski told Sommer he was complaining that his bonus was gone and he was in a jam waiting for his first paycheck of the season. He was "really drunk," he said, when one of these Miami friends offered to loan him money. He couldn't remember the amount, except that it was a lot. He asked when he would have to pay back the loan. His benefactor said not to worry about it. "We really like you and just want to help out," he explained. "You're going to be making a lot of money, and when you feel comfortable about repaying, just let us know. There are no strings attached."

Dalkowski knew better. "I never could have made the bigs," he told Sommer. "They'd have their hooks in me." Sommer concluded, "The mob had found Steve and he accepted their offer." Did Dalkowski get mixed up with gamblers as a player on factory teams earning money for his father? Did that cast of characters have anything to do with his Miami benefactors? After making a deal with strangers during a drunken stupor, Steve seemed unsure of where he stood or to whom he was in debt. Was organized crime a part of the picture?

These two accounts of Steve's mysterious financial dealings are the only ones uncovered to date. Other reliable sources might someday come to light, though the prospect of that lessens with every passing year. While Dalkowski seems never to have mentioned the subject elsewhere, the possible existence of some kind of shadowy benefactor bubbles to the surface once more later in his life.

NINE

Taming the Wild Man

"Get that clown out of there before he kills somebody!"
—Opposing hitter watching Dalkowski throw batting practice, 1960

Dalkowski reported to the Orioles minor league camp at Thomasville, Georgia, in the spring of 1960 to be sorted out with the other ninety-odd players among the various minor-league teams. The press considered this a make-or-break year for Dalkowski. Through three years and five teams, a small army of managers, coaches, and pitching experts had tried to tame Dalko's infamous fastball.

The Dalkowski sideshow continued as managers and coaches had him pitch for long stretches, throwing hundreds of pitches on the bullpen mound before games. Well intentioned though it was, this approach was thoroughly misguided and would never be employed today. The risk of injuring an arm is far too high. And by all accounts, Dalkowski threw only strikes on the sidelines. It was when he entered the game that everything changed. Everyone trying to help him still addressed the wrong problem: they kept fiddling with his mechanics.

While Steve did have some remediable mechanical issues, he also illustrated the point made by the legendary Yogi Berra, who said, "Baseball is 90 percent mental. The other half is physical." Steve's coaches told him repeatedly that he didn't have to throw smoke on every delivery. If he took a little velocity off the fastball, he would gain better control.

Some time around the beginning of 1960 spring training, coaches began working with Steve on a secondary pitch, the changeup. Though Steve resisted using it, observers as far back as high school coach Bill Huber said Steve had an excellent breaking ball. Numerous teammates and opposing players said the same thing. Why coaches didn't try to develop Steve's curveball remains a mystery. Teaching the changeup to a flamethrower is challenging, as their psyche and ego are tied to the gas. Regardless of how good Steve's breaking ball might have been, he was never focused on or committed to anything but the fastball. The result was that his off-speed pitches often got hit, which angered him because *no one* could hit his fastball.

Steve did not like hitters even making contact with his offerings. Every pitch was an all-or-nothing effort, an unhittable strike or an uncontrollable ball. Former scout and MLB executive Harry Dalton said that during a game in Johnson City, Tennessee, "Dalkowski was throwing a gem. In the fifth inning an opposing hitter hit a weak pop-up to the third baseman for the final out of the inning. Steve came into the dugout and said, 'Skip, you'd better get somebody up. I'm starting to lose it.' This was the only ball that had gone forward in five innings, fair or foul."

For all the evident power behind Steve's pitches, catcher Cal Ripken said they were easy to catch. He claimed he could have caught them barehanded. This assessment is confirmed by Andy Etchebarren, a fifteen-year major league veteran with two All-Star selections, who caught Steve in Elmira in 1962 and 1964. "Steve was easy to catch," Etchebarren said. "The ball was light, not heavy like some pitchers." These reactions are at odds with comments by Andy Baylock and Joe Ginsberg, who said catching Dalkowski was tough, and they had the black and blue fingers to prove it. Why catchers reported such vastly different reactions remains an open question.

During spring training for the 1960 season, Dalkowski worked with catcher Harry Dunlop, an Orioles minor league journeyman who played that year for the Tri-City Braves in Washington state. He was catching one day when Dalkowski was throwing batting practice. The first pitch hit the top bar of the batting cage fifteen feet off the ground with a loud ringing sound and bounced high into the air. As several heads turned to see what caused the racket, Dunlop heard a player yell, "Get that clown outta there before he kills somebody!"

John "Boog" Powell, who went on to a distinguished seventeen-year career in the majors (fourteen of them with the Orioles) including the 1970 American League MVP award and four All-Star appearances, played during the '60 season for the Fox City Foxes in Appleton, Wisconsin. Stepping into the batting cage one day during spring training, he hollered for Dalkowski to throw him his best stuff. "The next time I saw the ball," Powell later recalled, "it was rolling out of the cage. I never saw it. It was totally unhittable."

Steve was assigned out of Thomasville to the California League's Stockton Ports in California's Central Valley, the agricultural heartland of the state, featuring irrigated fields stretching to the horizon in every direction. This reunited Steve with manager Billy DeMars, who had managed at Aberdeen during Steve's first year there. The Ports were a Class C league team, up one notch from Pensacola. Dalko's arrival in the valley was big news. His pitching records and unpredictable performances were moving him into the national spotlight.

He made his debut with the Ports on April 22, 1960. It was a miserable night with intermittent rain and a temperature of forty degrees. Both the Ports and the visiting Bakersfield Bears built fires in their dugouts to keep warm. Steve started out somewhat cold himself, yielding two runs in the second inning. Then his fastball lit up, and he went on to an impressive 9–2 victory despite 15 walks, striking out 13.

DeMars believed that what Steve needed was game experience to improve his confidence. To that end, he planned to start him every fourth game. He also developed a training exercise to start him pitching fifteen feet from the plate then gradually increase the distance while maintaining his accuracy. At fifteen feet, every ball was right down the middle. Here DeMars might have been unknowingly on the right track. At fifteen feet Steve had something new and defined to focus on. However, as he moved back, he retreated into his old one-dimensional thinking: just rear back and throw hard. As the distance lengthened each pitch became more and more wild. Another idea was to position a wooden target over the plate and have him aim at that. The first few pitches missed completely. The next one shattered the target.

"This kid has the arm of a Bobby Feller, Rex Barney, or a Ryne Duren when it comes to speed," DeMars said, adding, "If I could sit in a chair behind the pitcher's mound and just tell him not to get nervous, he'd be a major leaguer right now."

As the season unfolded, DeMars sent daily reports on Dalko and the rest of the team to Orioles farm team director Jimmy McLaughlin and to Harry Dalton, who was now McLaughlin's assistant. DeMars spoke with them once a week or so by phone to fill in the details. The reports were a mixture of hope that Dalkowski was on the verge of turning the corner on his control problems and the realization that he hadn't. After losing 9 out of 10 games in April and May, the Ports and Dalkowski relished an 8–2 victory over the Fresno Giants on May 6.

The *Stockton Record* celebrated the win: "Flamethrowing Steve Dalkowski blazed a winning trail for the Stockton Ports last night as he fired a four-hit, 16-strikeout masterpiece. . . . The Giants were left swinging like a row of rusty gates in a stiff breeze. . . . Dalkowski, a young left-hander whose reputation for speed far preceded his arrival on these shores, was every bit as effective as the rumors said." Four days later, the Ports were trampled 11–3 as Steve gave up five hits, seven runs, and seven walks with five strikeouts in 3⅓ innings.

For all of his inconsistency and repeated relapses into control trouble, Dalko kept trying, kept training, kept doing his wind sprints, kept a positive attitude, and kept working as hard as ever. The number of pitches he sometimes threw in a game was unimaginable by later standards. By game's end he might have thrown 200 pitches plus eight warm-ups per inning. One night a teammate estimated he must have thrown close to 400. To put that into context, in today's MLB environment, once a pitcher gets his pitch count to one hundred—in a world where pitch count has become sacred—it's about time for him to be coming out of the game. Steve's arm was perceived as all-powerful, invincible, unstoppable. He seemed absolutely committed to making it do what he wanted it to.

The night of May 20, 1960, was a highlight of the season for Stockton. The game against the Modesto Reds started out on a moderately positive note until the fourth inning, when Dalko retired the side without a hit. He had the same success in the fifth, six, and all the way through the eighth. He made a conscious, concentrated effort to keep the ball low, liberally mixing sliders and curveballs in with his signature fastball. The result was a 4–0 shutout with only three hits allowed, nine walks, and 12 strikeouts. Dalko also shone on offense, knocking in a run on an eighth-inning double—a reminder of the outstanding athleticism Steve had been known for throughout his career.

Every Reds batter struck out at least once. Yet instead of running up the pitch count on batter after batter, Steve moved the game along at a pace that might have been a record to date for him—138 total pitches for the entire game: 83 fastballs and 55 breaking balls. This put Steve at a 15-pitch-per-inning average, which is quite good by MLB standards today. In his previous start he had thrown 210 pitches. For Steve to throw about 40 percent breaking balls was a very high percentage—for any pitcher. Typically pitchers throw 20–25 percent or so breaking stuff, and Dalko historically had thrown far fewer. Whether he was just experimenting, trying to save his arm, or was following his coaches' instructions, the higher mix was extremely effective.

At last, Steve saw and felt and understood that control and finesse were an essential accompaniment to speed. Something clicked. The message finally hit home. Ports catcher Ralph Larimore, who had also played with Dalkowski in Aberdeen, said the Modesto game on May 20 was the best he'd ever seen him throw. Larimore added, "His breaking stuff was sharp; he was fast, but not quite as fast as I've seen him, but way more effective than ever before."

Stockton sportswriter Al Goldfarb struck a joyful note in his write-up the next day: "Steve Dalkowski may have come of age last night. Not only did the fireballing left-hander pitcher pitch the Stockton Ports to a 4–0 victory . . . he also became a 'pitcher' in every sense of the word. . . . By his own admission, 'Dal' was a different man on the hill last night. . . . [He said,] 'I was a thrower before. But last night I tried to get them to hit the ball on the ground instead of striking them out. It helped my control.'"

Dalko held onto that attitude and that promise into his game on May 26 against Fresno. After one walk in the first inning, he pitched one clean frame after another. He had a one-walk shutout going through seven innings. Steve walked three in the top of the eighth but escaped without giving up a run. In the top of the ninth, the first batter to face him was Joe Laboy, the best hitter in the California League. Dalko struck him out, leaving the Ports two outs away from a 1–0 win. Then his nervousness returned. Steve walked the next two batters and was behind 2-0 on the third when DeMars pulled him for reliever Ken Temple. The game went downhill from there in a 4–1 loss for the Ports.

The greatest Dr. Jekyll and Mr. Hyde routine in baseball history continued. After losing 24 of their first 36 games, the Ports started improving. Dalkowski celebrated his twenty-first birthday on June 3 with a 7–5 victory with 18 strikeouts against the Visalia Athletics. Some opposing batters "flailed the air in futility," reported the *Stockton*

Record. "Others preferred to stand immobile before his blazing fastballs and his darting curves and sliders." Here again Dalko used a mix of breaking balls with his famous fireball to notable success.

There were times, of course, when the Ports' fielding influenced Dalkowski's performances—some helpful, some not so much. A reporter's account of a game later that month in Bakersfield conveys something of the excitement Dalko brought to the field and the thrill it was to watch him even when he lost: "Left-hander Steve Dalkowski provided the fans with another exciting, if unsuccessful, performance, and it was his best in several outings. In fact, the erratic fastballer deserved a better fate. . . . Dalkowski, who fires as if he were trying to launch a small, stitched satellite into orbit, must pitch the most exciting first innings in baseball. Displaying his usual first-inning nervousness last night, the bespectacled lefty walked Butch Miali, Connie Egan, and Gil Romero in succession to open the fray and went 3-0 to Dick Wilson before finding the range. With the crowd already on the edge of their seats, he blazed three strikes past Wilson. Rich Edwards departed with three more swings. . . . "

Dalkowski's next start on June 21 in Reno produced the kind of statistics Dalkowski was becoming famous for and which left baseball fans scratching their heads. Tying a league record for strikeouts with 19 even though he pitched only eight innings, he nonetheless lost 8–3. Holding a 3–2 lead in the eighth he faltered, walking two, hitting a batter, allowing two singles, and then giving up a grand slam to Bobby Cox (who after a short playing career with the Yankees would spend more than thirty years managing the Atlanta Braves and Toronto Blue Jays).

At the age of twenty-one, though still without a major league contract, Dalkowski was becoming a baseball sensation. The Associated Press story of his loss in Reno reflected some of the enthusiasm that infused the crowds watching Dalkowski on the mound as well as a touch of the dedication and innocent sincerity Dalko radiated in the clubhouse: "The American League figures Paul Richards' Baltimore

Orioles are loaded with strong young pitchers. But they ain't seen nuthin' yet! The Orioles have a 21-year-old southpaw . . . who has a fastball that's a blazeroonie. . . . Dalkowski . . . is an intense competitor. He was heartbroken after his loss. 'I let you down,' he told manager Billy DeMars. 'No you didn't,' DeMars replied. 'You're getting the ball over. That's all I ask.'"

Against the Fresno Giants on the Fourth of July, Dalko pitched a game that seemed like a continuation of the fireworks that kicked off the evening. He had lost his last four games in a row. In the first inning he gave up a run and walked in a second. The second and third innings were relatively quiet. Then in the fourth he walked two batters. His nerves were getting to him again. DeMars came out to talk to him, break the tension, and give his pitcher a minute to reset himself. Up to that point, with one out in the fourth, Dalkowski had already thrown 104 pitches. After that little pep talk, Dalko finished the game on only 48 more pitches with no more hits and no more walks. Still more evidence that nervousness and lack of confidence were key factors in Steve's unpredictable performance.

Buzzing with post-victory adrenaline, the next day's news lead-in read, "Sizzling Steve Dalkowski, hotter'n a Fourth of July firecracker, is back in the business at the old stand, and the high-flying Ports are still leading the California League as a result. Fireballing Steverino, the young man with a fastball whose 'whiff-'em-or-walk-'em' style has 'em talking to themselves in the circuit, twirled a one-hitter last night. . . . "

Time magazine, which didn't typically provide a lot of sports coverage, ran a story in its July 18, 1960, issue calling Steve Dalkowski the "hardest thrower in organized baseball." The account reported that he had thrown as many as six wild pitches in a row, torn off a batter's earlobe (the tall tales had already started), and "sent an unsuspecting umpire to the hospital with a stray fastball that popped him flush on the mask, knocked him eighteen feet, chest pad over whisk broom." The article mentioned the Cincinnati Reds exhibition game in Baltimore when Steve pitched the ninth inning and struck out the side on 12 pitches. But, "he was so wild that Oriole hitters disappeared when Dalkowski took his turn pitching batting practice." DeMars explained, "They were career men and they didn't want to wreck their careers through foolish bravery."

In the *Time* feature Dalko was quoted recalling a night when he threw three scorchers over the catcher's head and through the backstop screen. The next night as he was warming up, a fan yelled to ask if he was pitching that night. When Steve said it looked like he would, the fan yelled back, "Then I'm getting the hell out of here—and I'm taking my kids with me." As usual, Dalko was leading the league that summer in strikeouts (170) and walks (162). Summing up his thoughts on his unorthodox career thus far Dalko observed, "It's no picnic watching every other batter walk to first." The rest of the 1960 season was a mix of the same promise and frustration that had defined Steve Dalkowski. He shattered the league record for walks in a season with 262 (the old record was 202) and also chalked up a record 262 strikeouts.

After the World Series in October, Dalkowski joined the annual migration of American professional baseball players to the Mexican Leagues. There, where the temperatures were warm and the atmosphere was laid back, they could maintain their competitive edge, work on their game, and earn good money in the off-season. Sometimes major leaguers recovering from injury or needing special attention went to Mexico to escape the spotlight of the American press.

Steve played in the Sonora Winter League (later the Mexican Pacific League) for the Venados de Mazatlán, the "Deer of Mazatlán." The city name means "place of the deer" in the native Indian language. Mazatlán in the 1960s was a relatively isolated resort on the Pacific coast of Mexico. Ever since movie companies started shooting feature films there in the 1940s, Mazatlán had become a hideaway where some of Hollywood's biggest stars went to relax and escape the limelight. John Wayne, John Huston, Rock Hudson, and other leading men spent days sportfishing off the coast and nights drinking in the Belmar, the Posada, and other hotels along Olas Altas ("High Waves"), the beach-front boulevard where the action was.

Mazatlán was also a place where movie starlets came to vacation, to see and be seen by whatever producers and studio bigwigs might be in town. It was an ideal location for discreet romantic encounters as well. There were beautiful beaches, no gossip column paparazzi, and prices were low.

While Dalkowski was well known among his peers for after-hours partying, he had also become a ladies' man. Rattled and nervous as he often was on the mound, off the field he was gregarious, generous, easygoing, and never met a stranger. In Mazatlán that fall, Steve and Boog Powell caught the eyes of a couple of starlets on a break from the Hollywood scene. Connie Stevens was twenty-two, a young singer and actress who had a breakout role in the film *Rock-a-Bye Baby* starring comedian Jerry Lewis, then became a star as a featured player on the hit 1959 TV series *Hawaiian Eye*. At the age of twenty-nine, actress Angie Dickinson had already been married and divorced. She too had had a big career break in 1959, being cast in the now-classic western film *Rio Bravo* with John Wayne and Dean Martin.

During that fall in 1960, Steve and Boog dated Connie and Angie in Mexico. Evidently, it was all in fun and none of the group had any expectations of a more serious or lasting relationship. Presumably they made the rounds of the hotel bars and watering holes along the Olas Altas and went swimming in the Pacific. Since the baseball games were played during the day, Dalko and Powell and their lady friends had all night to paint the town. It seems that none of them stayed in touch. Both women went on to greater fame and famous husbands—Stevens married singer Eddie Fisher and Dickinson married singer/songwriter Burt Bacharach.

As hot as Steve's social life might have been that season in Mazat-lán, his best performance on the mound was even hotter. On Sunday,

October 23, 1960, Dalkowski pitched a game that fans in Mazatlán still talk about. It was the second game of a doubleheader against the Ostioneros de Guaymas. One member of the crowd that day was thirteen-year-old Eduardo Jimenez, whose excitement still comes through when describing the game more than half a century later. The pitches were "fast, fast, fast," he says, and sounded like the buzzing of a bee as they flew toward the mound. Steve "broke" batters like a cowboy breaking horses or burros, so fans called him "Burro Buster" along with his other nicknames. That afternoon young Eduardo and an astonished crowd watched as Dalkowski gave up a triple to the first batter, Gonzalo Villalobos, then retired 27 batters in a row.

At the end of 1960, Powell and Dalkowski played together again in the Arizona Instructional League in Phoenix. Steve's drinking had advanced by then to the point where his teammates knew they had to keep an eye on him and make sure he got back to the hotel at the end of the evening. Years later Powell remembered a night in Phoenix when, as usual, Dalko drank almost to the point of passing out. Powell was helping him back to the apartment complex where the team was staying. Approaching the building, Powell was literally carrying Dalkowski when he saw manager Earl Weaver also heading for the front door. Not wanting Weaver to see Steve so inebriated, he tossed him out of sight into a rose bush, scratching him up so that he "was bleeding like a stuck pig." After Weaver disappeared indoors, Powell retrieved Dalko from the bushes and got him up to his room, cleaned him up as best he could, then rolled him into bed. It was three a.m. The team had to be at the ballpark at nine.

Dalkowski woke up the next morning hung over and covered with scratches. He didn't remember getting home or taking a dive into the roses, and so he had no idea how he'd gotten hurt, only that he was scheduled to pitch that day. At first he considered telling Weaver he couldn't play, but decided to push ahead. As Boog later remembered, Dalkowski "got in the whirlpool, got a little rub, and threw the best game I ever saw him pitch. . . . That's how much talent the guy had."

By now Steve had developed the habit of spending his paycheck on drinks for friends and strangers alike, then having to borrow money from teammates. Every two weeks on payday, he'd ask each player how much he had borrowed and hand over the amount without question. But then, Herm Starette remembered, "before the day was over, he'd borrow it back."

On the mound, Dalko's unpredictability continued. During a typical game in Phoenix that November he struck out eight, walked five, and threw three wild pitches in 4⅔ innings of relief. Looking ahead to 1961, the Orioles had to decide whether to keep on trying to bring Dalko along or cut their losses. Every year the conundrum was the same. The young southpaw had a once-in-a-generation arm that, if he could ever control it consistently, would be a gold mine for the team. He would seem to be making steady progress, then implode on the mound for no apparent reason. How much longer could the Orioles afford to keep waiting for him to get it together?

Writing in his "Batting Around" column, Aberdeen sports editor Larry Desautels summed up the situation: "Dalkowski has probably become something of a headache to the Orioles. He had shown very little development after three [sic] years in the lower minors. Ordinarily a club would give up on him at this point, but Steve still throws a baseball harder than anyone in the game and could become a big leaguer overnight, simply by getting some semblance of control. So the Orioles are in the unhappy position of not wanting to hang on and being afraid to let go."

They were leaning toward letting him go. On November 19, 1960, Dalkowski was put into the expansion draft held by Major League Baseball scheduled for December 14 to field teams for the new Los Angeles Angels and Washington Senators. As a non-roster minor-league player, Steve was available to either team for $25,000. No one took him. Other Baltimore pitchers in the pool were Billy Hoeft, Gordon Jones, Roy Moeller, and Dean Chance.

On February 15, 1961, the Orioles announced that Dalkowski had signed his contract for the coming season. His record the year before with the Ports had been 7-15 with an ERA of 5.14. But he had struck out 262 batters in 170 innings. It was his best season yet. The Orioles management looked at that figure in hopes it was a sign of things to come. They tried not to concentrate so much on his number of walks— also 262, a league record then, which remains the California League record to this day.

TEN

White Lightning

"His speed has made him one of the best-known minor league pitchers and wildness has made him one of the most feared."

—Centralia *Daily Chronicle*, April 19, 1961

Dalko was invited once again to the Orioles major league spring training camp in Miami ahead of the 1961 season. It is during this time that we get one of the most detailed and revealing accounts of Steve Dalkowski and his celebrated fastball. The legendary "Sudden" Sam McDowell watched Steve throw batting practice to a group of reluctant Orioles teammates. His firsthand observations qualify Dalkowski's incredible raw talent:

"As to Steve Dalkowski, I can say he had the most perfect pitching mechanics I ever saw," McDowell said in a recent interview. "The most important component in the mechanical process is the way you rotate your shoulder back and load your throwing shoulder. That mechanical component must be perfectly aligned with your movement toward home plate. They are not separate pieces but precisely aligned pieces.

Maximizing the consistency of that load and coupling it with perfect timing allows the pitcher to harness his total physical energy as he moves toward the plate. Then, through the counter-rotation of his body, he delivers the maximum energy, power, and velocity to the hitter. Additionally, the pitcher will exhibit a greater ability to place the pitch in precisely the required location. Truthfully, when all of this occurs consistently, the process of throwing the baseball is completely effortless.

"Steve's mechanics were just like a perfect ballet, as free flowing as humanly possible. Just seeing his turn and movement toward the plate, you knew power was coming! Tragically, he never figured out the mental aspect of pitching. He had no faith in himself or his pitching.

"Steve couldn't get the wildness out of his head, and the media, coaches, and managers wouldn't let him forget it. During the time he played in pro ball, no one thought of the mental aspects of the game or of a player.

"Throughout my career and even now, many baseball experts try and determine the hardest thrower in baseball history—Koufax, Ryan, Feller, McDowell, Randy Johnson, Walter Johnson, etc. Whenever the conversation comes up, I always mention a guy named Steve Dalkowski, as I truly believe he threw as hard or harder than any of us!"

Steve pitched in an intrasquad game on February 26. Fans in the flamingo-pink stands gathered in the warm Florida sunshine to watch the famous fastballer in action. Two weeks later he pitched the last three innings of a so-called "B game" ahead of the first official game of the spring training season. Playing against the Pittsburgh Pirates, Dalkowski gave up a run but looked confident and in control.

Described by a reporter watching the Pirates game as "the wildest man in baseball captivity," Steve nonetheless made an impression on Orioles manager Paul Richards, who was also watching the action that day. Richards said it was the best he'd ever seen Dalkowski pitch, adding, "If he can keep getting the ball as close to the plate as he did today, he's going to be a great pitcher."

Dalko felt his confidence level rising. "Maybe I'll get the hang of this control business yet," he said. "There were days last season when I thought my control was as good as most pitchers. On other days it slips. Must be a matter of concentration. That's what people tell me." It was a typical Dalkowski comment—humble, courteous, showing an unflagging desire to learn and improve. It also marks Steve's tendency not to look too deeply within himself; he was more willing to let someone else figure out what to do than spend much time pondering the question on his own.

One of Steve's pitches that day sailed over the catcher's head and hit the canvas backstop so hard that it rebounded far enough toward the plate to drive the runner on third base back to the bag. The moment didn't sway Baltimore general manager Lee MacPhail from insisting that his club's investment in Dalko would eventually pay off.

"You've got to stay with anybody who has Dalkowski's kind of speed," he told a gaggle of reporters after the game. "I know how wild he has been. He even hit a man in the on-deck circle one day. But pitchers often mature late, and Dalkowski is young enough to acquire control."

Steve and his teammates were living at the McAllister Hotel in downtown Miami. It so happened that contestants for the annual Miss Universe pageant were also rooming there. Bo Belinsky was next door to one of the young competitors and her mother. (Belinsky remembered her as Miss Colombia, but it was more likely Miss Ecuador, Yolanda Palacios Charvert.) Dalkowski sneaked downstairs into an unlocked maintenance room and brought back a drill. In Belinsky's words, "Dalkowski drilled twenty holes in the wall, all at different levels, the entire length of the wall. He left nothing to chance."

Bo, Dalko, and teammate Steve Barber waited for the two women to come back from dinner, then spied on them through the peepholes. The next night, a dozen players huddled in Bo's room to see what they could see. One overeager spy shone a flashlight through a hole. Miss Ecuador screamed, her hidden audience scattered, and hotel security discovered the caper. The next morning Orioles manager Paul Richards confronted Dalkowski, who insisted he didn't intend to spy. "Why in the hell would you drill holes in a wall into a girl's room if you didn't intend to look through them?" Richards demanded. "Oh, I don't know, Skip," Steve answered sheepishly. "I just like drilling holes." Richards gave Bo, Dalko, and Barber a fierce tongue lashing but agreed to pay for the damage.

In spite of Steve's late-night hijinks, the Orioles brass evidently considered bringing him up to the majors that spring but couldn't quite make the leap of faith required. He was one of the last players cut from the Orioles roster on April 7, four days before the official Baltimore squad had to be set. He went from there to the farm club training camp in Thomasville, Georgia, as in past seasons, for assignment to a team in the Orioles organization. From Georgia he was sent to pitch for the Tri-City Braves of Kennewick, Washington, a new team affiliation in the Orioles network. He joined the Braves at their spring training camp in Rio Vista, California. The Braves were a Class B team in the Northwest League, one notch up from Steve's Stockton team of the year before.

As in the past, the southpaw's reputation preceded him. The Centralia *Daily Chronicle* heralded the arrival of "White Lightning . . . a Baltimore farmhand with a catapult arm. His speed has made him one of the best known minor-league pitchers, and wildness has made him one of the most feared." The Walla-Walla *Union-Bulletin* introduced him to local fans as "a fantastic young fireball pitcher . . . one of the hardest throwers in baseball . . . one of baseball's top attractions." The press also noted that at Sanders Field, Tri-City's home park, the screen behind home plate had been doubled.

Scouting reports from Steve's brief appearance at the Tri-City training camp were encouraging. Observers said they thought maybe at last he had tackled his wildness. Narrowly out of the running for the league championship the year before, the Braves looked like champions for sure with Steve ("The Flamer," "The Missile") Dalkowski added to their pitching rotation along with returning 20-game winner Fred Rick.

A profile of the new celebrity said in part, "Described as a shy, unassuming youngster with extremely strong arms and wrists, Dalkowski is tabbed as a real major league prospect. Reports say that in spring training [with the Orioles in Miami], when he threw—either in competition or just warming up—everybody stopped to watch, the way they'd do when Ted Williams stepped into the batting cage."

For all the preseason hype, Steve got off to a slow start and never recovered. He walked 10 in his first appearance then spent almost two weeks on the disabled list (whether due to injury, alcohol, or something else is not known). On May 14, the Braves and Lewiston Broncs played a game in Walla-Walla, the first regular season professional baseball game in the city's history. The biggest drawing card was the possibility that Dalkowski might pitch.

It was a too-familiar story that year for Steve. Fans, teammates, and coaches eagerly anticipated great things that never quite came to pass. He would show early promise in a game, but then his confidence would waver and the control disappear. Dalko ended the season in Kennewick with a 3-12 record and an ERA of 8.39, his worst since his last Class B assignment with the Wilson Tobacconists. There his ERA had been 12.21 with only eight appearances and no starts. In 103 innings for Tri-City he struck out 150, walked 196, and had 30 wild pitches.

In the wake of the 1961 season, a disturbing trend began to show in Dalkowski's performance statistics. Beginning the year before in Stockton, the number of hits allowed, runs allowed, and earned runs allowed all began to climb. This raises the question whether his velocity was beginning to decline, and whether his arm was still bulletproof and healthy. Though there's no solid evidence that arm issues were becoming a factor, Steve might have lost a yard off his heater by this time.

At least one report indicated Dalkowski might be drafted by the expansion Houston Colt .45s for the 1962 season. The story quoted Paul Richards, who knew Dalko well and was about to become general manager of the new team, saying, "From the pitcher's mound to home plate, he throws the ball faster than any man who ever lived."

But Dalko's poor performance still failed to shake Baltimore's resolve. On October 13 they assigned him to their Triple A Rochester Red Wings affiliate. This may have been a gesture to improve Steve's confidence, though it was weeks after the end of the minor league season. The Associated Press carried the announcement from Baltimore that Steve, pitcher Arnie Thorsland, catcher Frank Zupo, and outfielder Jim Liggett "have been assigned outright to the Rochester Red Wings," but Steve's official stats make no mention of Rochester in 1961. Maybe next year would be the year that White Lightning would finally strike.

It was a promising sign that Steve started the 1962 season back with Rochester. He reported to the Red Wings spring training camp at City Island Park in Daytona Beach. Rochester manager Clyde King was encouraged by Steve's performance and considered Steve his "special spring project." Dalko was throwing more strikes than balls for once, fanning more batters than he walked. Pat Gillick was Steve's roommate in 1962. He reports that during the season Steve "was throwing more breaking balls, which slowed his delivery, and this carried over into his fastball. The result is he was throwing more strikes."

In an intrasquad game, Steve struck out four and walked two in two innings while following King's instructions to slow down his fastball and mix in some curves. When King called him off the field, Steve asked to pitch another half-inning. "No, that's enough," King said. "Do your seventy-four pickups, then get in some good wind sprints. We'll try you again in a few days."

King worked on Steve's pitching technique during the spring. He told reporters that left-handed pitchers "can't throw a ball straight. . . . There's something about the way a left-hander throws the ball that makes it move differently. . . . Don't ask me why. . . . The good left-handers like Spahn and Ford learn to compensate for the fact that their ball is not going to be straight. The wild ones never learn."

To improve Dalkowski's performance, King changed Steve's mound position, having him pitch from the opposite side of the rubber. King explained that it was "the same theory as a golfer using the tee area to his own advantage on a hole where the woods are tight on the left side of the fairway." The press reported that "Dalkowski feels the change has helped him immeasurably already."

Pitching coaches today recognize that a pitcher's position on the rubber has no bearing on his ability to throw strikes. Pitchers need repeatability—timing, tempo, kinetic chain, the resulting movement and mechanics. What King was actually doing that helped Steve was unintended. Steve needed to park his wildness and create a refocusing plan. He wanted to believe that someone could and would help him. King's refocusing plan—changing Dalko's position on the rubber—allowed Steve to believe. But Steve still lacked confidence and became anxious and distracted. This increased the likelihood that he would make more mistakes and confirmed his reputation as a wild man who could not consistently throw strikes.

As managers before him had done, Clyde King took Dalko aside for individual instruction. In the dugout on Sunday, April Fool's Day, 1962, King "called his class in southpaw psychology to order" with a class of one. Steve had major league pitching speed but could not master major league control. As Chief Bender once said, "A pitcher who hasn't control hasn't anything." King was determined to spend whatever time it took to find Steve's problems and solve them. Like the rest of the Orioles brass, King was convinced that Steve was on the brink of major league stardom.

"Steve, there's no reason in the world for you to be as wild as you are," King said. "You have rhythm, a smooth motion, and a great fastball. There's more bases on balls given from here"—he touched himself on the head—"than from here"—indicating his arm. "Yeah," Steve answered. "I think I'm in the groove—like a golf swing—then all at once I lose it."

In addition to tweaking Dalko's position on the mound, King tried to help Steve "relieve the intense concentration on the target that has become an obsession with Dalkowski." He wanted Steve to relax, ease up, and throw three-quarters speed. "There are dozens of pitchers in our league whose fastball isn't as good as yours if you throw it at three-quarters speed."

As Dalkowski walked to the mound, Frank McGowan joined King in the dugout and the two kept track of Steve's pitches to the catcher in an otherwise empty batting cage. Of 24 deliveries, 19 were strikes. "Watch this now," King said, walking to the cage and standing behind it. Steve's next pitch bounced across the plate. The one after that went over the catcher's head.

"See, it's mental," he told McGowan. "He tries too hard, and the harder he tries—when he's conscious of the target—the wilder he gets." Other baseball greats would have agreed. Sandy Koufax once said, "Pitching is a static situation. You initiate the action. That means you must develop a special depth of concentration." Hitting legend Rod Carew observed, "A player must learn to relax, to accept things, to forgive yourself, not to expect to be perfect in baseball." The people around Steve were trying their best to convey these ideas.

King vowed to continue the private tutorials. McGowan compared Dalkowski to former Baltimore pitcher Ryne Duren, who labored for seven years looking for his control. After a season in Denver under manager Ralph Houk, Duren went on to a successful career with the Yankees and other major league teams. "Certain managers can get to certain players," McGowan observed. "Clyde has a way of doing it that's very effective. It's his sincerity. Dalkowski can win anywhere with control."

While Clyde King was correct to take Steve aside and work with him privately, it probably had the unintended effect of reaffirming to Steve that he was different from other players, and not in a good way.

This would further isolate him from his teammates and from responsibility for taking an active part in identifying his control problems himself. It separated him from the peers he desperately needed in order to feel like he belonged.

Still, it's only fair to give King, McGowen, Brecheen, and others credit for having the best of intentions. They genuinely valued Dalkowski and did the best they could to help him. There were no mental skills coaches, sports psychologists, or therapists available to players in the early 1960s. Most players were told simply to "figure it out." As Sam McDowell, Frank Kostro, Darold Knowles, and so many others have said, the problems that haunted Steve probably could have been fixed today.

Steve pitched in relief on April 5, escaping six walks in three innings with no hits and no runs. On April 12 Steve relieved starter Pat Gillick in the seventh and turned in an uneven performance, masterful in the eighth inning but hampered by control trouble in the seventh and ninth. He started off pitching half speed, then increased his tempo to three-quarters speed, which also improved his strike-throwing proficiency.

When Dalkowski went to the mound on April 19 against the Toronto Maple Leafs, his control seemed to evaporate completely. "Dalkowski's innings probably were his last," reported the *Rochester Democrat and Chronicle* the next day. "The less said about the exhibition match (or was it a mismatch?) with Toronto, the better." Pitching in relief, Steve walked three batters in a row, scoring two runs, and gave up seven runs, all in one inning.

With the deadline looming to cut his roster to the legal limit, Clyde King was faced with the reality that his "special spring project" was a failure. On Easter Sunday, April 22, 1962, Dalkowski and catcher Frank Zupo were sent back to the Orioles for reassignment. "The pruning job was particularly difficult for King," the press reported. Steve had come a long way with the help of King's one-on-one attention. But "Dalkowski's improvement, though remarkable, just wasn't enough."

ELEVEN

A Season to Remember

"He's been terrific. You just can't believe he's the same pitcher we've been watching for six seasons."

—Barney Lutz, Orioles scout, 1962

Steve Dalkowski found himself back in the Empire State when the Orioles assigned their troubled southpaw to the Class A Pioneers of Elmira, New York. Although never a major league city, Elmira had a long and distinguished baseball history. Local historians write that Union soldiers and Confederate prisoners played baseball there as early as 1865. The Elmira Babies played the first professional game in town in 1888. Baseball became immensely popular until New York Governor Charles Evans Hughes outlawed Sunday play. Without Sunday games, the league went bust at the end of the season.

Pro ball returned in 1908. In 1923 the Elmira Red Jackets became a charter member of the New York Penn League. Going back and forth between local public ownership and private owners, the Elmira team was affiliated for a few years with the Brooklyn Dodgers and later with the St. Louis Browns.

Dunn Field, with seats for fifty-three hundred fans, opened in 1938 and added lights for night play the next year. During World War II, when all able-bodied men were subject to military service, the Pioneers survived by combining players from the Philadelphia Athletics and St. Louis Browns systems into one roster. Dedicated fans who couldn't get gasoline to drive to the park because of rationing rode hay wagons, took bicycles, or walked. In 1950, the Brooklyn Dodgers organization returned to town but pulled up stakes five years later, leaving Elmira without a professional team. After brief associations with the Washington Senators and Philadelphia Phillies, Elmira welcomed Harry Dalton and the Orioles in the fall of 1961.

When Steve Dalkowski arrived in town in the spring of '62, so did his old mentor Earl Weaver, who'd coached him in Aberdeen and was now at the helm at Elmira. As a team in the Class A Eastern League, the Pioneers equaled the highest level of professional baseball Dalko had ever played, on par with the Knoxville Smokies four seasons before. He was heading steadily back up the ladder. Sports editor Bill Lee spoke for many when he suggested that Dalkowski "would be with Baltimore right now if he had the remotest idea where home plate is located."

Weaver was one of those in the coaching and managing ranks who had seen the Dalkowski magic up close. He'd coached the incredible shutout win in Aberdeen when Steve had 21 strikeouts and averaged less than a walk per inning. He had also seen Steve throw wild pitches completely out of the park. Though some commentators were starting to refer to Dalko's celebrity in the past tense, Weaver understood the young pitcher's nervousness, lack of confidence, and his frustration with his own stubborn failure. He still saw the potential of a focused and controlled version of White Lightning heading into Dalko's sixth year in the game. Steve's reputation as a player among his peers was as strong as ever. Darold Knowles, a teammate in 1962 who played sixteen years in the majors, recalled that Dalkowski was "looked up to by the guys on the team. Everyone talked to Steve to learn about players, pitchers, and managers."

Weaver believed that by the time Steve joined the team, "there was nothing I could tell him. Hell, he had gotten every piece of advice, tried everything, and had the best pitching coaches in the world talk to him. What was I going to say? So I didn't say anything. I just let him pitch." While that claim wasn't literally true, Weaver always tried to keep his instructions simple and the attitude positive. One coaching technique he tried was to order Steve to throw more breaking balls. He told Dalko not to throw his fastball until he heard Weaver whistle from the sidelines, which Weaver would do when Steve got ahead in the count. The whistle was the sign he could unleash his heater. The sound of it was music to Steve's ears.

Considering Pat Gillick's earlier assessment that Steve's delivery had slowed a bit, it is possible that Dalkowski was changing his arm speed to throw his breaking ball, which had an impact on his fastball arm speed as well. These changes are problematic and would be discouraged by knowledgeable pitching coaches today. To encourage or even allow a pitcher to have different timing, sequencing, and thus mechanics for different pitches is a recipe for arm trouble, especially a hard-throwing pitcher such as Dalkowski.

Weaver strongly believed that Steve should vary his pitch selection. "In order to be a consistent winner," Weaver explained, "a pitcher needs some type of slow pitch that he can get over the plate to keep the hitter from sitting on the fastball." Weaver believed that the faster the fastball was, the more effective off-speed pitches became. A good off-speed pitch keeps a hitter's timing off fastball mistakes—and all pitchers make mistakes. Hitting is all about timing. Pitching is all about upsetting a hitter's timing. Weaver recognized this because in a fourteen-year career in the minor leagues he hit .267. A hitter must set his timing on the fastball, respect the fastball, and then try to adjust to the off-speed pitch. If the spread between the fastball and the off-speed pitch is not significant enough, the bat is already in the zone and the pitcher can be hit.

If, for example, Dalkowski threw a 100-mph fastball and an 84-mph breaking ball, the differential in speeds is very difficult for the hitter to cover. Weaver understood this principle and preached it to Steve. Weaver especially loved sliders. "Earl wanted every pitch to be a slider," pitching great Jim Palmer said years later. "He loved sliders. . . . He had an unnatural attraction to them. But to me it is a dangerous pitch. . . . [I]f you hang it, it gives the batter a huge edge."

After talking with a number of former Elmira teammates, it still isn't clear who taught Steve the slider. The Pioneers did not have a full-time pitching coach. The Orioles had a roving pitching coach named George Bamberger, a journeyman minor league pitcher who appeared briefly in the majors with an MLB record of 0-0 and an ERA of 9.42. Knowles recalled, "I saw George Bamberger once very briefly during my five years in the minors. During that encounter he offered no advice and then he flew out." So if it wasn't the pitching coach who taught Steve Dalkowski the slider, it must have been Earl Weaver, even though according to Jim Palmer, "the only thing Earl Weaver knew about the slider was that he couldn't hit one."

Dalkowski may have thrown a curveball, a slider, or both. Generally, a curveball will have more break and a greater downward movement. A slider, originally called a "nickel curve," will have less break and downward movement, but more lateral movement. The slider movement appears closer to the batter and is therefore more deceptive. It also has greater velocity than a curve, and its spin more closely resembles a fastball. The purpose of both breaking balls—curve and slider—is to prevent hitters from sitting on a pitcher's fastball exclusively.

Writing in the *Elmira Star-Gazette* as the '62 season unfolded, sports editor Al Mallette affirmed that he was "anxious to watch Steve burn that famed (and feared) fastball across the plate." Mallette continued, "I'm also hoping this is one year he throttles the wildness and becomes the 'phenom' the Orioles once labeled him. It would sure help the Pioneers—both in the standings and at the gate. Baseball fans love a strikeout whiz almost as much as they like a home run swatter."

A hearty crowd of 734 braved the bitter cold at Dunn Field in Elmira for Dalkowski's first start on May 7 against the Springfield Giants. After the leadoff batter popped out to shortstop, Steve struck out the next eight batters. Then that mysterious switch flipped off again. In the fourth inning he walked four batters, forcing in a run. By the time he was lifted for a pinch hitter in the seventh, Dalko had struck out 15 but the Pioneers trailed, 5–3. In the bottom of the ninth, Elmira loaded the bases with no outs but could only manage one more run in a 5–4 loss. As Jack Wheeland asked his readers in the *Elmira Star-Gazette* the next day, "Wonder how it feels to strike out 15 batters in 7 innings yet lose the baseball game?"

Despite the loss and Dalkowski's seven walks in seven innings, Elmira fans were impressed with their new hurler. Of the 21 batters he retired over the seven innings Dalko pitched, he played a part in retiring 16 of them through either his pitching or fielding skills.

Ten games into the season, Dalkowski had started only once in Earl Weaver's five-man rotation. Even so, attendance so far was almost double any other city in the Eastern League. His next two appearances were struggles for Dalko. He started a game on May 20 but lasted only 4⅔ innings. "The Pioneer southpaw who serves mustard with each toss" fanned six, walked nine, and threw 121 pitches before an early trip to the showers. His next start was worse. He was lifted after two-thirds of an inning following a walk, a wild pitch, a triple, two singles, and three runs. Numbers like these raise the question whether Weaver's demand for more breaking balls was allowing for greater hitter contact and thus hits.

For Steve's next outing, pitching in relief of Herm Starrette on May 28 in York, Pennsylvania, the pendulum mercifully swung back the other way. Dalko pitched six shutout innings with two hits, 12 strikeouts, and—surprisingly—only three walks. He also hit a double.

Former teammates consistently recall Steve as a fine hitter. Knowles considered him "excellent." Starrette also noted that on the Elmira team that year, "Earl would take him out whenever he wasn't pitching good. He wouldn't let him pitch into jams. Wouldn't let him fail. And it was working. His control was coming and he was throwing strikes." Even so, the next night Elmira was pummeled 15–4 by the Williamsport Grays. Coming to the mound as the third pitcher of the night, Steve pitched 2⅔ innings including a disastrous eighth when ten Grays came to the plate. One batter flied out and another struck out, but Dalko walked four, forcing in a run. All in all he struck out three, walked six, and gave up four runs.

The *Star-Gazette* had a regular feature in the sports section titled "Meet Pioneers." On June 12 Steve Dalkowski was the player in the spotlight. The profile was mostly a listing of former teams and a collection of career stats, though it did mention that Dalko was single and his hobby was hunting. Fans continued to turn out for his games knowing that whether he was throwing bullets or sending balls over the backstop it would be a show worth watching.

One of the great performances of the season for Dalkowski was overshadowed by the circumstances of the game itself. On June 18 the Pioneers played the Williamsport Grays, the team that had steamrolled them 15–4 earlier in the season. Johnny Ellen started for Elmira and pitched six solid innings before being relieved with the score tied, 3–3. Dalkowski came to the mound in the seventh inning, then proceeded to pitch 10—count 'em, 10—shutout innings with five strikeouts, six walks, six hits, and no runs. It was a masterpiece of control, by Dalkowski standards at least, from beginning to end.

Playing for Elmira that night, Lloyd "The King of New Orleans" Fourroux recalled the game in glowing terms. "June 18, 1962, was the day that Steve became a pitcher," Fourroux declared. "He threw 178 pitches and was in complete control of the game. He gave up just six walks and had only one wild pitch. He even held Richie Allen in check. No easy task, as Allen was one of the top hitters in the Eastern League who went on to be National League Rookie of the Year and an American League MVP." Herm Starrette took over the pitching for Elmira in the 17th inning and labored away until the Pioneers finally chalked up a run in the 21st inning for a 4–3 victory.

The big news of course was a 21-inning game that lasted almost five hours. The great victory for Dalkowski was that he pitched his way out of trouble after walking the first two batters in the eighth and after loading the bases in the 16th. He didn't exhibit his usual compulsion to hurl bullets with every pitch only to see many of them careen out of control. Instead he "appeared to be working smoothly, just trying to get his good pitches over." Some fans detected a slight reduction in his average speed, but that was more than offset by improved control and consistency. The decrease in velocity is confirmed by future two-time All-Star and fifteen-year MLB veteran Andy Etchebarren, who caught every Dalkowski inning in 1962. Andy remembers that Steve was throwing "only" 95–97 mph that season and had thrown much harder when he first came into professional baseball. Darold Knowles confirms the observation: "In 1962 Steve began throwing a lot of strikes, but he was not throwing nearly as hard as in years past."

On June 26, Dalko won his first game of the season with a 3–0 four-hit shutout. Steve pitched the entire game with 11 strikeouts and only six walks. Of his performance Etchebarren recalled, "Steve was easy and fluid that day. His arm speed was faster than anyone I had ever seen, but his fastball was light as a feather and easy to catch." Pioneer fans, who wanted him to succeed as badly as Earl Weaver did, cheered him on with unbridled exuberance. He was their rising star.

Steve's exemplary performance continued. Pitching another complete game, the first matchup of a June 30 doubleheader against the Binghamton Triplets, he won 4–1 with eleven strikeouts and an almost unbelievable two walks. On July 4 he shut out the York White Roses with 10 punch-outs. Recalling the game more than half a century later, Etchebarren said, "Steve had a good slider working and he relied on that and the four-seam fastball to put hitters away." For the first time in his career, Dalko was really pitching. But an even more impressive victory was soon to come.

His win over Springfield on July 9 was his fourth in a row. It was yet another shutout, this one wrapped up in only an hour and thirty-five minutes with a mere 117 pitches. Steve had now allowed exactly one run in 46 innings on the mound. Far more significant in Weaver's eyes, and far more important for Steve on his way to a major league career, was that in the 1–0 win on July 9, Steve Dalkowski pitched a complete nine-inning game without a single walk. Eleven strikeouts, five hits, no walks.

All of Elmira seemed to join in celebrating the triumph. Dalko was finally "a winning pitcher and the hottest one now throwing baseballs for a living in the Eastern League." Reporters asked Steve what happened. What was he doing differently? "I wish I knew," he told them in the locker room after his no-walk shutout. "I think I'm throwing the same but I'm not pumping as hard as I used to. Maybe that's good. . . . Maybe that's the answer. . . . I just don't know. . . . I wish I did" [ellipses in original text].

Weaver was beside himself. "It's unbelievable," he declared. "It's simply amazing." Barney Lutz, an Elmira native working as a Baltimore scout, had watched the game. "He's been terrific every time I've seen him this year," Lutz said. "You just can't believe he's the same pitcher we've been watching for six seasons in the organization." Since June 4 Steve had thrown 56 innings of baseball with 67 strikeouts and 28 walks. Over that span he had allowed two earned runs. Dalkowski was knocking on the door of the major leagues at last.

Unlike other promising moments in Dalko's career, this streak of great playing went on and on. By the time of the All-Star break in mid-July, Weaver considered Dalkowski one of the top players on the team, including him in a hypothetical ten-man staff that could "win today in the majors with a four-run cushion." On July 25 Steve pitched a three-hit, 6–0 shutout over the York White Roses with four walks. Four days later he walked one in 3⅓ innings with five strikeouts.

The solid performance slipped a bit after the four wins in a row, then recovered by mid-August. On the 16th he shut out the Binghamton Triplets 4–0 with 14 strikeouts and eight walks in "his most brilliant performance of the season." He also hit a double and scored a run. Steve started against Binghamton again on August 20. After walking the first two batters, he retired 15 in a row. By the end of the night Elmira had won 6–0 and Dalko had pitched back-to-back shutouts against the Triplets on a mix of curveballs, sliders, and his signature fastball. As opposing first baseman Ken "the Hawk" Harrelson, a future All-Star (1968 with the Boston Red Sox) who would play nine years in the majors, observed, "He's the best in the league when he has his control."

Steve Dalkowski ended the regular season at Elmira with a 7-10 record including six shutouts, eight complete games, and a 3.04 ERA. For the first time in his career he walked fewer batters than innings pitched: 144 walks and 190 strikeouts in 160 innings.

Weaver sent him to the mound for the first game of the league playoffs at York on September 10. Steve pitched 8⅓ innings of the 11-inning contest, which the Pioneers finally won 5–1 after a flurry of runs in the top of the eleventh went unanswered. Their second playoff victory came on the 14th. Dalkowski started again and pitched a masterful complete game, a five-hit, 2–0 win that marked his seventh shutout in eight victories. It was a study in control, with four walks, six strikeouts, and 130 pitches thrown.

Elmira went on to win the playoff title for the first time since 1943. The first week in June they had been in the league basement, and now in September they were champions. Sports editor Al Mannette called it the greatest comeback for the team since 1935. Each player received a playoff bonus of $46.14 from a pool funded by a twenty-five-cent surcharge on playoff tickets. Pioneers management rounded the award up to fifty dollars per man.

Weaver said it was Dalkowski's best year ever. "He's always had the stuff," he declared. "It simply developed this season." There was no talk that fall of trading Dalko or making him available for the draft. The Orioles were still smarting from their decision to trade Steve's old roommate Bo Belinsky to the expansion Los Angeles Angels after four years in the Orioles' minor-league organization. Though even more of a carouser off the field than Dalkowski, Belinsky made his mark in the majors early on by pitching the first no-hitter in Angels' history a few weeks after being called up.

What could account for Dalkowski's incredible improvement with the Elmira Pioneers in 1962 after five long years of frustration? It wasn't that Steve suddenly had a great pitching coach after being without one in his previous professional seasons. In the 1950s and '60s, minor-league teams didn't typically have dedicated expert pitching coaches. A coach did what he could to help pitchers improve, although most coaches had only general baseball knowledge and very little firsthand pitching knowledge.

Sometimes even the major league coaches were a mixed blessing. Despite his reputation as a pitching mentor during the years Dalko played for the Orioles organization, Harry Brecheen ended up being fired for developing a string of promising young pitchers who later had arm problems. (Whether he had any long-term negative effect on Dalkowski is unknown.)

Weaver was in his seventh season of minor-league baseball at Elmira in 1962, his sixth with the Orioles. On the field, he had played second base. He had no training as a pitcher. As Palmer later observed, "Earl never pitched, never caught, and wasn't much of a hitter." Even so, he had a way with pitchers, eventually coaching and developing great hurlers including Palmer, Dave McNally, Pat Dobson, and Mike Cuellar.

Weaver's great gift was his overall technical mastery of the game. Palmer said, "While Earl couldn't coach pitchers, he could find them. He could spot them, trade for them, stick with them. He might drive them crazy, but he knew the ones to drive crazy." Weaver had the ability to assess a young player's strengths and weaknesses in order to build up one and minimize the other. Throughout his career and afterward, Dalkowski said that Earl Weaver helped him master his control and improve his game more than anybody. Earl's greatest strength, especially in the minor leagues, was that he encouraged players by saying things that were supportive. He learned to recognize what it took to motivate a particular player and that one size does not fit all.

Weaver believed that Steve was easily distracted and confused, and that the reason his performance didn't improve is that coaches were trying to tell him too much at once. They fiddled with his pitching motion, his arm movement, his leg kick, his follow-through. They told him to concentrate. They told him not to panic when the going got rough. They had been a part of building his reputation as a flame-thrower for the ages, an amazing specimen who could throw a baseball through a backstop or bean a fan standing in line to buy a hot dog. By now, the fans expected a show everywhere he went, and management expected impressive stats. There was a lot of hype to live up to. Steve was so eager to please that his natural reaction was to overreach, try too much, throw too hard, worry about the game ahead, and thus slip back into old habits and old results. He had no support to help him reconcile the three people each of us has inside: the one others see, the one you know you want to be, and the one you know you are.

Coach Weaver responded by keeping it simple, working on one variable at a time, building up Dalko's confidence. It's also likely that Weaver sincerely wanted his young pitcher to succeed because he saw something of himself in him. As much as Weaver loved the game, he never made the big time as a player. He sensed that Steve loved the game as much as he did. Maybe he could help this youngster to the Show where he himself had failed. The proof of his approach is in the results. The year 1962 was by far the best of Steve Dalkowski's career to that point. As his coaching under Weaver continued, the best was yet to come.

Weaver also had a big heart when it came to overlooking Dalkowski's increasingly pervasive drinking problem. He took midnight phone calls telling him that Crazy Steve was sleeping in the street again or was in the drunk tank downtown. Weaver would crawl out of bed and go after him. When Steve was intoxicated, he resented Weaver as an authority figure, referring to him as "that friggin' midget." When he was sober, he credited Weaver above all others with his budding success.

Aside from the question of his effectiveness as a pitching coach, one fair criticism of Earl Weaver is his claim that he arranged IQ tests for his players and that Steve's score of 60 was the lowest of the group. (Orioles scout Jim Russo considered Dalko "dumb, awfully dumb. . . . He was a flamethrower, though I'm not sure he could spell flame.")

It is time to put the fiction of Dalko's low IQ to rest.

A score of 60—and there seems to be no concrete proof of this with Steve—would classify Dalkowski in the lowest 3 percent of the population in intelligence. People in this range were variously labeled in the 1960s as "morons" or "mentally defective." If he took the test at all, Steve likely scored low because he considered it a joke and paid no attention to it. A star quarterback who led his team to back-to-back undefeated seasons is not a moron. A ballplayer who can throw seven shutouts in a baseball season is not mentally defective.

In September 1962 Steve signed a contract to play winter ball for the Orioles in Puerto Rico, and the Orioles announced his assignment on October 22. Plans changed, however, because Dalko began the winter season on the roster of the Cardenales de Lara in the Venezuela Western League. A likely reason for the change was that Earl Weaver was managing the Cardenales. Based on their outstanding success during the regular season, one or both of them wanted to keep working with the other.

Dalkowski pitched 38 innings over 10 games in Venezuela and produced a 3-3 record. On a percentage basis it was his best effort to date, the first where the losses didn't outnumber the wins. He struck out 56 batters and walked 44 to go with an ERA of 5.21. In January he moved on to Puerto Rico, where he played for the Indios de Mayaguez.

One of Steve's teammates in Puerto Rico for the 1962 winter season was Frank Kostro. "I hadn't seen Steve since I faced him in the Sally League in 1958," Kostro said. "By this time he had lost his 100-mph fastball and was only throwing around 90 mph. Rumor was that they had him throwing relentlessly on the sidelines to tire him out during the season and he had hurt his arm. His arm bothered him enough that he left Puerto Rico and the team and went home early. I never saw Steve again. We became real good friends in Puerto Rico. He was a great guy—just a plain good guy that everyone liked. But I will say this: he was easily influenced by the guys around him. If someone suggested something stupid, like jump off a bridge, Steve would lead the way just to fit in with the guys."

Meanwhile back in Elmira, the fans were still enjoying the afterglow of their first postseason championship in nineteen years. Many considered the pitching staff to be the best since 1937. Also in the news was the move up from Class A to Double A for the Pioneers. Club director Harry Dalton figured that Dalkowski and other top players had "earned a boost" to Baltimore. Dave McNally, John Miller, and Dalkowski had the best chance of making the Orioles in Dalton's view, though if they were far down in the bullpen it would be better for them to go to Triple-A Rochester in order to play more regularly. On February 20, 1963, the Orioles announced that Steve Dalkowski had signed his contract for the coming season. Within the next few days he packed his bags and headed for the Orioles spring training camp in Miami, ready for what was bound to be his breakout year.

TWELVE

On Deck for the Show

"1963 Rookie Stars: Steve Dalkowski, Baltimore Orioles"
—TOPPS Baseball Card #496

On top of the experience Steve Dalkowski had gained with eight minor-league teams in the Orioles organization (one of them twice) over the past six years, he had two other big advantages going into the 1963 baseball season. The first was his long run of instruction under the eye of manager Earl Weaver—a full season in Elmira immediately followed by most of the winter season in Venezuela. More than any other coach, Weaver had figured out how to help Dalko improve his pitching performance. Now they had been together longer than Steve had ever worked for a single stretch with anyone else in his professional career.

Dalkowski would also collect pointers this spring from manager Clyde King of the Orioles' Triple-A Rochester Red Wings. It was King who experimented with corralling Steve's wildness by putting a batter on both sides of the plate and having him throw at half speed. When Steve fired one strike after another King encouraged him to do the

133

same thing during a game. If he could do it facing two batters at once, he could do it with one.

The other advantage for Dalkowski besides coaching was a change in the strike zone for Major League Baseball. The top of the zone had been lowered in 1950 from shoulder level to the level of the batter's armpits. For 1963 the strike zone would return to its pre-1950 level, opening the top edge for business and accepting high heat. American League president Joe Cronin believed it was a change for the better because it would encourage batters to swing more. He added, "The new strike zone is good for a pitcher with a hard, high fastball." It was tailor-made for Steve Dalkowski, whom Cronin singled out as one of the best-looking big-league rookies of the year.

Rochester Red Wings general manager George Sisler Jr. hoped the umpires would strictly enforce the new strike zone. "Because if they do," one New York sportswriter predicted, "Sisler and the Red Wings (and Baltimore) will come up with a gangbuster of a new pitcher in Steve Dalkowski. . . . If the strike zone goes up, so will Dalkowski . . . " Dalko was evidently assigned briefly to the Red Wings some time during the spring of '63.

Throughout the baseball world, coaches, managers, sportswriters, and fans were already thinking of Dalko in terms of the big leagues. Orioles manager Billy Hitchcock believed he had "a good chance of making the staff" as a big-league rookie during the coming season. This assessment was confirmed by Eddie Watt, who spent that spring with Dalkowski and would have ten solid years in the Orioles bullpen. "Steve was coming off a very good year in Elmira," he said. "He seemed to have conquered his control issues. His mechanics were good and easy. He never looked like he was working hard at all when he was pitching."

Not that his trademark wildness was completely gone. Pitching batting practice at the beginning of spring training, Steve's first hitter was Gene Woodling. The first pitch missed the batting cage completely.

The second went over Woodling's head and tore a hole in the netting at the back of the cage. The third pitch followed the same track as the second. Before Steve could wind up again, Woodling left the batting cage and refused to return.

In spite of this encounter, first impressions at the Orioles training camp in Miami underscored the shared sense that this was Dalko's year. In an intrasquad game on March 7, Steve pitched two scoreless innings, striking out four including future Hall of Fame shortstop Luis Aparicio and second baseman Jerry Adair, who would spend thirteen seasons in the majors. Steve was taken out after being hit on the wrist while trying to bunt. The injury seemed not to bother him, though a few days later Rochester sportswriter George Beahon reported the "bad news" that Dalkowski was "out with a severe sore arm." (Some accounts say it was Eddie Watt who hit Dalko during this game. Though Watt doesn't remember throwing the errant pitch, he said he might have: "I was just so darned excited to be in the major league camp I could have hit Mickey Mantle and I might not remember!")

Looking for a pitcher to round out the Orioles bullpen, Hitchcock believed Dalkowski had earned a place on the roster. It seemed like the organization would have the chance to unleash the famed Dalkowski fastball in Baltimore at last. As Hitchcock told reporters, "His chances depend on whether he can get the ball over the plate."

Five days later, Dalko pitched three innings in an exhibition game against the Detroit Tigers without giving up a hit. On March 17 he pitched three more hitless innings against major league sluggers, this time against the Dodgers, with five strikeouts: Bill Skowron, Wally Moon (future National League Rookie of the Year and two-time All-Star), Maury Wills (1962 National League MVP), Tommy Davis (reigning National League batting champ), and Don Drysdale (known as a fine-hitting pitcher). He punctuated that success by hitting a single off of Drysdale, the year's National League Cy Young winner. By the next week Dalkowski had pitched nine innings of major league exhibition baseball without giving up an earned run. The last six innings he had not given up a hit. Fans in Miami loved him, cheering encouragement every time he walked to the mound and roaring their approval with every strikeout. Steve "Wild Man" Dalkowski was a hero on his way to major league stardom.

A story on the UPI wire announced, "Dalkowski seen as possible Oriole bullpen ace." Writers began referring to him more regularly as an Oriole rookie. A Topps baseball card titled "1963 Rookie Stars" featured him along with three other pitchers, Fred Newman of the Angels, Carl Bouldin of the Senators, and Jack Smith of the Dodgers. The other three had actually played in a handful of major league games before the '63 season. All three would pitch in the majors during the coming season though only Newman would have a sustained major league career, playing six years with the Angels.

Covering spring training in Florida, Hartford sports editor Bill Lee asked Billy Hitchcock about Dalkowski's chances. Hitchcock replied that for the first time in what Lee called Steve's "meteoric baseball life," he had a real shot at a major league contract. "I think he has a good chance to make our staff, especially to come in from the bullpen for three or four innings," Hitchcock explained. "We've always known how hard he can throw. All Steve has to do is get the ball over. In the past, he hasn't been able to do it. This spring, he drops the ball right in there around the plate."

In past instances when Dalkowski was on a hot streak, he didn't seem to know why he was doing so well or how to keep it up. This time it was different. A more mature and self-aware Dalko assessed his recent performance, telling Lee that he'd "been around long enough to learn a little about pitching" and was coming off a relatively good year at Elmira with 192 strikeouts against 114 walks. What he emphasized most of all was playing winter ball in Venezuela under Earl Weaver. "Pitching winter ball helped a lot," he said. "I've got confidence now. I just hope I can keep it up."

Lee concluded, "[The Orioles] are definitely planning on taking him back to Baltimore. He may be ready, finally, to blossom into the authoritative pitcher he has always promised to be." On Friday, March 22, 1963, before one of the last exhibition games of the season in Miami, Hitchcock told equipment manager Clay Reid to measure Dalkowski for a Baltimore uniform. "He's staying with us," Hitchcock said.

That night the Orioles squared off against the high-flying New York Yankees, back-to-back winners of the World Series in 1961 and '62. It was a beautiful night, breezy and clear with temperatures in the mid-sixties. The Orioles beat the Yankees, 7–6, coming from behind to score their third win in a row over New York in exhibition play. Accounts of the game noted that Wild Man Dalkowski relieved former Elmira teammate Dave McNally in the sixth inning. Fellow southpaw Steve Barber, watching Dalkowski from the sidelines, remarked, "This kid is faster than I am."

Dalko struck out two batters, then left the game with "a pinched nerve in his pitching arm." The Associated Press added, "There was no report of how serious the injury would be for the bright rookie prospect." A later syndicated report reassured fans that Dalkowski's injury was "not serious." *The Sporting News* repeated, "It isn't believed to be serious." Some reports said he had strained a tendon.

This brings us to another crucial moment in the legend of Steve Dalkowski when the story was scantly reported at the time and, in the absence of solid facts, has morphed over the years to the point where the truth is elusive. What is true beyond a doubt is that in the spring of 1963 Dalkowski was pitching better than ever before. On March 22 something happened to his elbow in the sixth inning of an exhibition game against the Yankees, and from that moment on the trajectory of his life and career were never the same.

Steve started the inning by striking out Roger Maris and Elston Howard, both Yankee All-Stars. Sportswriter George Vecsey, watching the action that night, later wrote that Maris, who in 1961 had set the all-time record for home runs in a season with 61, "was theoretically standing near home plate in Miami, but his fanny was more or less in the Bahamas" when Dalkowski struck him out on three pitches. (Yankee batters teased each other in the locker room afterward about their various dance moves to keep out of Dalko's way.) After Howard also went down swinging, Hector Lopez singled.

The next batter up was Phil Linz. As Dalkowski threw him a slider, he felt something pop in his elbow. Herm Starrette, watching from the dugout, recalled that there was no doubt that night that Steve had made the Orioles. "He was throwing great," Starrette said. "And then he threw one pitch that went way wild, and he looked over at the dugout like something funny had happened, and everyone just sat there and watched. They thought it was just one of his [wild] pitches. Then he threw another pitch that went funny, and I said to Harry Brecheen, 'Cat, you better go out there. I think he's hurt himself.'" It was his elbow. By the time Brecheen got to the mound, Vecsey added, a knot had formed on Steve's arm "the size of a handball."

Oriole pitcher Dick Hall, who spent sixteen years in the majors, was also watching from the sidelines. "Steve was throwing real well," Dick remembered, "throwing like a guy who belonged on the staff. He was blowing away the fabled New York Yankee lineup and making it look easy. Then a pitch sort of popped out of his hand, went ten feet up in the air and harmlessly rolled over the first base foul line. Everyone on the bench looked at each other and seemed to say, 'What was that?' Steve's next offering looked the same and went about twenty feet up in the air and, again, rolled harmlessly over the first base foul line. Brecheen jumped off the bench and headed to the mound to check on Steve. That was the end of the night for Steve. Ultimately it was the end of his dream of playing in the majors and the end of his baseball career."

Eddie Watt added that the team trainer went with Brecheen to the mound. But, he said, "Remember in those days 'trainer' was simply a title. They had no medical training at all. The resume of our trainer was that he had changed the numbers on the scoreboard and then been our batboy!"

Retelling the story himself five years or so after the fact, Steve said he struck out Joe Pepitone and Roger Maris, then popped his elbow throwing a pitch to the next batter. In another retelling, he said his hand went numb after the pitch. According to teammate Boog Powell, Steve had "hurt his arm a little" playing in Puerto Rico that January. He was also hit on the wrist during a plate appearance March 7 in Miami, but neither of these injuries seemed to be affecting him at the moment. Steve later said he had never had arm problems in his life, but that night against the Yankees he felt something let go or "pop" in the elbow."

There are many variations to the story. A 1970 *Sports Illustrated* feature by Pat Jordan claimed that Dalkowski "fielded a bunt and threw off-balance to first base. He got the runner but also pinched a muscle in his elbow." Another source claims the bunt was by Joe Pepitone. An account years later said the injury happened when Steve was fielding a bunt from Jim Bouton. Yet another version claims the batter was Bobby Richardson. Other accounts have various batters facing Steve in various other innings, but the newspaper story published the day after the game makes it clear that Dalko pitched only the sixth inning. George Vecsey's report of that night, an expert eyewitness account printed the next day, is surely the most credible and reliable version of them all: Maris and Howard went down swinging, Lopez singled, and Linz was up when Dalkowski threw a slider and popped something in his elbow.

Fred Valentine, playing with the Orioles that spring, believed well-intentioned coaching was part of Dalkowski's problem. Dalko had learned from his years of experience and was "throwing very well," Valentine said. "Everyone knew that Steve would finally make the majors." Yet on the mound in Miami that night, Steve was "a totally different pitcher from the guy I saw in 1958," Valentine recalled. "His velocity was down, his mechanics were completely different, and his motion was not as fluid as it once had been." All the "random" changes various coaches had made in his delivery, Valentine believed, "had been leading to the arm problem that showed up against the Yankees. . . . It didn't just show up all of a sudden."

The Orioles faced a dilemma. After six years and counting, their legendary fireballer had finally found the handle: at the end of the '62 season he had turned in his best performance ever. In his last 57 innings he struck out 110 and walked 21, giving up a grand total of one earned run. Now in spring training he'd struck out Roger Maris on three pitches. At the same time, he was at least temporarily damaged goods, and the Orioles had to get their roster down to the required number of players for opening day. Three players were shipped back to the minors on March 28, but the team held on to Dalko. On April 5, the last day to cut players, Dalkowski and fellow pitcher John Miller were optioned to the Rochester Red Wings.

Four days later Dalkowski appeared in the bullpen for the first time since his injury. Red Wings Manager Darrell Johnson planned to have him throw in practice every other day for two weeks, pitching fastballs only. Onlookers thought his deliveries carried as much heat as other pitchers' at their peak. Still the elbow gave him trouble. On April 15, Dalkowski went on the disabled list. He had not pitched since his injury on March 22. The same day Steve went to Rochester, the Orioles announced he had been advised by an orthopedic surgeon not to throw his breaking ball for another ten days. As Pat Gillick wryly explains, "Fifty years ago 'rest' was the treatment for everything. Put whatever ails you under hot water. Very few medical operations."

Though Steve's seemingly sudden arm trouble was a setback, no one considered it a threat to his career. On the contrary, praise and encouragement kept coming. In his syndicated column "The Scorecard," Harry Grayson doubled down on Dalko's recent improvement and future prospects: "The Orioles' phenom this spring is Steve Dalkowski . . . wilder than the man from Borneo on and off the field. . . . Like nearly all kid left-handers, Dalkowski couldn't find the plate with a telescope. The result was that . . . managers and coaches [worked] on him until he was so confused he had a hard time finding his way to the park." With Elmira in 1962, Grayson pointed out, Dalkowski's innings pitched (114) were more than his bases on balls (110) for the first time. Grayson wrote that Steve credited Clyde King and Earl Weaver with the improvement. He also reported that Orioles pitching coach Harry Brecheen said Dalko could be "called back from Rochester at any time," the implication in the wording being that Brecheen thought of the young southpaw as essentially a member of the Orioles squad.

On April 20 Steve's former teammate Dave McNally, an $80,000 bonus baby from Montana who would go on to win 181 games for the Orioles, started for Baltimore in place of an injured Chuck Estrada, notching an 8–1 victory with nine strikeouts. According to the *Elmira Star-Gazette*, the ex-Elmira lefty, "it is believed, made the Oriole squad this spring only because of an injury to the pitching arm of Steve Dalkowski." Without that pop in his elbow, Dalko would almost certainly have been the one covering for Estrada on the mound that night.

The Red Wings played their home opener on April 24. Dalkowski remained on the disabled list, though reports indicated he could be recalled to the active roster in a day or two. He was finally restored to the lineup on April 30. But any chance Dalkowski might start that night was dashed when the game was called on account of snow.

On May 2, George Beahon surveyed the scene in his regular column for the Rochester *Democrat and Chronicle*. The fact that Dalkowski's long struggle on and off the mound was old news by then did nothing to dampen the writer's interest or dim his hopes that this might finally be Dalko's moment.

"Dalkowski is a valuable property," Beahon wrote, "not for sale at any price." He noted that Steve had injured his arm throwing a slider, "which is what some baseball men call a censored mixed breed consisting of a nickel curveball and a ten-cent fastball." Red Wing manager

Darrell Johnson "maintains the slider causes more serious damage to young pitchers (right down to Little League level) than all the wine, women, song, and nicotine in sight."

"Some night he might walk all of Red Wing Stadium," Beahon continued, but at no time "did Baltimore brass ever waver on this kid. . . . Dalkowski's projected range for 1963 . . . started with the Orioles and ended in Triple-A Rochester. He would go no lower. Billy Hitchcock, the Daddy-O, said last winter he had big plans for the young left-hander." Hitchcock said that what he wanted Dalkowski to do was "walk into the clutch spot with one or two runners on base, to strike somebody out. He will do it with his fastball." Once again, the key to success was building up Steve's confidence.

Beahon pointed out that the year before and in this year's spring training, managers worked to cut back Steve's speed and improve his control. "With his firepower, three-quarters speed is more than plenty. As some great phrasemaker once said, Dalkowski could throw a strawberry through a battleship. . . . Before he decided to go pitching instead of throwing, Dalkowski was a one-man baseball show. Today he doesn't insist on striking out everything that waves a bat."

The same day Beahon's column ran, Steve pitched the bottom of the tenth inning in relief for Rochester against the Richmond Virginians. He walked the first batter on four pitches, then gave up a hit and was charged with the loss. By May 12 Dalkowski was back in Baltimore for more treatment on his elbow. When he returned, his manager decided against putting him on the mound because of game-time temperatures in the thirties. Dalko was moved off the disabled list and back on to the active roster May 27. Two nights later he made his first appearance for the Red Wings at home, pitching two shutout, no-hit innings "with consummate ease."

After that performance, the road turned rocky. On June 3 Dalkowski registered his second loss when he relieved starter Nelson Chittum. He opened the final inning with two walks, then gave up a run. On the 19th, Steve faced the very situation Billy Hitchcock had described in George Beahon's column earlier in the year. On the road against Toronto, Dalko went into the game with two outs in the ninth and runners on first and third. His first pitch to pinch hitter Joe Hannah was a wild pitch. Catcher Joe Pignatano scrambled to retrieve it as the third base runner, Ty Cline, sprinted for home. Dalko beat Cline to the plate, fielded the throw from Pignatano, and tagged the runner out. The play was a success, though not the sort of success Hitchcock had in mind.

On June 29, Herm Starrette and another Rochester teammate, outfielder Fred Valentine, were called up to Baltimore. Before the week was out, on July 2, Steve Dalkowski was sent back down to Double-A Elmira in exchange for lefty Dick Tetrault. Dalko was "solidly unhappy about the switch" according to the Rochester press. His record at Rochester was 0-2, nine strikeouts, and 14 walks over 12 innings for a 6.15 ERA—a disappointing showing compared with his stellar results in spring training barely three months earlier, before his injury. Red Wings manager Darrell Johnson explained that the decision to reassign Dalko didn't mean the team was abandoning their big plans for him. Rather, they were looking for a way to give him more time on the mound. "If Steve can get enough work to get his control in shape, he's a major league pitcher," Johnson said. Whether that work was in Elmira or Rochester didn't matter to the franchise.

Many years later, Fred Valentine suggests that the team should have taken a different tack: "I always felt that they should have turned him into an outfielder to take the pressure off him as a pitcher," Valentine said in a recent interview. They could have brought him in once in a while to pitch and see if the anxiety went down and the control went up. He was a good teammate, a good hitter, and he had a cannon for an arm. Who in the hell was going to go first to third on Steve's arm? No one!"

Although Dalkowski was unhappy to be going back to Elmira, the fans there were delighted. They cheered him as the "hero returning," the "fireball hero of last year's Pioneer staff" who "saw limited action in Rochester after getting a good look from Baltimore in the spring." He would be reunited with his mentor Earl Weaver, "who brought him along slowly last season to become one of the standout pitchers in the league." Their reunion was delayed slightly while Weaver finished a three-day suspension for "a run-in with an umpire."

Steve's appearances in Elmira were the familiar mix of brilliance and frustration. Some days were good. In a 3–1 loss to York on July 12, Steve pitched four innings in relief with seven strikeouts, four walks, three hits, and no runs. Some days were not so good. On July 24 he came on in relief in the sixth, loaded the bases with three walks in a row, and was pulled. Dalkowski made his first start since returning to Elmira on July 28 in the second game of a doubleheader. The home team lost the first game 8–2. In 3⅓ innings Steve allowed six earned runs on five hits with three walks and three strikeouts, taking the 9–0 loss.

On the sidelines and away from the pressure, Steve's arm seemed as powerful and precise as ever. After a game was rained out one day, catcher Andy Etchebarren bet some of his teammates that Dalkowski could throw a ball through a split log wall at the end of the bullpen. Bets were placed, Steve went into his windup, and the ball crashed through the wall. Yet by the middle of August, Steve's elbow was giving him serious trouble again. He returned to the disabled list August 21.

As part of an end-of-the-season wrap-up in early September, Johnson spoke of how the team missed Fred Valentine's "infectious spirit" and hitting ability along with Herm Starrette's pitching skills after they were both called up to Baltimore. He listed several other players whose departures had sent the Red Wings' fortunes downhill at the end of the season. He made no mention of Steve Dalkowski. Nonetheless, at the very end of the season, on October 12, Dalko was sent back up to Rochester. More than anything else, this move was a show of confidence on the part of the Orioles organization that allowed Dalko to end the 1963 season on a higher rung than he started, only one step away from the major league debut that hovered tantalizingly just out of reach.

Even so, by this time the Orioles were less enthusiastic than before about their troubled pitching sensation. At the end of the 1963 season, professional baseball was preparing to institute its first comprehensive player draft system, which would start in 1965. Teams could protect existing players by putting them on their major league rosters. Any non-roster player who had completed his first full year of pro baseball could be drafted by another team for only $8,000. The big question was which players a team should protect. Paul Richards, by this time general manager of the National League expansion Houston Colt .45s (later the Astros), said, "The hardest part is trying to consider the value of these players two, three, four years from now."

The Orioles evidently didn't think Dalkowski's future was promising enough to protect him from the competition. He was not added to the major league roster, yet there were no takers. At the start of the season he was Baltimore's No. 1 rising star. Now they were willing to let him go for $8,000, but no other team would make room for him. The vision and momentum for Dalko's path to stardom began to waver.

THIRTEEN

On the Bubble

"By all odds this must be a make-or-break trip back to Elmira for the fun-loving fireballer."

—*Elmira Star-Gazette*, April 21, 1964

arl Weaver arrived in Elmira near the end of February 1964. To local fans this meant baseball spring training was right around the corner. Some of the first questions and conjectures about the upcoming season focused on the future of Steve Dalkowski. Would he be back in Elmira? Or would he move on up to Baltimore as he'd seemed certain to do before he hurt his arm? While Weaver thought Steve Barber was the best-performing pitcher he'd coached, he still believed Dalkowski had more potential than anyone else. "Let it suffice that he is the greatest unharnessed pitching talent ever to set foot on the mound," he said effusively. Even so, he wasn't sure where Steve would end up at the beginning of the regular season. He thought it likely that Dalko and teammate Frank Bertaina would move back up to Triple-A Rochester or to the Orioles.

Accounts of Steve's arm injury sometimes say he pinched a nerve that night in Miami or that his arm went numb. From the descriptions, it's also possible that he damaged the ulnar collateral ligament in his pitching arm. This is a thick ligament on the inside of the elbow that connects the humerus or upper arm bone to the ulna, the larger of the two lower arm bones. The ligament can be damaged by overuse or misuse. In Steve's case, one scenario is that he tried to throw too many breaking balls without being taught how to throw them properly. The repetitive stress on the elbow eventually caused the ligament to tear. Based on current studies by the American Sports Medicine Institute, the ulnar collateral ligament (UCL) should not be able to handle the rigors of throwing a baseball at all, let alone throwing a baseball 100 mph or throwing hundreds of pitches every fourth day.

In 1974, California surgeon Dr. Frank Jobe would develop a surgical procedure to repair ulnar collateral ligament damage by replacing the torn ligament with one taken from elsewhere in the patient's own body. Named after its first patient, Dodgers pitcher Tommy John, the surgery not only extended the careers of many big-league pitchers, but it sometimes allowed them to throw faster than they had before the operation. Had Tommy John surgery been available ten years earlier, it might have relaunched Steve Dalkowski's career. As it was, Dalko approached the 1964 season on the bubble, with advancement to Baltimore on one side and a trip back down the minor-league ladder on the other.

Dalkowski was one of fourteen pitchers on the squad when the Rochester Red Wings opened their spring training camp in Daytona Beach on March 19. The Orioles hoped to keep Steve in Triple-A ball if there was any way to do so. Manager Darrell Johnson had to choose nine members of the pitching staff to take back to Rochester. The rest would go to Thomasville for reassignment or be released. In early practices Dalko seemed to be getting the ball over the plate. His control looked good. His first outing, pitching in relief against Seattle, was promising. Before the game was called because of rain, Steve pitched to eleven batters, allowing one hit with one walk and one strikeout. Johnson commented, "Steve threw more strikes than I expected he would."

Rochester sustained its first loss of the training season against the Dallas Rangers on March 31 in Daytona Beach. Pitching in relief, "woefully wild" Dalkowski "walked half the ballpark" including three in the fifth to force in a run, then gave up a single that drove in two more runs. In the seventh he walked two and allowed two hits for another run. The unbeaten Rangers won, 7–5.

As spring training progressed, there was more bad news than good about Steve's performance and control. To coaches, reporters, and writers who knew him, Steve Dalkowski was no longer the rising star they'd eagerly watched come up through the ranks, the fireballing southpaw who was *this close* to the Show. Reporting from Daytona for the Rochester *Democrat and Chronicle*, Bill Vanderschmidt gave a measured yet frank assessment of Dalkowski's present situation and future prospects. Headlined "Crackers Stop Wings: Dalkowski Blows Up," his story began, "Steve Dalkowski, his golden left arm tarnished with disuse, pitched himself a giant step nearer Elmira yesterday [April 8] as the Atlanta Crackers beat the Red Wings, 7 to 6, at blister-hot City Island Stadium.

"Elmira—spelled S-I-B-E-R-I-A by ballplayers hoping to win Triple-A jobs in Rochester—was home to Dalkowski last year after a sore arm ruined his first real shot at the majors. Just twelve months ago Dalkowski was throwing as hard as any pitcher in baseball and seemed to have found the control which had always been lacking before. 'He had made our club,' said Billy Hitchcock, last year's Orioles manager. 'He was throwing aspirins and tearing up the Yankees in an exhibition game when he popped something in his elbow. He hasn't been the same since . . . He just isn't throwing,' said Hitchcock. Because the Red Wings still have to lop at least four pitchers from the staff, Dalkowski's chances of remaining are slim indeed."

The very next day, Steve was sent to the Orioles' Thomasville, Georgia, camp for reassignment to another team because of his "poor effort." This short description carries a big meaning. Up until now Dalko was universally described as a tireless worker, constantly trying to improve his craft. However drunk he was the night before a game, he was the first one running wind sprints the next morning. One of the reasons everyone stuck with him and rooted for him tirelessly over the years was because he tried so hard, wanted it so badly, and by any reasonable standard deserved a place on the Baltimore Orioles roster.

After the Red Wings sent him packing, for the first time in his career Dalkowski left the impression that he'd quit trying. He was assigned to Thomasville on Thursday, April 9, and expected there by coach Earl Weaver over the weekend. He didn't make it then, or the day after. He arrived at Thomasville five days late. By that time Weaver and others in the Orioles system wondered if—with his drinking increasing and his performance decreasing—Steve Dalkowski had finally gotten to be more trouble than he was worth.

The Orioles fined him $20 a day, $100 in all, for failure to report to Thomasville and decided to leave him in Georgia "until he proves his intentions to play," according to the *Elmira Star-Gazette*. "It was felt he wasn't putting forth the effort expected of him." This drastic change in attitude was likely the toxic result of disappointment and frustration over his elbow injury combined with the accumulated effects of years of alcoholism.

When he showed up in Thomasville at last, Dalko arrived with fellow pitcher Frank Bertaina. They were both drunk, swigging from bottles of beer as they climbed out of a taxi at the training complex. Staggering uneasily toward the clubhouse, the two looked like they had stopped at every bar between Daytona and Thomasville. They certainly had the time. Tim Sommer, a second-year player who recalled meeting Dalkowski that day in his book *Beating Around the Bushes*, helped

Dalko to bed: "I tucked him in and rushed to tell all about Superman who looked more like a choir boy."

Pitcher Eddie Watt, whose trajectory that season was the same as Dalko's—spring training with the Orioles, then Rochester and on to Thomasville—clearly remembered Steve's arrival more than fifty years later.

"I had my car in Daytona, so Ricardo Delgado and I jumped in and made the two-hundred-mile drive to Thomasville. When Ric and I arrived, Weaver asked us where Steve was. We shrugged our shoulders and said that we didn't know. It was five days later when Dalkowski showed up. He looked disheveled when he arrived, with just a tooth-brush in his shirt pocket. He had no suitcase as, he explained, it had been lost somewhere on the trip. Then Weaver asked him why he didn't report immediately, and Steve glibly responded that he was 'told to report. No one said anything about when.'

"In Thomasville we were all housed in Quonset huts. Each hut had six army cots. There was a vacant cot next to me, and Steve took it. The next morning at about 5:30 a.m., our coaches came in and told the play-ers to get up to get ready for the day. I heard a loud pop and *shuuuuuush*. I turned around to see Steve drinking a warm beer for breakfast."

Weaver announced on April 20 that Steve Dalkowski would be suiting up with the Elmira Pioneers for the third time. As the local press reported, "The man with the 'golden' left arm is headed back to Elmira for the third time. . . . By all odds, this must be a make-or-break trip . . . for the fun-loving fireballer." Dalkowski called Elmira his favorite baseball town, and the fans were excited about having him back. To make room for him on the roster, the team put lefty Dick Tetrault on the disabled list with a sore arm.

Trying to help Steve manage his life off the field, Weaver assigned first baseman Joe Altobelli as his roommate. Altobelli was a level-headed, thirty-two-year-old veteran in his thirteenth year of profes-sional baseball who had played parts of three seasons in the majors.

Maybe some age and experience would give Dalko an example to live by. It didn't turn out that way.

Steve's demotion back to Elmira hadn't dulled his sense of humor or his willingness to show off. Some time at practice during the spring, Dalko was running in the outfield and stopped by teammate Davey Johnson. Like everyone else on the team, Johnson had heard stories of Steve's legendary pitching power. "Hey, Steve," Johnson said, "can you throw the ball through the fence?" The outfield fence was made of 1 x 6 lumber.

"I don't know," Steve answered. He then picked up a baseball and threw it through the wooden fence. Everyone who tried to duplicate the feat saw their ball bounce off the boards. Another time, supposedly on a ten-dollar bet, Steve threw the ball from the center-field fence over a 40-foot-high backstop behind the plate.

This was also the season of Steve's notorious encounter with the police in his teammate's car. Herm Starrette, fellow pitcher and some-time roommate, shared his version of the Dalkowski vs. traffic cop story in a history of the Orioles, *From 33rd Street to Camden Yards*:

"One night in Elmira he got pretty lit after a game, and he was driving around in Ray Youngdahl's [beautiful new] Cadillac" with Youngdahl asleep in the back seat. The cops stopped him right near the stadium. Though Steve was obviously drunk, the policeman was a Pioneers fan and decided to let him go. But then "Steve threw the thing in reverse and just slammed it into the cop's car. . . . Tore up the Cadillac. . . . [T]hey took him down to jail and called Earl . . . and they said, 'We got Steve down here,' and Earl said, 'God dammit, let him stay there tonight.'"

It was unclear whether Steve rammed the police cruiser on purpose or by accident. He seldom drove and around this time stopped driving altogether after having his license revoked. Whatever the truth was, even Weaver—who'd brought Steve along with such care and atten-tion for so long—had had about all of Dalko's behavior that he could stomach. He was tired of retrieving Steve, hung over and remorseful, from jail every month or two.

Starette later claimed that rooming with Steve Dalkowski was like rooming with a suitcase. (This comment was attributed to several of Steve's roommates over the years.) Steve was never in their room because he was always out carousing. Dalko continued borrowing money from his teammates to get through the week, faithfully paying it back every payday. Ray Youngdahl started holding onto Steve's paycheck and giving him an allowance, hoping to keep him from spending every dime on alcohol.

To Weaver's credit, he kept trying to pull his once-promising fireballer back into shape. Dalkowski appeared several times in relief with credible results—despite pitching with temperatures in the low thirties—before his first start of the regular season for Elmira on May 25. Sick with a virus, he nonetheless carried a one-hitter into the fifth inning before his control vanished. On June 4 Dalkowski started the second game of a doubleheader, striking out nine in six innings with four walks in a 4–1 loss.

The last straw for Weaver and the Pioneers came on June 8, 1964, when Elmira was pummeled 13–3 in the first game of a homestand doubleheader against Springfield. Dalkowski was relieved with one out in the first by outfielder-pitcher Gerry Gilbert after ten men had batted and four had scored. Three days later the club sent Steve packing back to the Stockton Ports, where he had played the 1960 season. Weaver told the press Steve was cut "because he couldn't get enough work to get his arm back into shape." That was the public story, and it was true. What was also true was that Steve's after-hours antics had become too distracting to the whole team and were affecting team morale.

Orioles director of farm operations Harry Dalton asked Stockton skipper Harry Dunlap if he wanted the troubled lefty. "Maybe it was the ego that made me say yes," Dunlap later admitted. "A manager always figures he could be the one to straighten out a guy who's had problems."

This reassignment was the beginning of the end for Steve Dalkowski. As the local press reported, "One of the most promising careers in Oriole baseball history has apparently ended." But Steve wasn't ready to give up. He headed west to California determined to prove them wrong. He may have been distracted and distressed, his performance might have been off, but baseball was the only life he knew.

On June 13, 1964, the Stockton Ports announced Dalkowski was rejoining the team. His return, and his previous Stockton record of 262 strikeouts and 262 walks in 170 innings during the 1960 season, were big news in town. Dalko was a legend in the eyes of his new teammates. He was older than most of them, had been on the team before, and was known coast to coast for his speed and unpredictability on the mound and the endless partying in his private life. Young players looked up to him and asked him for advice. He was unfailingly nice and willing to help everyone. For all his seasoning, he still sometimes showed a glimpse of underlying naivete. Stockton teammate Frank Peters heard him refer to a manager as "coach." The manager corrected Steve, saying, "Legion ball, high school, and college have coaches. The pros don't."

Dalkowski met the club on the road at San Jose. His first appearance was three days later against the Fresno Giants, relieving starter Pat McMahon in the fifth inning. He struck out the first batter he faced, walked three in a row to fill the bases, then pitched himself out of trouble by fanning the next two. In the seventh he struck out one before again loading the bases with walks. Manager Harry Dunlop pulled him for Ricky Delgado. On June 18 he did better against the Bakersfield Bears, pitching two no-hit innings with five strikeouts and only one walk.

The Stockton bullpen was in center field. One day somebody dared Steve to throw the ball as far from there as he could. Without warming up, he threw a ball from the bullpen to the top of the backstop behind the plate 420 feet away. "Nobody could do that!" one astonished witness said. (This story is so much like the Stockton tale that the two could be different versions of the same event. Regardless, it raises the question of how badly his arm was hurt.)

Fans loved Dalkowski. Bruce Babcock, a lifelong baseball aficionado, spoke about seeing Dalko as a wide-eyed nine-year-old during the 1964 season. "Steve was pitching against the Santa Barbara Dodgers at Laguna Park," Babcock said. "His reputation for throwing hard and being wild got to the park long before the game between Stockton and Santa Barbara was to start. Everyone was talking about Dalkowski when we arrived, but I was a Dodger fan and equally excited about seeing Don Sutton, Bill Singer, Wes Parker, and a young LA kid named Willie Crawford in his first professional game. Steve threw a baseball harder than anyone I had ever seen then or since. It was an experience that I will never forget."

"Dazzling Dalkowski" was in top form on Independence Day 1964—it was also Little League Day—when he pitched a superb complete game at home against the San Jose Bees for a 3–1 victory. Before a small but exuberant crowd of 998 fans, "Steaming Steve" chalked up seven scattered hits with 14 strikeouts and only two walks, making this statistically one of the best games of his career. Whatever frustration or resentment he felt earlier was at least temporarily under control.

As his improvement on the mound held steady, he continued to enjoy his postgame adventures. One night after he was relieved in the fourth inning, he showered and left the clubhouse with four dollars in his pocket. He came back to the hotel the next morning with his face covered in lipstick, fifty dollars in gambling winnings, and a pound of bacon in his hand that he was eating raw. As Frank Peters remembered years later, "The whole team was amazed but excited about being part of the Dalkowski legend and seeing a new tale with their own eyes."

Steve had long since developed a reputation as a ladies' man. Though he didn't have matinee idol looks, he did have a boyish attractiveness that gave him tremendous appeal. Some time during his months on the west coast, he established a relationship with a woman his friends called the Blonde Bomber. She was a buxom young lady with a slinky walk, peroxide hair, and a preference for form-fitting clothes. She and Dalko may have become an item when he first played for the Ports in 1960 and then reconnected when he returned to Stockton in 1964. He seemed sure she would still be around even though they had not stayed in contact during the four years he was away. He bragged to his friends that she would show up when they were barhopping, and she did. One of his teammates compared the Bomber's glamor and sex appeal to actress Elizabeth Taylor.

Whatever understanding he had with the Blonde Bomber didn't keep him from chatting up other attractive girls. The Ports lived in the Pershing Apartments in Stockton. It was a decent but modest complex in a town where housing was in short supply. In addition to the Ports, railroad engineers lived there in apartments maintained for them by the railroad. Between the engineers and the ballplayers, there was a lot of coming and going at the complex.

Another resident at the Pershing Apartments was Linda Moore, freshly graduated from the College of the Pacific in Stockton and waiting to start her first year teaching in the nearby town of Manteca. Though her family lived within walking distance of the campus, Linda moved in with some older friends at Pershing for the summer. With short black hair, a winning smile, and an outgoing personality, Linda struck up casual friendships with the young ballplayers. She did housekeeping for them as well. "I was their Wendy," she later explained, "and they were definitely Peter Pan boys."

Linda recognized some of the same maturity in Steve that his teammates had sensed, and for the same reasons. Though Dalko was only twenty-five that summer, she saw him as an elder statesmen of the team, partly because he was older than many of the others (the average age was twenty-one) and because he had spent a season with the team years before. There was a trace of chemistry between Linda and Steve, but Linda didn't expect any sort of romantic relationship to develop. She had heard all about, and seen, the Blonde Bomber. She herself had gone all the way through college without a steady boyfriend.

It was in Reno, where Steve and Herm Starrette were loosening up before a game one night, when Dalko told Herm he was going to throw his first warmup pitch over the press box. True to his word, he fired the ball over the press area and out of the stadium, sending sportswriters scattering. When manager Billy DeMars asked Starrette if the crazy shot was thrown on purpose Starrette answered, "I don't think so; that's just Steve."

Steve continued to run hot and cold through the month of August: strikeouts and walks, Dr. Jekyll and Mr. Hyde. Dalkowski, who along with teammate Ed Barnowski had been christened the Ports' Pitching Poles, turned in a solid performance on August 14 with 12 strikeouts and three hits in a 4–1 win over Bakersfield. By mid-August Barnowski led the league in strikeouts, fanning 280 in 189 innings. Had Steve started the season in Stockton, he might well have given Barnowski a run for the title. Dalko had 107 strikeouts over 85 innings to date for a 6-3 record and an impressive 2.33 ERA. Some observers saw the old Steve back on the mound during his outing against Bakersfield. The lead in next day's *Humbolt Standard* began, "One of baseball's most storied pitchers, Steve Dalkowski, is back with the Stockton Ports and seems to be sharper than ever."

Steve turned in some excellent performances in the weeks that followed. He pitched a complete game, 5–0 shutout against Modesto on August 19. Though the Ports lost to Bakersfield, 6–1, on August 28, he delivered one of his most controlled games of all time. In 8⅔ innings, he struck out 18 and walked only one. However, he gave up 12 hits, which bolstered his contention that his slower, more controlled pitching was getting hit. Perhaps he was trying to protect his arm and, as a result, was tipping pitches. (Not everyone agreed that his pitching was slower. Jay Johnstone, who played twenty years in the majors, watched one night from the on-deck circle as a member of the San Jose Bees. To him the pitches smacking into the catcher's glove sounded like they were being thrown "nine hundred miles an hour! I didn't want to face him.")

The last home game of the season for the Ports was a doubleheader on September 1 against Reno. It was Player Appreciation Night, with players receiving shirts and wallets before the game. Steve's friend Pat McMahon, with help from what the press called Pat's "tantalizing, unhittable curve ball," pitched a five-hit, 1–0 shutout in the first game. The victory was McMahon's second shutout in three starts and evened his record for the year at 10-10. Relieving starter Ron Kotick in the second game, Steve struck out seven of the eight batters he faced and notched the 2–1 win. This victory gave Dalkowski an 8-4 record for the season with an ERA of 2.83.

The uptick in Steve's pitching was too little too late. As Ports manager Harry Dunlop would later say, "Everybody loved him. He was just easily led astray and couldn't stop drinking." On September 2, one day after his win against Reno, the Orioles announced they had traded Steve Dalkowski to the Pittsburgh Pirates' Triple-A Columbus Jets in Ohio. This was part of a deal that brought Jets righthander Samuel "Sad Sam" Jones to Baltimore as a player/coach. Jones started as a Negro League pitcher in 1946, broke into the majors with the Cleveland Indians in 1951, and played big-league baseball for eleven seasons. He and Dalko had a key pitching strategy in common: throw hard. For three years in the 1950s, Jones led the National League in both strikeouts and walks.

The press back in Elmira, which continued to follow Dalkowski's career, took this latest move as a bad sign. The *Star-Gazette* reported, "One of the brightest prospects the Baltimore organization has ever had will try to pick up the pieces of a shattered career with the Pittsburgh Pirates. . . . Steve Dalkowski, southpaw flame-thrower, . . . was victimized by wildness in a long minor-league career including his victorious '62 Elmira campaign. He apparently cured that flaw in spring training with the Orioles in 1963 before a pinched nerve kept him out of a big-league uniform."

Steve announced to his roommates and neighbors at the Pershing Apartments in Stockton that he was moving to Ohio and asked Linda Moore to take him to the airport. She was glad to oblige, driving him in her new blue MG. As they said goodbye, Steve told her, "I'm coming back for you." Having some hint of Steve's lifestyle off the field and having gotten an eyeful of the Blonde Bomber, she answered, "Oh, yeah. Sure."

She never expected to see him again, though she did hear that his first night with the Jets he pitched a shutout victory and hit a grand slam. The next night in Columbus the old wildness was back. Steve got drunk after the game, knocked over some streetlamps, and got arrested.

In the short time left during the 1964 season, Dalkowski pitched 12 innings for Columbus, yielding a 2-1 record. These two victories were Dalko's only career wins in Triple-A baseball.

Steve went home to Connecticut at some point after the end of the season. It's uncertain how long he was there, but it was long enough to be arrested again. In the local crime report for January 16, 1965, the *Hartford Courant* noted that Steve Dalkowski, twenty-five, of 67 W. Main Street, was arrested for breach of the peace. He was sentenced to thirty days in jail suspended and probation for six months.

Dalkowski's return to Columbus for spring training with the Pirates organization the next season was short-lived. On March 30, 1965, the Jets announced that he would go back to Baltimore. The previous season's trade with Pittsburgh was reversed: Dalkowski returned to the Orioles and Sam Jones rejoined the Pirates. Jones's brief appearance with Baltimore in '64 was his last outing in the major leagues; he finished his professional career three years later in Columbus.

The Orioles spent the spring of 1965 deciding what to do with their fading fastballer. Dalko was back with Elmira in April and May, where manager Earl Weaver judged his fastball a little slower than before. Steve evidently didn't appear in a game for Elmira that season. In May he was once more on the Tri-City team—now called the Atoms instead of the Braves—in Kennewick, Washington. Dalkowski spent two and a half months with Tri-City and manager Cal Ripken, who'd been Dalko's catcher in Aberdeen and since then had moved on to a new stage of his career. Ripken was only three years older than Steve, knew his story, and wanted to keep him going in professional ball if he could. He would be Dalko's last chance to remain part of the Orioles organization.

Steve appeared in 16 games with the Atoms, posting a 6-5 record. By this time his onfield performance had become secondary to the disaster of his personal life. As much fun as Steve was to be around and as legendary as his reputation was as a pitcher, the tipping point was soon to come when the Orioles would finally throw in the towel on the fastest pitcher in baseball history.

FOURTEEN

Final Out

"Living Legend Released, Dalkowski Eyes New Life"
—*The Sporting News*, May 7, 1966

When Steve moved back to Kennewick, Washington, to rejoin the Atoms, he lived away from the rest of the team. Instead of moving into the apartment complex where Cal Ripken and several other players lived, he found some cheap rathole nearby. Only the people who gave him rides ever knew where it was. Dalko was a fount of knowledge about local bars and hangouts from his time there in 1961. It seems he also reconnected once again with the Blonde Bomber. Some of his teammates had heard about her, but nobody believed the stories until she came to pick him up at a bar one night. When she walked in and stood in the doorway, he got up and followed her out without a word. The rumor that she was married further added to the mystique.

Since the Kennewick team couldn't afford a bus, they traveled to away games in a parade of worn-out station wagons. Tim Sommer remembered riding to a game with Steve in the middle of the back seat,

161

drinking bottles from a case of beer and throwing his empties out the window. The men were listening to the *Joe Garagiola Sports Show*, a popular syndicated radio program, when Joe announced that the show tonight would be about "the legendary Steve Dalkowski." Introducing the segment, Joe said, "I don't expect you to know who this person is, but you should understand his importance to professional baseball." The commentator spoke of Dalko in the past tense, yet there he was riding home from a game. It must have been a strange feeling.

When Joe got a fact right in the broadcast, Dalkowski nodded his head between pulls on his bottle of beer. When he got something wrong, Steve set the record straight then and there. When Joe repeated the story about a batter's ear being torn off, Steve exclaimed, "I didn't rip the guy's ear off; just hit him on the earlobe and there was a lot of blood!"

Tri-City teammates also remember coming up on Steve when he was supposed to be in the dugout logging pitches. Ripken's orders were that the day before a pitcher was scheduled to pitch, he was supposed to watch the game and log what pitches were thrown and how opposing batters responded. That would give Tri-City pitchers a better idea of how to throw to those same batters the next night. But rather than sit in the freezing dugout, Steve hid in the clubhouse and listened to the game on the radio. If the announcer didn't call the pitch, Dalko wrote down whatever he would have thrown under the circumstances. Ripken always accepted his log sheets without a word.

Steve's teammates were of two opinions about him by now. On the one hand, he stayed drunk and embarrassing much of the time. He was taking up a valuable slot in the rotation and also a place on the team roster. On the other hand, he was the friendliest and most honest person any of them knew. He still borrowed heavily between paydays, then every two weeks he would ask each player what he had borrowed and return it on payday without question.

The wives of married players couldn't believe the wild man they heard about was the quiet, polite Steve Dalkowski they met. At dinner at one player's house, Steve was a good conversationalist, drank frugally, and absolutely charmed all the ladies. The wives later accused their husbands of being jealous of Steve's polished personality.

Steve evidently hadn't had a driver's license since around the time he crashed Ray Youngdahl's Cadillac in Elmira, so he was always angling for a ride. His friends seldom left him stranded. On the contrary, there was general agreement that somebody would make sure he got home and in bed every night. Yet no one wanted to be his driver because he always stayed at the bar until the last drink was poured. Players took turns handing him off and ferrying him from one bar and party to the next.

In *Beating About the Bushes*, Sommer shares a detailed account of Dalko's last days with Tri-City and the Orioles organization. It was July 1965. The Atoms finished a home game and would drive to Lewiston, Idaho, the next day. After the game Steve hitched a ride from the ballpark to the Playboy Tavern in Kennewick, which supposedly served the best pizza in town. Steve asked for a ride from there to a club to see a new dancer he'd heard about. After watching her for a while, he joined in with a big group in the club and got invited to a party at somebody's house. Of course he needed a ride there, too, and convinced Sommer to drive him. After a while at the house party, Tim decided to leave because he had to get some sleep before the drive to Lewiston in the morning. Steve swore at Tim for abandoning him, but Tim figured Steve would work out his transportation somehow.

Tim woke up somewhat the worse for wear. Dalko arrived at the hotel five minutes before departure, driven in a convertible by a young woman from last night's party. They parted after a long kiss, and Steve was ready to go. Well supplied with cans of beer, he took his place in one of the station wagons and the team left for Lewiston. Along the way, Steve mooned a traffic coordinator at a construction site, although it took some doing to move the baseball gear around in the back of the wagon to give the worker the appropriate view.

Emboldened by the alcohol, Steve yelled out the window, "My ass is better looking than your face!"

The station wagon caravan arrived at the Lewis and Clark Hotel in Lewiston three hours before leaving for the park, as usual. Some players used the time for a nap. Others went to a movie or did something else to pass the time. Dalko knew the hotel barber from previous visits and that he was a reliable drinking buddy. He convinced the barber to close up early and have a few drinks before the game. Steve's usual plan of attack was to drink several double martinis followed by all the beer he could consume before the bar closed or trouble broke out.

Later at the ballpark, Sommer scanned the field an hour before game time and didn't see Dalkowski warming up, even though he was scheduled to be the starting pitcher. Tim headed for the clubhouse, where he found Steve in the shower, vomiting and miserable. He helped him clean up, get into his uniform, and stumble out to the dugout. Between the beer and the vomit Steve smelled terrible on this hot, humid afternoon and was left to himself on the end of the bench.

Against all odds, the game was a triumph. Sommer recalled, "From the start, Steve was in command of every pitch and throwing harder than any of us had ever seen, except for [manager] Cal [Ripken]. Between innings his catcher quietly, and respectfully, complained about pain in catching Steve's fastball. The curve ball was downward and biting, resulting in a complete game with double-digit strikeouts and few walks."

One of the strikeouts was against Rick Monday, who had recently signed with the A's organization for $104,000. Striking out Monday for the fourth time on a rising fastball, Dalko yelled, "$104,000 my ass!" Monday started to charge the mound, but backed off when none of his teammates joined in.

Lewiston was a tough town filled with real-life cowboys who were not impressed with baseball players. With that in mind, Ripken placed the entire town off-limits to the team. That little inconvenience did not deter Dalko from choosing to celebrate his stellar victory at a big nightclub a block from the hotel that had a live band, a dance floor, and plenty of attractive women.

Within minutes after he arrived, Steve was chatting up two attentive young ladies near the dance floor. When sober, Dalko was an excellent dancer whose moves usually cleared the floor as admiring onlookers watched him in action. Suddenly, there was the sound of a scream and then a slap. His judgment clouded by alcohol, Steve had simultaneously propositioned one of the women and grabbed her where she didn't want to be grabbed. As Sommer later wrote, "Within seconds we were surrounded by a group of large, square-jawed cowboys wearing great looking white Stetsons."

Sommer scooped Steve up by the belt and the back of his shirt and whisked him out the door. On the way through, Dalko purposely smashed the round glass window in the door with his fist. Tim was afraid he couldn't control and protect Steve and left him just long enough to sprint to the hotel for help. No one was around at that late hour, so he ran back to the nightclub. The police arrived and tried to sort out the story. Steve blamed the broken glass on a homeless man who was at that moment relieving himself against the side of the building. When the truth came out, the club owners agreed not to press charges if they were paid immediately in cash for the damages. Tim gave them $20, all he had on him, and they let the matter drop.

Sommer wrestled Dalko back to the hotel and into the elevator. On the way up, Dalko pushed the button for another floor, got off, and started going up and down the hall banging on doors and yelling, "Come out! I know you're in there and want me!" Sommer finally got his arms around Dalko, pulled him back into the elevator and into his room.

The next morning the Lewiston police called on Ripken at the hotel and told him what had happened. Ripken was under strict orders from Baltimore to report any serious misbehavior by Dalkowski. He had just pitched his best game in years, but once again it was too little, too late. When the front office heard the news, they ordered Steve's unconditional release. As much as he liked Dalko, Cal knew the time had come. Later he would say that Steve "got to the point where he didn't want to stop drinking and go to bed." The Orioles announced Dalkowski's release on July 16, 1965.

To save him embarrassment, Ripken bought Dalko a bus ticket back to Kennewick so he wouldn't have to ride with the team. He called someone to open the clubhouse for Steve to collect his gear. As usual, he owed a number of his teammates money, which they assumed they would never see. To their surprise, when they finished the road trip and returned home, Steve was in the locker room their first day back with a handful of cash.

"Line up you sons of bitches!" he ordered. "Here I am." He went from man to man with the same question: "How much did you give me?" and paid everyone back without question. Comparing notes later, the players realized that all of them had given Dalko a figure that was ten cents on the dollar.

After almost nine seasons, all but one of them with the Orioles, it seemed that baseball had finally given up on Steve Dalkowski, the likeable southpaw with the miracle arm.

But Steve Dalkowski wasn't ready to give up on baseball.

Harry Dunlop, who brought Dalkowski to the Stockton Ports in 1964, moved to the California Angels organization the next year to head up the Quad Cities Angels in Illinois. It may have been through Dunlop that Dalko made a connection with the Angels and landed a spot on the roster of the Class-A San Jose Bees. The Bees manager, Rocky Bridges, announced on July 28, 1965, that Steve had joined the team. The exact chain of events that brought Dalko from the Tri-City Atoms to San Jose is not clear. Ripken and others might have gone out of their way to find one more opportunity for their troubled teammate.

Whatever the details, Dalkowski made his first start for the Bees against the Salinas Indians on July 29. It was a rocky debut described succinctly in the local press with the headline, "Dalkowski Wild." Steve, "famed for his ability to fire the ball and notorious for his wildness," had "lived up to his reputation." He walked the bases loaded in the first inning and gave up a run on a sacrifice fly. Before being relieved in the fifth inning, he had walked seven and allowed four runs.

Steve pitched an impressive game against Santa Barbara on August 5, a three-hit, 10–0 shutout. Leaning more on his slider than on his fastball, he walked nine and struck out seven while maintaining firm control from beginning to end. After chalking up his second win for the Bees on August 12, Steve was in good form on the mound August 19 against the Bakersfield Bears until his control evaporated in the seventh. Coming to the mound with the bases loaded, reliever Dick Sevde threw his first pitch to right fielder Dennis Wagner, who clobbered it for a grand slam.

In keeping with the many other misses of his career, Dalkowski narrowly missed being part of a league championship team twice in the fall of 1965. The Tri-City Atoms, where Dalko had played less than two months before, won the Northwest League championship. Meanwhile, the San Jose Bees played the Stockton Ports for the California League trophy. The Ports won their second game of the best-of-three series in a close 6–5 victory, with Steve's old teammates defeating his new ones. Dalko entered that game as a pinch hitter and threw one inning in relief, giving up one walk.

The last batter he faced was infielder Frank Peters, who vividly remembered the encounter more than fifty years later. Approaching the plate with trepidation, Peters stood in the far rear corner of the batter's box and watched Dalkowski's "compact windup and electric release." The first pitch was a great breaking ball for a strike, but was called a ball by the umpire. The next four pitches were all four-seam fastballs: two balls, a strike, and a final ball for a walk. Peters was happy to have survived the at-bat. "I got to first with a big smile on my face and was happy to have survived," Peters said. "I turned around to witness a broken ballplayer leaving the mound. . . . A nice guy, always proud, but done." It would be Dalko's last pitch in American professional baseball.

Steve ended the season at San Jose with a 2-3 record and an ERA of 4.74. His first win for the Bees had been a terrific 10–0, three-hit performance. In Tri-City he had won his last three games. His combined record for the 1965 season was a respectable 8-8. He was only twenty-six years old. The Angels nurtured a glimmer of hope that Steve might yet live up to the potential the world had seen in him for so long.

After the season ended, Steve went south again to play in Mexico, pitching once more for the Venados de Mazatlán on the Pacific coast. His highly anticipated Sonora Winter League debut that season was October 12, 1965. It was the first time in league history that an American pitcher had received the honor of starting a team's season opener. Dalko, known as "El Velocista" to his Mexican fans, lost 5–2 in an exciting pitching duel that saw Dalkowski throw far more pitches than his rival Vicente Romo de Guaymas. Billed as "*el lanzador más veloz de todos los tiempos*" (the fastest pitcher of all time), Steve reportedly hurled the baseball at 108 miles per hour.

Seemingly on his last legs as a professional ballplayer, Steve Dalkowski was a genuine sports hero south of the border that year. Residents of the Mexican state of Sinaloa, which includes Mazatlán, boasted that "If you don't love baseball, you're not a Sinaloan." Every day at the local stadium, a few minutes' walk from the beach, fans could find a party, carnival, and baseball game all rolled into one. The locals loved baseball, and they loved El Velocista. Opposing teams came to town simply hoping to avoid a *blanqueo* (shutout), and their hitters approached the plate every time fearing another *poncho* (strikeout).

Dalko's performance that fall and winter in the Sonora Winter League was the polar opposite of the struggling player who seemed on his way to washing out in California. Steve was a master on the mound. Fans loved his passion for the game, his intensity, and his protestations whenever he was relieved—he never wanted to leave the job undone.

He was still their "burro buster." Teammates loved him because he was so kind and easygoing, always eager to help younger players improve their game. He still sometimes lost control, but invariably gained it back. Fans saw one catcher after another massaging his sore hand after a session behind the plate with Dalkowski.

Since all games were played in the daytime, Steve was chronically sunburned because of his fair Polish complexion. Players and fans teased him, saying his red face made him look drunk and nicknaming him *el borracho*, "the drunkard." Though fans may have heard rumors that Steve loved his booze, there is no account of a single incident of Dalkowski being drunk in Mexico. Ballplayers in Mexico were (and are) under far less pressure than in America. The combination of less stress, admiring fans, and respectful teammates likely allowed Steve to build the confidence that kept his pitching on track and the bottle at bay.

An account from the newspaper *El Regional* of a game in Hermosillo on December 8, 1965, conveys some of the excitement Steve generated when he was on the mound in Mazatlán. Under the headline that translates, "The Sugarcaners Fall Before Steve Dalkowski," the paper recounts a 4–1 victory over the Cañeros. A crowd of more than six thousand cheered El Velocista as he led the Venados to victory despite 10 walks in the game. It was surely a thrill for Steve to play in front of such a large and enthusiastic audience, when in San Jose the crowds were often in the low hundreds.

(Young American players still play in Mazatlán and still thrive on the lack of stress and the enthusiastic local support. Pitcher Mitch Lively is one of many who love the "big-league attention," the good money, and the relaxed lifestyle. In 2017 Lively broke the league record for consecutive wins with eight in a row, besting the mark set in 1948 by Yankees legend Whitey Ford. "I love the game and I love the way it's played down here," he says. "I love the enthusiasm, I love the crowds, I love the will to win." Teammate Nick Struck agrees that Mexican fans are wild about the game. "They come up and ask for pictures," he says. "Down here it's a different world." Of his American teammates he observes, "Everybody wants to be here. Nobody wants to go home." Every time he walks to the mound to deliver his 95-mph heater, the PA system blasts "Fireball" and the stadium erupts in cheers.)

Steve appeared in 20 games for Mazatlán during the 1965 winter season, with a 7-9 record. In 98 innings he allowed 41 runs on 72 hits with 85 strikeouts and 77 walks, for an ERA of 3.30. He pitched five complete games, all of them shutout wins. By the end of the season on January 16, 1966, Dalkowski was tied with pitcher José Peña for the most shutouts in the Sonora League. Though somewhat erratic, these are not the numbers of a baseball has-been. They show a pitcher with serious talent and at least a few years of remaining potential. Given his successful 1965 season in Mexico, it is clear that, far from being a baseball basket case hopelessly compromised by an elbow injury and alcoholism, Steve Dalkowski was a solid performer and one of the best, most popular players in the league.

Yet the momentum failed to carry. North of the border the elusive magic disappeared. Coming off his shining season in Mazatlán, Dalkowski reported to the California Angels' minor-league training camp in Fullerton, California. There he was assigned to the Seattle Angels, a Triple-A club. Pittsburgh had played him with the Triple-A Columbus Jets in 1964 and now, coming off of a year in Class-A ball and an impressive season in Mexico, he was headed back to Triple-A, one rung down from the majors. Then there was a change of plans. The farm club manager asked him to start the season with a Triple-A team in Guadalajara, Mexico, instead of the Seattle squad. Steve resisted. In spite of his recent success, he didn't want to play in Mexico during the regular season and didn't want to be the only American on the team.

Hearing that, the Angels said they would send him back to Class-A San Jose. Steve thought it over and decided that, faced with the choice between Class-A ball in California and Class-AAA action in Mexico, he was willing to go back to Mexico after all. But by the time he told the Angels he'd changed his mind, they had already sent another player to Guadalajara in his place. The Angels then gave Steve Dalkowski his unconditional release.

In a front-page feature bordered in black, the *Sporting News* issue of May 7, 1966, announced, "Living Legend Released, Dalkowski Eyes New Life." The story reported that Dalkowski, "a baseball legend in his own time, apparently has thrown his last professional pitch." The article went on to summarize his career stats and note some of the tales that were told about him: tearing off a batter's ear; knocking down an umpire; throwing balls through backstops and wire fences. It also mentioned the lengths his managers had gone to in trying to tame his fireball: throwing at a wooden target; practicing with a batter on both sides of the plate; standing fifteen feet from the plate.

At twenty-six years of age, Steve Dalkowski had thrown a baseball almost every day for half his life. Now it seemed his professional career was ended and the rest of his life was about to begin. Steve headed back to Stockton where he still had friends and allies in the Orioles organization. And where he had last seen a cute young schoolteacher with a blue MG.

FIFTEEN

Love and Loss

"He was in some ways a lost soul. After baseball he never found another thing to do."

—The former Mrs. Steve Dalkowski, 2017

By the spring of 1966, Steve was back in Stockton, hanging around the ball field for a chance to talk to his old teammates. Sometimes he would stand at the fence looking for a familiar face. Other times he would send the Ports batboy to find someone he wanted. When the player appeared, Dalko would cheerfully insist he join him for a drink after the game.

A few weeks before the end of the season, he invited Tim Sommer to go with him to his girlfriend's apartment. He evidently had found a companion and was staying with her in a nice place furnished and decorated with a feminine eye. The three of them didn't have any particular idea about how to spend the evening until Tim mentioned he was leaving on a road trip to Reno the next morning and had always wanted to learn to play craps.

"Don't worry," Steve exclaimed. "You've come to a master, and when you hit the tables there will be a fortune to be made!" The two men moved furniture aside, got on the floor in the dinette, and started throwing dice against the wall. Drinking excessively, Steve was soon drunk and wanted to switch to blackjack. Though they played only for points, Steve was so dissipated that he lost heavily then insisted his girlfriend write Tim a check for the actual amount. He handed Tim a check for $300, which Tim slipped back to the girlfriend as he left.

One night Steve was at a bowling alley in Stockton, when he thought he recognized a familiar face in a group of young women at the bar. He made his way over to them, walked up to the one he'd seen, and asked, "Are you Linda?"

"Yeah," she answered, immediately recognizing her old neighbor from the Pershing Apartments even though they hadn't spoken in two years. Linda Moore's father owned the bowling alley, and it was one of the few places in town where she and her girlfriends felt comfortable drinking on their own.

"Wanna dance?" he asked.

"Yeah!" she answered. He was an even better dancer than she expected. The two left together that night with an unmistakable sense of romance in the air.

Linda Moore was in her second year teaching language arts and math at the middle school in nearby Manteca and lived with her mother in the house on Oxford Street where she'd grown up. Her father was a successful commercial builder who had moved to town from Winnipeg when he was three. She saw some similarities between Steve and her father in their personal habits: they liked to drink and they swore a lot. Linda noted how imaginative Steve was in applying what she called "the f-word" as a noun, verb, adjective, and otherwise.

Linda's mother was born in Stockton. Her mother's father was an itinerant actor from the original Dutch stock on Manhattan Island. Her maternal grandmother, who raised eleven siblings after their mother died and their father became mentally ill, taught school for forty-eight years and passed down her love of teaching to Linda.

Steve rented a small apartment on the west side of town, and he and Linda saw each other every day. Sometimes they cooked meals together at Linda's house. Steve was a surprisingly good cook. He made goulash, kielbasa, and other Polish dishes, though one of his favorites was hamburgers, which he fixed often. They ate out frequently and went barhopping almost every night. One favorite joint was on El Dorado, a bar owned by their friends Ray and Phil.

With one exception when she saw him drink a glass of blackberry wine, Linda never saw Steve drink anything but beer. While he drank a lot of beer and drank it all day, he never touched hard liquor or wine in front of her. He was mildly inebriated virtually every night. However, she never saw him violent or out of control because of drinking. He enjoyed the conversation and the friendly atmosphere of bars as much as or more than the alcohol. He liked to talk to people, sit in at cards, shoot pool, play pinball, and take in the scene.

It's possible that the stories about his drunken days and nights on the road as a baseball player were exaggerated. Ray Youngdahl, among others, said later that he thought stories of Dalko's drinking were overblown even though Steve had a widespread reputation as a boozer. Regardless of how much he drank in the past, Steve found in Linda someone he cared about enough to clean up his act—at least in relative terms. He left the Blonde Bomber and his most recent girlfriend behind to make Linda Moore his steady companion.

Linda had loaned her blue MG to a friend who crashed it. She replaced it with a small Yamaha 60 motorcycle. Since Steve didn't drive, the two of them rode double around town and on their nighttime adventures. Soon there was another passenger added to the list. Linda had gotten to know and like Steve's friend and former teammate Pat McMahon. The three of them fell into the habit of going places together on the motorcycle with Steve on the back, six-foot-four

McMahon in front, and Linda sandwiched in the middle driving. They were three young musketeers full of life enjoying themselves and looking for adventure together on warm California nights.

Steve still wanted to get back into baseball, and still thought he had a chance. After it became obvious he was not getting anywhere with the Ports, he decided to move to San Jose and try to land a spot with the Bees. That was where he had last played ball, and where he had turned down a chance to play with the Triple-A team in Guadalajara only a few months earlier. Maybe they could work something out.

Linda, who had never been out of Stockton, thought it would be fun to go to San Jose with him. Her parents didn't share her admiration for her new boyfriend. From their point of view, she had a college degree and a successful career ahead. He was unemployed, drank too much, had no apparent prospects, and didn't seem the least interested in getting married. She was dating far below her station; her parents thought she could do better and told her so. Her friends warned her, too. From the first night Linda and Steve danced at the bowling alley, her girlfriends cautioned her that he was bad news.

But Linda was in love. She loved Steve's broad shoulders and sparkling eyes. She loved his graceful, panther-like way of moving. She loved his energy and enthusiasm for whatever he did. She loved his kindness and easygoing personality. And he had the most beautiful eyelashes she'd ever seen.

Steve left Linda in Stockton during the spring of 1966 to try his luck in San Jose. Linda finished out the school year at Manteca, then followed him to a new city where one of baseball's "living legends" would try to restart his career. Linda had another car by then, which they named "White Lightning" after one of Steve's nicknames. The two of them loaded Linda's motorcycle into the back seat and took it with them. Linda got a contract to teach elementary school in Berryessa. Steve had never had a full-time job in his life besides baseball.

Steve Dalkowski doing some sideline work with the Stockton Ports, his sixth team in four years of pro ball. His "rep" and legend status were now secure, as a 1960 *Time* magazine column, "The Wildest Pitcher," stated that Dalko was "the hardest thrower in organized baseball." CREDIT: FORREST JACKSON/*TIME*

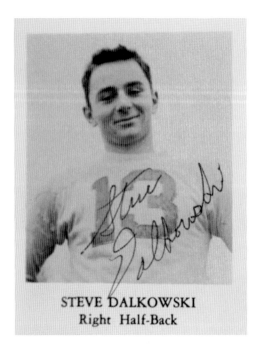

STEVE DALKOWSKI
Right Half-Back

Try to take it away from Steve Dalkowski. You've got your work cut out for you.

As shown in these pictures from the 1957 *Beehive* yearbook, Steve was a highly respected two-sport letterman for the Golden Hurricanes of New Britain High. He was a star in the backfield for the undefeated football team and a menacing force on the hill in baseball. CREDIT: NEW BRITAIN HIGH SCHOOL YEARBOOK, 1957

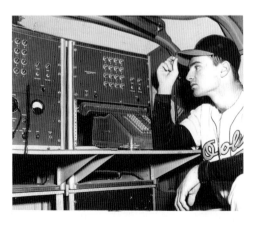

These historic images prove that when Dalkowski tested the speed of his fastball at the army's Aberdeen Proving Ground in Maryland, he pitched off a mound, wore a full uniform including cleats, and threw to Orioles catcher Joe Ginsberg.

Photos were taken for the *Baltimore News-Post & Sunday American* by James Kelmartin at Aberdeen on June 5, 1958.

(top) Brecheen, Dalkowski, and engineer John E. Bedwell examine the army's sky screen system. Photographer's note: "Bedwell points to slit in box that ball must pass over to record speed of Dalkowski's pitch."

(center) Dalkowski fires away to Ginsberg over the two boxes that calculate pitching speed. The truck at right houses the system electronics. Photographer's note: "Steve Dalkowski, pitching. Joe Ginsberg, catching. Dalkowski's speed checked by Army Velocity Measurement Section at Aberdeen Proving Grounds."

(bottom) Steve inspects the control panel of the sky screen. Photographer's note: "Steve Dalkowski, Orioles pitcher, inspects board in Army truck that recorded speed of his pitch." Credit: Hearst Communications, Inc.

(left) Dalko anticipating spring training in Scottsdale, Arizona, 1958. The following year the Orioles moved spring training to Florida.

(below) Billy Loes and Dalko watching the action, spring training 1959. CREDIT: HEARST COMMUNICATIONS, INC.

Under the watchful eye of pitching coach Harry "The Cat" Brecheen, Dalko does some bullpen work at the Orioles spring training camp in Florida, February 1959.

Brecheen left a controversial legacy as a coach, with some suggesting that his techniques, though well-intentioned and perhaps based on the best practices of the era, were harmful to young pitchers' arms.

CREDIT: HEARST COMMUNICATIONS, INC.

Harry Brecheen Introduces Rookie Hurlers to 'Iron Mike'

John Papa, left, and Steve Dalkowski watch the "Cat" load up the mechanical marvel.

MIAMA, FLA. Feb. 21—PITCHERS LOOK OVER THEIR REPLACEMENT—Baltimore Orioles' pitchers John Papa (left) and newcomer Steve Dalkowski (center) watch as Coach Harry Brecheen loads the mechanical pitcher for the intra-squad game today. Papa doesn't seem concerned but Dalkowski wonders if he should switch to the outfield.

Again in 1961, Steve was invited to Orioles spring training in Miami. The inference that Dalkowski is an Orioles "newcomer" implies he's on his way to *The Show*. CREDIT: AP PHOTO

Dalkowski warms up before a spring training game c. 1962. CREDIT: NATIONAL BASEBALL LIBRARY, COOPERSTOWN, NEW YORK

Dalko pitched 12 innings over 12 games for the Rochester Red Wings in 1963 after his arm injury, his only Triple-A appearances in the Orioles organization. CREDIT: NATIONAL BASEBALL LIBRARY, COOPERSTOWN, NEW YORK

Steve at home after the end of his playing days. This may be the apartment in Bakersfield, California, that he shared with his wife, Virginia, for about ten years beginning in 1981. CREDIT: PHOTO BY GARY KAZANJIAN

Brian Vikander's extensive memorabilia collection includes the auto-graphed photo reprint (above) and baseball (below) signed "Fastest Ever" by Dalkowski.

Also pictured are autographed baseballs signed by manager Earl Weaver and team-mate Bo Belinsky.

Bottom Row, left to right: Koepf, Hinckley, Barrier, Loninger (bat boy), Youngdahl, Gilbert, Rushing. Middle Row, left to right: O'Neil, Dalkowski, Clarke, Rick, Heron, Dewald. Back Row, left to right: DeMars, Marchbanks, Kristinik, Chincholo, Barraclough, Olson, Smith.

(above) 1961 Tri-City Braves team photo from a game program.

(right) "1963 Rookie Stars" Topps card signed by Dalko.

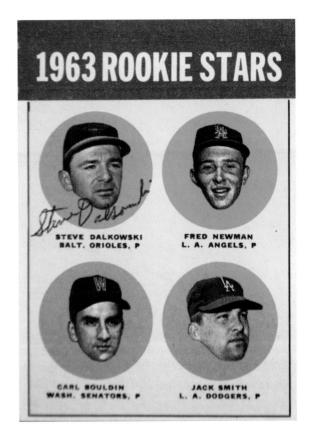

1963 ROOKIE STARS

STEVE DALKOWSKI
BALT. ORIOLES, P

FRED NEWMAN
L. A. ANGELS, P

CARL BOULDIN
WASH. SENATORS, P

JACK SMITH
L. A. DODGERS, P

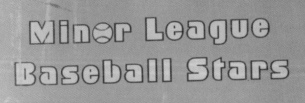

Minor League Baseball Stars

Career Records Compiled
by
the Society for American Baseball Research

STEVEN LOUIS DALKOWSKI

Born, June 3, 1939, at New Britain, Conn.
Threw left. Batted left. Height, 5:10. Weight, 170.

Steve Dalkowski

Had great potential as pitcher but suffered from notable lack of control (see BB totals relative to hits and IP).

YEAR	CLUB	LEA	G	IP	W	L	H	R	ER	BB	SO	ERA
1957	Kingsport	Appal.	15	62	1	8	22	68	56*	129*	121	8.13
1958	Knoxville	So. Atl.	11	42	1	4	17	41	39	95	82	7.93
	Wilson	Carol.	8	14	0	1	7	19	19	38	29	12.21
	Aberdeen	North.	11	62	3	5	29	50	44	112	121	6.39
1959	Aberdeen	North.	12	59	4	3	30	43	37	110	99	5.64
	Pensacola	Ala.-Fla.	7	25	0	4	11	38	36	80	43	12.96
1960	Stockton	Calif.	32	170	7	15*	105	120	97	262*	262	5.14
1961	Kennewick	No'west.	31	103	3	12	75	117	96	196*	150	8.39
1962	Elmira	Eastern	31	160	7	10	117	61	54	114	192	3.04
1963	Elmira	Eastern	13	29	2	2	20	10	9	26	28	2.79
	Rochester	Int.	12	12	0	2	7	8	8	14	8	6.00
1964	Elmira	Eastern	8	15	0	1	17	12	10	19	16	6.00
	Stockton	Calif.	20	108	8	4	91	40	34	62	141	2.83
	Columbus	Int.	3	12	2	1	15	11	11	11	9	8.25
1965	Kennewick	No'west	16	84	6	5	84	60	48	52	62	5.14
	San Jose	Calif.	6	38	2	3	35	25	20	34	33	4.74
	Minors		236	995	46	80	682	723	618	1354	1396	5.59

Dalko's minor league career stats compiled by the Society for American Baseball Research, signed by Dalkowski.

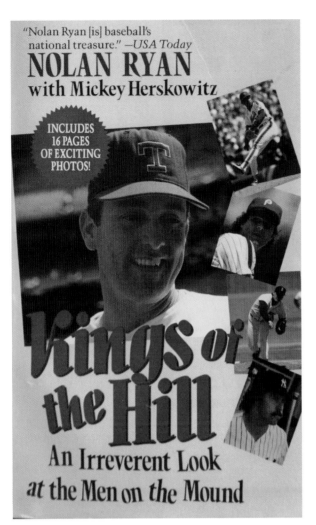

"Nolan Ryan [is] baseball's national treasure." —*USA Today*

NOLAN RYAN
with Mickey Herskowitz

INCLUDES
16 PAGES
OF EXCITING
PHOTOS!

Kings of the Hill
An Irreverent Look
at the Men on the Mound

Nolan Ryan had a modestly dismissive attitude about the Dalko legend. However, he graciously devoted five pages of his book *Kings of the Hill* to Steve Dalkowski. CREDIT: HarperCollins, 1992

ing who was the fastest gun, you kept hearing about one pitcher whose legend grew to almost Paul Bunyan proportions but who never won a game in the major leagues.

Steve Dalkowski

His name is Steve Dalkowski, and you heard it wherever you went, even in the low minors. There was no one who could touch him, they said. The myth was that he threw his fastball at 120 miles an hour, and only one thing kept him from going on to Cooperstown. He couldn't get the ball over the plate.

He had an almost cult following, an underground fame, that must have been something close to what Tom Wolf wrote about Chuck Yeager in *The Right Stuff*: his name was virtually unknown to the public, but every pilot who felt the wind beneath his wings knew who he was.

Some of the characters who played a part in the Dalko story.

(top left) Harry "The Cat" Brecheen in an autographed St. Louis Photo Pack Picture (note his misspelled name) and an autographed 1986 reprint of 1951 Bowman card.

(middle) Steve Barber in an autographed 1961 Topps card and Bo Belinsky in an autographed 1963 Topps card.

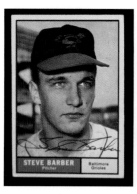
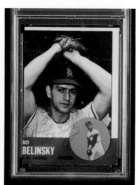

Pictured (left to right) Dalko's high school football coach John Toner, Dalko, Dalko's high school baseball coach Bill Huber, and friend and teammate Andy Baylock c. 2000. CREDIT: PHOTO COURTESY OF ANDY BAYLOCK

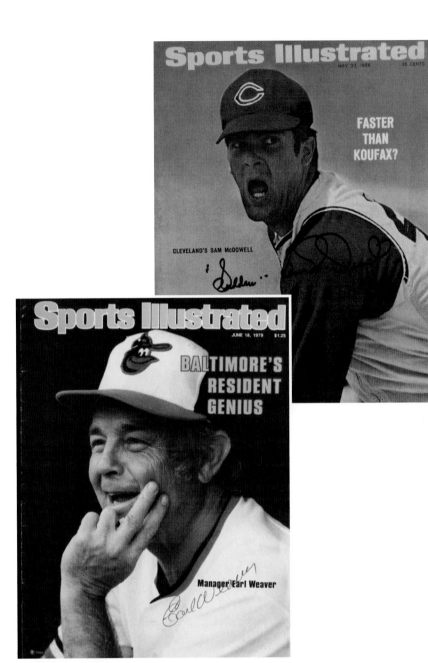

(top) Considered by many to be the hardest throwing pitcher in MLB in the late 1960s, Sam McDowell, in the foreword to this book, claims that Dalko threw a lot harder than he did. CREDIT: PHOTO BY JACK SHEEDY & GEORGE LONG/*SPORTS ILLUSTRATED*

(bottom) Earl Weaver, "Baltimore's Resident Genius" was the guy who got Dalko in position to make the Big Club in 1963. CREDIT: PHOTO BY JAMES DRAKE/*SPORTS ILLUSTRATED*

Dalko eyes the future.

By the time Linda joined him in San Jose, the fastest pitcher in baseball history was working in a match factory.

They rented a house and settled in. They went out to bars and restaurants almost every night. Steve always drank beer in abundance but not to excess. Steve also loved card rooms. Linda didn't play cards, so when Steve was at the table Linda spent the time reading. They made weekend trips to Lake Tahoe. They got two cocker spaniels: Doctor, who was black, and Nursie, a golden. As in San Jose, Steve tried to leverage his old baseball connections into one more season, but without success.

Eight months after Steve started work at the match factory, there was an explosion and he quit his job. Whatever he earned wasn't enough to risk being blown to bits. From then on they lived off Linda's teaching salary, and Steve spent his days on projects around the house. He started every morning with beer for breakfast, then tackled whatever job he would do that day. Steve was a good and meticulous worker, sanding floors, planting in the garden, and cooking hamburgers and his Polish specialties. He was fastidious about cleanliness and his appearance. His standard uniform for the day was a clean white T-shirt, a fresh one every day, and jeans. He also had a large collection of sweaters with leather patches (later stolen) that he had picked up over the years in places where he had played.

When the two of them weren't out on the town, they spent a lot of time sitting outside. "We never lacked for words," Linda remembered years later. "We just talked. He wasn't interested in intellectual things. He was interested in nature. He liked being outside. And he liked bars. We both liked them." Original Joes was a favorite place to hang out, as was the High Life.

Linda was surprised that with so much of Steve's life and personality tied up in baseball, he didn't play in a recreational league or otherwise keep his skills sharp while he was looking for a new team. The two of them never went to games together. She believed it was because he'd played baseball year round since he was a teenager and was worn down by the physical demands of the pace he had set for himself.

"Baseball was his job. It was not his passion," Linda believed. "It was something he could do well and make money at it. If it had been his passion, he would have wanted to go to baseball games. It was just something he fell into because he had the talent."

Without any prospects for restarting his career and now without a job, Steve grew restless spending the days at home alone while Linda was at school. He was at loose ends, with no direction or specific plan of action. The couple had lived together in San Jose for about a year when Steve decided to go home to Connecticut. Maybe there he could reconnect with old friends and stir up some baseball opportunities. Linda had already signed her teaching contract for the 1967–68 school year. Neither of them thought he would be away for long, so they agreed that he would go back to New Britain alone and she would wait for him in San Jose. In midsummer of 1967, Steve and Linda made the rounds of all their friends and favorite watering holes so Steve could say goodbye. She drove him in White Lightning to the airport, where he took a cross-country flight east.

New Britain welcomed Steve as a returning hero. He was home again, surrounded by friends and family, back at the scene of his historic early triumphs when the sky was the limit and Steve Dalkowski was destined for stardom. Some old friends gladly put him up in their garage apartment while he mined every lead and prospective opportunity to play baseball again. He and Linda corresponded long distance, she writing in her schoolteacher script and Steve answering with his bold printed style.

Late in the year, Linda was shocked and delighted to hear that the Boston Red Sox had invited Steve to their winter camp in Daytona Beach. Though he hadn't played baseball in more than a year he was still in excellent physical shape. The question, as always, would be whether he could throw his fastball over the plate.

Linda flew to meet him in Connecticut so they could drive to Florida together. The entire East Coast was blanketed by a winter storm. They crept through Washington, DC, with a heavy layer of snow on the ground. In North Carolina they decided to stop for a drink. When they walked in, they realized it was an all-black bar. That made absolutely no difference to Steve or to Linda. Steve had played with black players since high school and never had a prejudiced bone in his body. He was as cordial and chatty to that roomful of strangers as he would have been in New Britain or San Jose. Everybody was his friend.

The couple arrived in Daytona Beach on New Year's Eve 1967. Not surprisingly, they went to a local bar that was packed to the rafters to ring in the new year. After a few beers, Steve had to use the restroom. Seeing the long line at the men's room door, he went outside to do his business on the beach. Police officers patrolling nearby spotted him and arrested him. He was escorted to the Daytona Beach jail and Linda went back to their motel alone.

The next morning Linda was startled awake by a knock at her door. It was the police again, with news that the credit card Steve used to pay for their room was no good. Steve had told Linda that someone he called his "sponsor" had given him the card with instructions to use it any way he wanted. Steve had used the card throughout their trip from New England. Linda had no idea there might be some sort of problem.

It seems possible that this sponsor was connected somehow either with the people who had paid him to play ball as a teenager in New Britain or the shadowy network of benefactors who reportedly loaned him money in Miami early in his career. The source of the card and the identity of its owner remain unknown.

Steve had spent the night in jail. Now Linda was hauled down on suspicion of credit card fraud and also held behind bars. She called her family back in Stockton, filled them in on what happened, and told them to call her school to say she would be late getting back from Christmas vacation because she was sick. Her family was shocked and angry—they had warned her this guy was no good—but made the call and bought Linda the extra time she needed.

Linda and Steve spent that night in the Daytona Beach jail. The next day they were both released. Whatever story they told the police about the credit card convinced the judge to let them go. Steve reported to the Red Sox training camp and Linda flew home to California.

Steve still wanted to play baseball. He had evidently cut down on his drinking since meeting Linda, remained in good shape, and had convinced the Red Sox management to give him a shot. All the pieces seemed to be falling into place for a restart. But it was not to be. A few days after he arrived, Steve got into a fight at the Red Sox camp with another player who Steve said insulted him. He punched the offending player and a brawl broke out. The Red Sox sent Dalkowski packing. Sometime during the first weeks of 1968, Sizzling Steve Dalkowski walked off a professional baseball diamond for the last time. He rejoined Linda in San Jose and resumed the task of trying to figure out what to do with the rest of his life.

After the school year ended in the spring of 1968, Steve and Linda moved back to Stockton and stayed with Linda's parents. Though the family still didn't like Steve, Linda's mother told him that if they were going to live together, he should marry her. Steve resisted, saying, "I can't take care of myself. I sure can't take care of Linda."

Linda's mother answered, "If you'll get married, I'll make sure you're taken care of."

That changed Steve's mind. Linda's father was furious at the news she and Steve were getting married, but her mother still believed it was better than living together unwed. The couple married in Carson City, Nevada, in the summer of 1968. Linda wasn't interested in a traditional wedding with a fancy white gown; she got married in a suit. After the ceremony she, Steve, and the friends who came to the wedding headed for the casinos. "We gambled and partied and had a good old time," she later recalled. As far as she was concerned, her mother would never have to worry about making good on her promise to support them. "I was a worker," she said. "I always had a job and could pay the rent."

She never resented Steve for not bringing in a paycheck. Neither of them worried about money or cared about making a fortune. They were young and in love, and Linda was content to pursue the career she'd always wanted while Steve took the time to find a new direction for his life. During the summer, when Linda wasn't teaching, the two of them spent the days visiting friends, dining out, going to their favorite card rooms and bars, and occasionally visiting Linda's mother at a pet shop she bought after she and Linda's father divorced.

Still restless and unsettled, Steve wanted to move again, this time to Pasco, Washington, in the Tri-City area. It was another place where he had played baseball near the end of his career and where he thought he might yet pick up the thread of a comeback. He couldn't give up the idea of playing again. At the end of the year they moved north, and Linda got a job teaching at Pasco Elementary.

In Pasco the Dalkowskis rented the guest house behind a fine old mansion in town. They got a job painting the inside of the big house and made $450 for the work. Though it was less than Linda earned from a month of teaching, it gave Steve something to focus on. He was a careful and diligent worker; the two of them produced impressive results.

When the painting job was finished, Steve wanted to move again, this time back to Stockton. They had only been in Pasco six months and Linda was in the middle of the school year. Nevertheless, Steve wanted to go back to Stockton right away. When he left Stockton for San Jose in the spring of 1966, Linda had finished out her teaching contract and then followed him. Now that they were married, she decided to leave Washington in the middle of the spring semester and go with Steve back to Stockton. She could easily find another job in her hometown.

They moved into a two-level townhouse at the Adobe Hacienda Apartments in Stockton. They reconnected with their friends there and visited Linda's mother on Oxford Street. It was a quiet summer for

Mr. and Mrs. Dalkowski until the day Linda was sunning herself by the apartment pool and a neighbor invited her and Steve out to dinner. The three met in Steve and Linda's apartment later to drive to the restaurant. While Linda and the neighbor waited for Steve to come downstairs, the neighbor told Linda she was "too classy" for Steve and shouldn't be with him.

He implied that Linda should leave Steve for him. Linda was speechless for a minute. In spite of her friends and family warning her away from Steve, she loved him without reservation. He was the only man for her, "the only guy in my eyes."

Steve heard the conversation from upstairs. Momentarily blinded by jealousy, mild-mannered Steve Dalkowski stormed down the staircase in a rage and literally threw the neighbor out the front door. It was the most unexpected and violent act of his life. Except for what happened next. The offending neighbor had scarcely hit the ground before Steve threw his wife out, too, and locked the door behind her. She landed hard on the pavement. The impact broke her left elbow. Locked out of her own home and with a broken elbow, Linda went back to her family. Steve's behavior was proof to them that Linda should never have married him. "This is it!" her mother exclaimed. "You've been in jail. Your elbow's broken. What do you want next?"

Her friends and family pressured her to file for divorce. But she still loved Steve, believed in him, and understood his increasingly desperate quest for focus and direction in his life. She went back to him and they reconciled. Some husbands would have brought their wives flowers under the circumstances. Steve bought Linda a bottle of Four Roses bourbon. (At some point along the way he had also told her she had better legs than Connie Stevens.)

Since it would be fall before Linda could start teaching, the two had to earn some money until then. Stockton, in the middle of one of the biggest agricultural regions in the world, had plenty of work available harvesting crops. The Dalkowskis got jobs picking cherries, the first time either of them had done that kind of labor. For Linda, who worked that summer on a ladder with one good arm and a broken elbow, it was also the last.

As the summer ended and the school year began for Linda, Steve said he wanted to move again. He had exhausted all hope in the cities where he had played without getting an offer. Now his idea was to go to other teams in the league—Fresno, Visalia, Bakersfield—to stir up an opportunity.

But Linda had had enough. She had to settle somewhere, had to get her life straightened out and her career firmly on track. She was staying put in Stockton. She moved out of the apartment at Adobe Hacienda, took her name off the lease, moved in with her family, and started the academic year teaching at a nearby middle school. Steve stayed in their apartment until the end of the month, then left because he had no way to pay the rent.

Steve drifted from place to place over the next few months, ending up in Bakersfield sometime around Christmas. Writing in the *Bakersfield Californian* on January 27, 1970, sports editor Larry Press reported that Steve Dalkowski was in town with hopes of returning to baseball:

"Bob Williams, president of the Bakersfield Dodgers, tells us that Steve Dalkowski is now living here and wants to try for one final fling in baseball. . . . He never could lick his control problems and dropped out of the game. Now he wants to try it once more, and told Williams he plans to test himself at the Dodger Stadium winter workouts." These are open workouts where unsigned players can show their skills in front of team managers in hopes of getting back in the game.

Later in 1970 Linda filed for divorce. Steve wrote her a letter saying he was working and trying to get himself together, but she never wrote back. She didn't know what to say. He called and left phone messages for her. Her family advised her not to answer them and she didn't. After the divorce papers were signed, they never saw each other again.

Linda never had any hard feelings toward Steve and their failed marriage. Almost fifty years later she reflected on the time they spent together:

"He was a really simple, complicated person. He didn't want big stuff. He wasn't wanting to rule the world or have a lot of money. He just wanted to get along and go along. Once baseball was over, he didn't have any overarching goals. He was lost. . . .

"I think Steve lacked confidence in himself. He was out playing year round. That can't be easy. And he was always nervous. . . . If he had been able to stay with Earl Weaver, I think Weaver could have [tamed his fastball]. Earl had the discipline and the love for the game and Steve had the talent."

Along with that talent, beyond the rough language and bravado of a pro ballplayer, Steve was a kind, generous man. "He was basically a Christian," Linda said. "He believed in the Golden Rule. He was good to people. . . . When we'd go into a place, he would talk to people. He would buy them a drink. He was generous. Anything he had you could have." Linda also defended Steve against claims that he had low intelligence. "He was not the low IQ that people think it was. And I would know, being a teacher."

Yet as a player and as a person, Steve Dalkowski never really found his path. "He was in some ways a lost soul," Linda said. "After baseball he never found another thing to do. He went where life pushed him. . . . Maybe he should have stayed in Connecticut [when they were there together at the end of 1967] because they really loved him there. I think he never felt at home anywhere else."

Linda taught in Stockton until 1978, then branched out into careers in real estate, magazine publishing, and fashion design. She traveled the world from Europe to the South Pacific, returning eventually to California and school teaching. In the summer of 2017 she was retired, continuing to travel widely, and keeping up with former students, the oldest of whom still called her Mrs. Dalkowski.

By 1970, Steve was settled in Oildale, California, a working-class community on the northern edge of Bakersfield. There is no evidence he attended the winter workouts in Dodger Stadium that year. On the contrary, Steve Dalkowski was on his way down to a long, agonizing season of misery and neglect.

SIXTEEN

Fading into History

"You can't cry over spilled milk, can you?"
—Steve Dalkowski, 1979

After Steve Dalkowski officially retired from professional baseball, sportswriter Pat Jordan published a *Sports Illustrated* retrospective on October 12, 1970, titled "The Wildest Fastball Ever," summarizing Steve Dalkowski's career. Several of what eventually became legends about Steve appeared for the first time in this story. Some have become the most-repeated stories about Steve's life. They may well be true, but finding independent confirmation of them has, in some cases, proved difficult. The legend of Steve Dalkowski is secure, and there is much solid evidence to confirm his legendary feats. For some parts of the Dalkowski legend, however, the evidence is more sketchy.

Consider, for example, the often-repeated story from Pat Jordan's article about Ted Williams taking batting practice against Dalko in Miami. Williams is reported as not connecting with any of Dalko's pitches, and saying afterward that Steve was "the fastest pitcher he had ever faced and that he would be damned if he would ever face him again." It seems that such a historic standoff between two legends would leave a bigger paper trail. Yet the *Time* magazine article about Dalkowski in 1960 didn't mention it. Likewise, the 1966 story in the *Sporting News* announcing his release from baseball didn't mention it.

A credible variation of the story comes from Orioles scout Walter Youse, who said decades later that Ted Williams once stopped what he was doing to watch Dalkowski throw batting practice (rather than actually take batting practice from him) before a game against the Red Sox. When Williams was asked about taking batting practice from Dalko after Jordan's article appeared, Williams claimed not to remember it happening. Did Williams not remember the incident to preserve his own legend at the expense of Dalkowski's? Did he not remember it because his memory let him down? Or because it didn't happen at all?

Other commentators, including Baseball Hall of Fame broadcaster Ernie Harwell, quoted Williams as saying Steve was the fastest pitcher he ever faced. Jordan's source for the story was several players "who were there [when] the legend began ten years before, on a hot spring day in Miami, Fla." Who were these observers and what additional details about the Ted Williams incident might they have been able to share? These are mysteries lost in time.

Although Jordan's 1970 story in *Sports Illustrated* about Dalko raises many interesting historical questions that invite further scrutiny, it constitutes a historically significant contribution in its own right. Especially insightful is Frank McGowan's assessment, as reported by Jordan, of why Dalkowski never made it to the big leagues. It was McGowan who recruited Dalkowski for the Orioles and whose hopes for his success rose and fell over the years. McGowan gave three reasons why Dalkowski ultimately failed.

First, according to McGowan, he was "always terrified of hitting someone" after hitting a batter (Bob Beavers, who isn't named by McGowan) in the head playing for Kingsport in 1957. This was likely true, though McGowan also said of the player who was hit that "the boy never played ball again" and that he "was never quite right in the head afterward," neither of which was true.

McGowan's second explanation for Dalko's failure was right on target: "he was too easily led" and "seemed always to be looking for someone to follow, and in the minors he followed the wrong guys" such as Bo Belinsky and Steve Barber. McGowan added, "I think Steve could have made it if he was ever led by the right guys."

The third reason for Dalko's decline, McGowan believed, was that "the Orioles made too much of a fuss over him. They were always billing him as the 'fastest pitcher alive,' and I think the publicity hurt him. Stuff like taking him to the Aberdeen Proving Grounds, and conducting all those experiments. I think he would have been a lot better off if they just left him alone." This conclusion is supported by facts and stories from many players and managers who interacted with Dalkowski over the years, and by comments from Dalko himself.

Jordan's 1970 *Sports Illustrated* feature describes a ballplayer who is a hero even in defeat. Jordan suggests that Dalkowski's real fame lies not in statistics or even the legendary stories about him, but in the scruffy minor-league towns where players "still struggle toward the major leagues. To these minor-leaguers Dalkowski always symbolized every frustration and elation they had ever felt. His successes and failures were theirs and, though he failed, they look with pride on that, too. Because his failure was not one of deficiency, but rather of excess. . . . His talent was too superhuman. In a way, Dalkowski's failure softened the grimness of their own possible failure." Even so, few players would have cared to share the true grimness of Steve Dalkowski's life after baseball.

After moving out of his apartment in Stockton because Linda would no longer pay the rent, Steve went to Bakersfield hoping to try out with the Dodgers organization. He also evidently attended a union-sponsored landscaping school there, possibly as early as the fall of 1969. He might have had a landscaping job when he wrote his last letter to Linda. He continued with landscaping work off and on, but for the next five years he spent most of his time picking crops up and down the Central Valley of California. After his divorce from Linda in 1970, and with his last hope of getting back into baseball flickering out, Steve joined the transient army of farm workers in the region. Some of them followed the seasons from Arkansas, Oklahoma, and Texas into Bakersfield and the surrounding communities each year. Many were families of Mexicans and other Hispanics who had regular work every season up and down the state harvesting citrus, vegetables, cotton, nuts, vineyard grapes, and other produce.

Steve lived mostly in Oildale, a suburb north of Bakersfield, where block after block of cheap basic housing had been built for oilfield workers and their families early in the twentieth century. He rented a succession of small one-bedroom or efficiency apartments with a patch of dirt for a yard and bare-bones furnishings inside. The worst job he had during those years was chopping cotton, thinning and weeding between cotton plants as they matured over the season. He used a short-handled hoe—later outlawed in the fields—which made the backbreaking work even harder and more uncomfortable. He was paid by the hour for ten hours a day under a blistering sun where temperatures routinely topped one hundred degrees. The hottest day he remembered was 117. Hoeing stirred up clouds of dust. It also disturbed rattlesnakes that lashed out without warning and had to be scared away or chopped to death.

Picking fruit was easier. It paid better too, because pickers were paid based on production and not by the hour. Steve picked apricots, lemons, oranges, and other similar crops though he didn't always earn the money he should have. He harvested oranges by climbing a ladder under a tree with a bag, filling the bag with oranges, then dropping it into a bin. At the end of the day, he made seven or eight dollars a bin. But big families of Mexican children would sometimes pilfer his bags undetected while he was still high on a ladder.

"I just tried to forget the past and work hard," Steve later remembered. At various times, he said, he earned between $40 a day and $15 an hour.

Steve was usually the only white picker on his crew. They rode from town out to the fields before dawn in the back of a truck. When they arrived, they built a fire to stay warm until the sun came up. Steve noticed that other men bought cheap fortified wine to drink while they worked. Always a follower and always ready for another excuse to drink, Steve adopted their tradition. He carried his bottle into the field and set it on the ground at the end of the row as an enticement to get that row harvested and have a swig. Where his baseball days had been a combination of liquor and beer and his years with Linda were beer only, he now turned to working-class wine to satisfy his cravings.

He may have continued to get landscaping work once in a while, and might have worked as a stevedore in a packing house. But most of the time he was a farm laborer, living alone in a squalid Oildale apartment and drinking up his meager wages. He was arrested repeatedly for drunkenness and sentenced ninety days at a time to a road camp, where prisoners worked off their sentences doing roadwork and other hard, menial jobs. Steve's job was mixing cow and chicken feed for twenty-five cents a day. He was paroled in order to attend Alcoholics Anonymous meetings. Then he would miss a meeting and be hauled back to the camp.

Sometimes he would go to Sam Lynn Field in Bakersfield and stand in the shadows near the bullpen fence along the right-field line. It was a long, hot walk down the dingy main street south from Oildale, across a bridge spanning a marshy creek, then to the ballpark. Because the stadium faced due west, by tradition afternoon games were halted for a few minutes at sunset when the batter looked directly into the sun setting behind the center-field fence. The small grandstand held a few hundred seats, and there were two sections of aluminum and plastic seats along the baseline to first. Gripping the chain-link fence, Steve called to players he knew. Occasionally, they would come over to talk for a minute. He often asked them for spare change.

The change went for more wine. At least once he was so poisoned by cheap alcohol that he had hallucinations and delirium tremens bad enough to be admitted to the hospital.

Late in the 1974 season, the baseball world was buzzing about the upcoming scientific test to measure the pitching speed of California Angels fireballer Nolan Ryan. The twenty-seven-year-old right-hander had thrown two no-hitters the year before and also set the single-season record for strikeouts with 383. He would go on to become one of the greatest hurlers in the game's history.

Ryan was already recognized as one of the fastest pitchers of all time. North American Rockwell, an aerospace company, came up with a way of testing his speed with a new technology that would later be known as the radar gun. The system was first tested on August 20, 1974, at Anaheim Stadium, where two of Ryan's fastballs were clocked at 100.9 mph near home plate. On September 7, Ryan's speed was measured again. In the ninth inning of a contest between the Angels and the Chicago White Sox, the third pitch to ninth inning leadoff batter Lee "Bee Bee" Richard was officially timed at 100.8 mph just in front of the plate.

This was the first time radar had been used to time a baseball, and the first pitch officially ever to fly faster than Bob Feller's famous 98.6 mph scorcher, timed by light beams in 1946. (Later pitches were measured closer to the pitcher's mound. Had Ryan's pitch been timed there, physics tell us it would have been going 108 mph, a speed that has never been equaled in major league baseball.) The story of Ryan and the radar gun revived interest in fastballs in general. Sportswriters and fans who remembered him started asking themselves, "Whatever happened to Steve Dalkowski?"

He was still in Oildale, still working in the fields, getting drunk, and panhandling at the ballpark. In September 1974 the *Long Beach*

Press-Telegram reported that Dalkowski's "last-known address was the Kern County jail in Bakersfield." Days later, however, the *Bakersfield Californian* sports editor Larry Press interviewed Dalkowski in person. "Not only does he not look like a fireballing pitcher," Press reported, "but, from his appearance, you could be excused for not even knowing he was an athlete. . . . That southpaw slingshot is not particularly muscular, nor do the hand and wrist appear especially impressive."

In the interview with Press, Dalkowski said his nerves were what had kept him from the success everyone expected. "If Harry Brecheen could have stood right behind me when I pitched, I would have been all right," he said. This is consistent with what others said about him. Asked about the famous IQ test given by the Orioles, Dalko answered, "All the psychiatrist did was have me look at a couple of pictures and tell him what they looked like to me." Steve believed he could have made it to the majors if his teams "had stuck with him just a little longer."

Bleak as his present state and future prospects were, Dalko did not linger in the past. "[H]e says the memories aren't important," Larry Press wrote. "He has worked in the fields around here and now is looking for work. He's not particular but he'd like 'something better than working in the fields.' Anyone wishing to contact him should call [phone number]."

The Orioles organization tried to keep up with Dalkowski during these years without success, despite his occasional newspaper interviews. They had reported they lost his trail when he was released from Kern County Jail in 1974. The California League put out a newsletter appeal for information about him but got no response, even though he still turned up at ballparks from time to time. Bakersfield manager Ron Midal, a former teammate, sometimes let him into Sam Lynn Field to watch.

Dalkowski called old friends back in Connecticut once in a while, hoping to reconnect. In 1975 he talked with Hartford sportswriter George Smith about a new book on baseball players that gave Dalko a chapter all his own: "The Living Legend." (Smith, a Vietnam veteran who died in 2017, wrote four books of military history after retiring from the *Hartford Courant* in 1995. There is no record that his baseball book was published.) He remembered that during high school there were "more scouts than people at the games I pitched." His speed, he told Smith, was "a gift from the Lord."

Sometime in the mid-1970s, Steve met Virginia Greenwood when they were picking oranges together in Bakersfield. Virginia had been born in Oklahoma in 1931. She was divorced and had five children from her previous marriage. Steve and Virginia became a couple and then evidently married in 1975, though at times afterward they had separate addresses. In 1977, for example, the Bakersfield city directory reports that Virginia lived on E Street in Bakersfield. The address there is a beautiful Spanish-style duplex with a graceful palm tree in the front. Steve, on the other hand, had a rundown rental on El Tejon miles away in Oildale. Is seems likely that they separated when Steve's drinking got to be too much, then reconciled later on. They may have split up and reconnected more than once in the late 1970s.

In the first week of December 1977, *Hartford Courant* writer George Smith published a survey piece on former athletes he had written about over the past two years. All of the subjects he called were willing to talk to him, and most of the conversations were upbeat and enjoyable. "The saddest experience of all, however," Smith wrote, "was talking to New Britain native Steve Dalkowski, a kid pitcher fifteen years ago with a blazing but errant fastball and now a young man beset with personal problems."

Recalling their 1975 interview, he continued, "I got in touch with him in Bakersfield, California, where he is a hotel desk clerk. He wasn't feeling well and he apologized for his speech, which he fought to control. He told me a lot about himself and his problems. A little bit about baseball, too. 'Please don't hang up,' he asked me several times."

Steve drifted out to various ballparks from time to time watching his old teammates from the shadows, brown bag in hand. Herm Starrette later remembered seeing him at Candlestick Park in San Francisco in 1977. Herm was a pitching coach for the Giants that year. Warming up a pitcher in the bullpen, he looked up to see Dalkowski leaning over the railing. "The poor guy looked seventy," Starrette recalled. Steve was thirty-eight. "He was staying at Ray Youngdahl's place, and Ray had him in rehab, but he'd go to rehab during the day and come home and get drunk at night. He had the beer stashed somewhere."

Youngdahl was the former teammate and roommate from Elmira whose Cadillac Steve had infamously smashed into a police car. Youngdahl had founded a Christian outreach for incarcerated minors and also worked for the California probation department. He had wanted to find his old friend and help him if he could. To partner with him on the search for Steve, Youngdahl called Chuck Stevens, head of the Association of Professional Ball Players of America (APBA), a charity founded in 1924 for retired baseball players and supported by volunteer contributions from active players, coaches, and other baseball professionals. (Stevens played parts of three seasons with the St. Louis Browns in the 1940s and led the APBA for thirty-eight years. At the time of his death in 2018, two months shy of his one hundredth birthday, he was the oldest living Major League Baseball player.)

Youngdahl found Dalkowski in Oildale and offered to help his old teammate get back on his feet. Youngdahl and Stevens explained to Steve that the APBA would pay for substance-abuse treatment and provide direct financial assistance. They were willing to help him as long as he was willing to help himself.

Steve agreed. Youngdahl and Stevens found "a fourteen-foot-long medical sheet" and "thirty-five common drunk arrests" tracing the hard years since Dalkowski had left his first wife, Linda, in Stockton and started picking crops. The two men got him through the Project 90 alcohol rehabilitation program and helped him find a job. "We had him absolutely dry for three months," Chuck Stevens said. Ray even took Steve into his own home to give him some stability and keep an eye on him.

Unfortunately it didn't last. Steve went back to the bottle, and the Association withdrew its assistance. "We went through lots of heartache and many dollars," Stevens recalled, "but Dalkowski didn't want to help himself, and we weren't going to keep him drunk." He added, "We did everything humanly possible. . . . We had Dalkowski on his feet and if he chooses to destroy his life, we cannot change that desire. . . . We worked our tail off for this man. It's heartbreaking."

During an interview in 1982, Youngdahl summarized the frustration and sadness he felt: "I had lost track of Steve for ten years. When I found him in 1978, he was about ready to die. He smelled so bad. I . . . drove him to my home in San Mateo, where I got him in a detox program. They had to strap him down for four-and-a-half days. . . . When he finally got out of detox, I got him into a landscaping school. He lived with us for a time. He was sober for 110 days, and then we began to find wine bottles around the house. Then he went on a bus to Bakersfield to see Virginia, and somehow he got off in San Jose and started drinking again."

In the spring of 1979, Steve's father died in New Britain. Dalkowski wanted to go back for the funeral but didn't make the trip. He spoke later about maybe visiting his family at Christmas but didn't travel then either. Steve was working that year for a landscaping service as a laborer. He also had operated a forklift and a road grader. He and Virginia were back together by then. She had a job at the local bowling alley, and the two were settled into an apartment on McCord Avenue in Oildale.

Around the time Steve's father passed away, Steve Jacobson wrote a feature for *Newsday* about the Dalkowski legend. "It will be a legend," he declared, "as long as anybody who saw him pitch, or merely heard about him, is around." He quoted Yankees outfielder Paul Blair saying he had hit against Nolan Ryan and Sandy Koufax and that Dalko was faster than either of them.

Jacobson expanded on the story of Dalko pitching against the Cincinnati Reds in spring training. He claimed Reds manager Birdie

Tebbetts demanded that Paul Richards take Dalko off the mound or he wouldn't play. Richards held his ground and Steve famously struck out the side on twelve pitches. Later, after moving from the Reds to the Orioles, Frank Robinson confirmed that Tebbetts had threatened to fine any batter $100 who stood close enough to swing. "I got them this far," Tebbetts supposedly said. "I want to open the season with them." Jack Fisher remembered the fine being $100 per swing; batters were warned to take a walk or strike out.

Jacobson said that Earl Weaver remembered how no matter when Steve fell into bed the night before, he was always up and eager the next day. "He had to be put to bed at 3 a.m. Saturday night and then had to be told to stop his wind sprints Sunday morning."

Two months after the *Newsday* story, Mark Fleisher, assistant sports editor of the *Elmira Star-Gazette*, tracked down Dalko in California and had a long telephone conversation with him. He published the interview June 17 in a feature article headlined "Dalkowski—the fastest ever." A big cartoon on the page showed Steve with his glasses and wearing an Elmira Pioneers uniform, swinging an enormous bottle instead of a bat. The story was a mixture of old statistics and Steve's current life. Some facts in the account were incorrect. Fleisher reported that Steve lived with "his second wife and their six-year-old daughter," but Dalkowski never had a child with Virginia or anyone else.

Steve told Fleisher that he worked for Charlie Earley's Handyman Service and hadn't had a drink in two months. He also said that in the past he never drank on a day when he was scheduled to pitch, though plenty of accounts dispute this. Dalkowski told Fleisher he had been through two alcohol rehab programs in the past eighteen months. Another article two weeks later in the *Sporting News* quoted Chuck Stevens as saying Steve had gotten rehab help four years before.

Maybe Steve's sense of time was off regarding the rehab, or maybe he was trying to spin his story in a more favorable light. He did admit to Fleisher that after he popped his elbow in 1963, "Everything seemed to come unglued then. My arm hurt, and then I really started drinking." (And yet two seasons later he was a star in Mexico.)

By this time Steve Dalkowski had been out of professional baseball longer than he had been in it. Looking back on his playing years, he told Fleisher, "What bothered me was every time I'd go to a different league, people would say, 'Holy Christ, there he is.' Like I was a freak or something. I look back at it all and I'm a little disgusted. All those damn years. The travel, the lousy ballparks, the long bus rides. All for nothing. I'd have a team made and then there I'd go again.

"But you can't cry over spilled milk, can you?"

Though Mark Fleisher won a 1979 Associated Press award for his story, its subject continued drifting further into obscurity. Steve went to work for Miller Construction Company in Bakersfield and, in 1981, moved with Virginia to an apartment on Douglas Street in Bakersfield. That move was the beginning of some of the most settled years in Dalkowski's adult life. Steve now had a caring wife, a job, and a stable home environment. For a while at least, his post-baseball journey had finally taken a turn for the better.

SEVENTEEN

Nice to Be Remembered

"I wonder whatever became of Dalkowski? I dream of finding a pitcher like him someday."
—Charlie Wagner, Red Sox player and coach, 1981

The new apartment in Bakersfield was a big step up for the Dalkowskis. It was a two-bedroom ground-floor unit in a subsidized complex operated by a private nonprofit organization. It was the newest, nicest housing in town in its price range, with spacious lawns, tasteful landscaping, playgrounds for the children, central air conditioning, and modern bathrooms and kitchens. Steve alternated among various outdoor jobs—laborer, construction worker, welder's helper, equipment operator—and periods of sitting at home all day drinking beer. Having returned to domestic life, he also went back to beer, leaving the rotgut wine of the harvesters behind. Virginia started a job as a clerk for Galland's Bakery, which she kept until she left California years later. She also continued part-time at a nearby bowling alley, where she worked as a babysitter.

Once in a while Steve's name still popped up in the sports pages. In the summer of 1981, Red Sox player and coach Charlie Wagner gave an interview about pitchers he had worked with over his career. The fastest he ever saw, Wagner said, was Steve Dalkowski. "He had the greatest arm I ever saw," Wagner continued. "I wonder whatever became of Dalkowski? I dream of finding a pitcher like him someday. What a find!"

The *Baltimore News American* ran a story about Steve on the front page of the sports section on August 28, 1981. Sports editor John F. Steadman wrote that he and Dalkowski had a good talk during a recent phone conversation. "He will tell you he wishes he didn't drink so much," Steadman reported, "and that his wife, a compassionate and understanding woman from Keota, Oklahoma, saved him from total destruction. At forty-two, with baseball only a memory, he works as a welder's helper in the oilfields near Bakersfield, California." According to his wife Virginia, the men he worked with around the oil rigs had a hard time believing Steve was "the one-time phenom of the Orioles who could fire a ball so fast it defied tracking."

Dalkowski had called Steadman to "check out a reporter for a national magazine who was planning to write a story on him. He hopes it won't be another downer." Steve said he was "sitting around having a few beers" during the call. "Out here in California we ain't got no clams," he told Steadman. "We don't have any oysters or crabs. And we don't even have an Earl Weaver." Weaver, Steadman said, blamed his prematurely gray hair on "all those Dalkowski bases on balls, plus worrying if Dalkowski was going to make room check."

"A lot of people put words out about me that aren't true," Steve declared. "And another thing, I never lie. Me and 'Booger' Powell don't know how to lie."

Like so many writers before and since, Steadman searched for reasons why Dalkowski came so close to the Show without ever making it. He quoted Billy DeMars, by this time coaching for the Philadelphia Phillies: "I think now there was a problem deep within him. I remember one time he was pitching in 1958 at Aberdeen in the Northern League, on a cold night when the temperature was around the freezing mark. By the second inning, his uniform was a different color of gray because of how he was perspiring. I wonder if the wildness came from nerves."

It was another in a long line of expert eyewitnesses who believed nerves and lack of confidence were major stumbling blocks throughout Dalko's career. (Years later DeMars added to his thoughts, telling another interviewer that Steve was "a very, very nervous kid. He knew he could throw hard, but he didn't have that confidence, that cockiness. I thought that hurt him. On nights when he pitched, he could hardly speak to you. But on nights he didn't pitch, he was the life of the party.")

Steadman ended his article by noting that Steve continued to forget "the frustrations and disappointments with a few drinks. He gets up early almost every morning and heads for another day in the oil fields. There's still an almost child-like gentleness to him, without a trace of regret or bitterness at the rest of the world."

In July 1982, *Inside Sports* published a long feature about Dalkowski by Pat Jordan. As in his past writing on the subject, some of Jordan's narrative repeats familiar but inaccurate accounts (tearing a batter's ear off), misstates various facts (that he lived in a "tiny" apartment, which it wasn't), proposes alternate versions of events (that Steve and Virginia met when she was working in a hotel), and seems to spin stories out of thin air (that Steve left his first wife by driving off in her mother's Thunderbird to get a pack of cigarettes and disappearing forever, despite the fact that Steve never smoked and by then likely hadn't driven a car in years).

To be fair to Jordan, by 1982 Steve Dalkowski was no longer an accurate source of information about his own life. Alcohol had clouded his memory, and he had heard apocryphal stories about himself so many times that he'd started to believe them. The article is valuable, however, for the viewpoints it captures from Dalkowski and others.

According to Jordan, Steve's mother credited well-meaning friends with starting Dalko on the road to alcoholism. "It was the adults who started him drinking," she said. "New Britain was a town for all sports. The old-timers would grab a kid who was good in sports and buy him shots and beers. Whether a kid was good or not, he turned out to be an alcoholic."

Jordan spoke with Steve's friend Charles Garrett. Steve and Charles met in 1973 when they were serving ninety days on a road crew for drunkenness. Garrett later become a detox program counselor who helped treat Steve during his stints in rehab. "Steve is a helluva nice person," Garrett explained to Jordan. "He's slow to release anger, which is why he drinks. Most alcoholics have a low opinion of themselves, and a low frustration level. They generate anger over the slightest insult, but they can't release that anger. So they drink. . . . During all the times [Steve has] been here, he never mentioned his baseball failure as a cause for drinking."

Jordan reported that Steve worked for the city maintenance department cleaning public parks. He was up by 4:30 a.m. and fortified himself with wine until his ride came to pick him up at 7:00. He got home at 4:00 then drank until bedtime around 7 p.m. Virginia had her jobs as cashier at a bakery and babysitting at a bowling alley. She cooked dinner after work every night, but Steve seldom ate.

"Why the hell do we ballplayers drink so much?" Dalko wondered aloud.

A year after the *Inside Sports* article, Earl Weaver was reminiscing about his first season coaching in Elmira. The game that turned that 1962 season around for the Pioneers, he said, was the famous 21-inning marathon when Steve was the star of the moment. Dalkowski took the mound in the seventh inning "and proceeded to pitch 10 shutout innings in what Weaver still believes to be the best pitching performance during Dalkowski's short, explosive, controversial professional career."

Steve kept the lines of communication open, albeit barely, with old teammates from his playing years in California. Players swapped stories of seeing him once in a while hanging around at ballparks. The conversations typically ended with Dalko asking for spare change.

"Look at that," players would say, pointing out Dalko's stooped form to younger teammates. "That's Steve Dalkowski, the fastest pitcher of all time." The comment was both a mark of distinction and a cautionary tale. *That could be any of us.*

Steve evidently held onto the same construction job in Bakersfield until going to work for the parks department. His first years with Virginia on Douglas Street with relatively stable employment, a forgiving and understanding wife, regular visits from Virginia's grandchildren, and a clean, cheerful neighborhood, were the best of times during this season of Steve's life. He kept a job of one sort or another for extended periods. Still the alcoholism pulled him down time and again.

Former teammate Boog Powell would get a call now and then from Steve asking for money: "Hey, brother, can you help me?" Then, as Powell related, "His wife or whoever he's with says, 'Don't help that son of a bitch; he'll just drink it up.' You know, I can hear her in the background. Then all of a sudden, click, the phone hangs up."

Dalko kept in touch by phone with some of the old New Britain High gang as well. He especially remembered his former catcher Ken Cullum and Ken's brother Jack, along with next-door neighbor and one-time catcher Andy Baylock, and high school baseball coach Bill Huber. Ken had made it briefly to Class A with the Braves organization in 1960. Andy Baylock captained both his football and baseball teams in college and went on to become the head baseball coach at the University of Connecticut.

In 1986, Jack Cullum contacted Steve's sister, Pat, in New Britain. She helped him track down Dalko in Bakersfield. Steve's childhood friends knew he was struggling and wanted to extend a helping hand. Cullum called with an offer from his old New Britain teammates of a job back in Connecticut and treatment in a private substance-abuse clinic.

Steve turned them down. He said he was comfortable where he was. Twenty years earlier he had gone home looking for a fresh start and left empty-handed. Now when he had another chance, he decided against it. Home these days was with Virginia in California. Steve did return to New Britain briefly and quietly in 1987 for his mother's funeral. The family kept his trip under wraps because they didn't want the occasion to become "a media event." Only his closest friends knew he was in town.

One year after Steve slipped in and out of New Britain, Cullum decided to visit him in California. To Cullum, Dalkowski had "literally dropped out of sight." He asked himself, "How many times have I heard, 'Whatever happened to Steve Dalkowski?' Where was the southpaw phenomenon reputed to have thrown a baseball faster than any other human? . . . I was determined to see him."

Jack and his son Jason arrived in Bakersfield on a scorching July afternoon in 1988. The temperature was 102 degrees when he rang the doorbell on Douglas Street. Though Jack had set up the visit by phone days earlier, Steve "opened the door and just stared for what seemed like minutes." Finally he asked his visitor, "Jack, is that you? What the hell did you put on so much weight for?" Steve motioned Jack and Jason into his apartment, its floor littered with toys for Virginia's grandchildren. Over a long conversation that afternoon, Jack got the impression that Steve was truly happy and content.

"My memory of Steve is a fun-loving, partying person and this antithesis—a caring grandfather figure with all of the attendant responsibilities—was not lost on me," Jack recounted, describing a "staid, semiretired Dalkowski who could not be defined by his past." Cullum continued, "He never lost his love of baseball and feels no bitterness over what happened to him . . . for several hours, he vividly recalled the people, places, and dates from over thirty years ago as if it happened yesterday." Steve told Jack he sometimes went to the Bakersfield Dodgers games with a season pass from team manager Gary LaRoque, a former University of Hartford baseball and basketball star.

"He admits to making some mistakes, primarily off the field," Cullum said. "[But] he's come to terms with his problems. . . . I would have preferred that he had a full-time job and that things were better for him financially, but he seemed genuinely happy, and I'm glad for that."

Jack echoed the feeling often expressed by Dalkowski's family and close friends that unfortunately, the public was interested in Steve only for stories about his wild pitching and wild living. They weren't interested in what Jack considered to be the real Steve, and Dalko had the right to be left alone if that's what he wanted. "He's been exploited—abused isn't even too strong a word," Cullum wrote after returning to Connecticut. "There is a side to Steve Dalkowski that people have never heard about," a "warm, kind, generous side" that the world ignored in favor of tales about throwing balls through backstops and alcoholic meltdowns.

As Jack and his son were driving back to their hotel, Jack tried to summarize his thoughts to Jason about their visit with Dalko. "I couldn't explain what it meant to me to have seen Steve, with roots firmly planted . . . a loving wife, baseball still part of his life—an ordinary man. This athlete, who had the most natural ability I ever witnessed, found outside of baseball that which eluded him during his career—an inner peace."

It is a rare and welcome vision of relative calm and contentment among all the reports of alcoholism and despair that punctuate this era of Steve Dalkowski's life. Even allowing for Jack Cullum's natural bias in favor of his old friend, the story of his 1988 visit is an encouraging one. It's the only solid eyewitness account of Dalko's home life during his years with Virginia.

A phone call with Hartford newspaperman Bob Sudyk a year later seemed to confirm the picture Jack had painted. Steve told the writer that his drinking had settled down. "I just do a few beers," he said, "just get a little high, and I'm eating pretty good right now." He asked Sudyk to remember him to his old friends in Connecticut. "I miss them a lot. Just tell them this old Polack has no regrets. He took the good with the bad and did the best he could. Tell 'em he's doin' OK." Steve added that he was working part-time for a landscaping company, and Virginia was a clerk at a bakery. He said he also received "a small pension check from a national baseball players association," and admitted to weighing 220 pounds. "I look like the back end of a beer truck. Too many golumbki," he explained, referring to Polish stuffed cabbage, "but they don't make them here like back in New Britain."

Sudyk added his musings to the long list of speculations about why Steve Dalkowski came so close to stardom without breaking into the big leagues. "Some said it was his romance with beer and all-night partying. Some said it was his poor eyesight, or his fear of killing a batter. Others say he was intimidated by his gift." Now, however, Dalko had his "guardian angel" in Virginia, the company of her five children and their families, a steady (if part-time) job, and the joy of reconnecting with his sister, Pat, his old teammate Jack Cullum, and others from his glory days as a New Britain star.

Around this time, Dalkowski's name made a short but impactful reappearance in America's sports pages. The news about timing Nolan Ryan's fastball with a radar gun in 1974 had earlier revived public interest in Dalkowski's life and career. Now another media event rekindled the world's curiosity about the one-time flamethrower in the Orioles organization. Screenwriter, director, and former Oriole minor-league second baseman Ron Shelton scored big in 1988 with a movie about a gifted but troubled pitcher that reminded many fans of Dalko's career. In fact, Steve was part of the inspiration for the character Nuke LaLoosh in the Hollywood hit *Bull Durham*.

Shelton started his professional baseball career with the Bluefield Orioles of the rookie Appalachian League in 1967 at age twenty-one. Later in the season he moved up to Class-A ball with the Stockton Ports. That was where he first heard of the legendary Steve Dalkowski. Dalko had last played there only three years before, and his exploits were still vivid memories for everyone who'd seen him. As Shelton later wrote, "[I]n the wake of the great players who preceded me—Brooks Robinson, Boog Powell, Jim Palmer, and the rest—the stories passed on by bus drivers and groundskeepers and minor-league players and managers were not about the exploits of those Hall of Famers, they were about an obscure pitcher named Dalkowski."

In 1970 and '71, his last years in baseball, Shelton played for the Rochester Red Wings, where Dalko had pitched in 12 games in 1963 after hurting his arm in spring training. The manager in '71 was Joe Altobelli, the player Oriole brass had tapped to be Dalko's roommate in hopes that the older and more mature team member could be a calming role model to the wild, young southpaw. Shelton was fascinated with the idea of the older player whose best years were likely behind him being paired with a promising but untamed new prospect. Joe explained that he loved Steve and wanted to help him, but he was never in his room. "I roomed with a suitcase," he recalled (a phrase also used by Herm Starrette). Steve would come home wasted in the middle of the night but somehow be on the mound throwing his fireballs a few hours later. As he had at Stockton, Shelton heard the legendary stories about Steve throwing incredible numbers of pitches, setting records for strikeouts and walks, the unbelievable wildness on the field and off, and the rare and wonderful talent underlying it all.

Ron also saw Steve occasionally when he played in Stockton. He wrote, "I would see a figure standing in the dark down the right-field line at old Sam Lynn Park in Oildale, a paper bag in hand. Sometimes he'd come to the clubhouse to beg for money. . . . Altobelli would talk to him, give him some change, then come back and report, 'That was Steve Dalkowski.' And a clubhouse full of cocky, young, testosterone-driven baseball players sat in awe—of the unimaginable gift, the legend, the fall." (Likely this was in 1969 at the end of Shelton's time in Stockton, after Dalko and his first wife, Linda, had separated.)

Shelton watched a lot of movies during his baseball years, he said, because the movie theater in whatever little town they were playing was the one place where you could be sure there was air conditioning. Years later he became a screenwriter and made his debut as a director with *Bull Durham*. "There were elements of Dalkowski I used in Nuke," he explained. "This relationship—the veteran who loved a game more than the game loved him, and the God-gifted rookie who was otherwise a lost soul—was the inspiration for *Bull Durham*," though nothing in Altobelli or Dalkowski's character is applicable. "He had it all and didn't know it. That's why Steve Dalkowski stays in our minds. In his sport, he had the equivalent of Michelangelo's gift but could never finish a painting."

Bull Durham, starring Kevin Costner, Susan Sarandon, and Tim Robbins as rookie pitcher Nuke LaLoosh, was a solid hit that went on to become a classic favorite. It earned Ron Shelton an Academy Award nomination for best original screenplay and in 2003 was selected by *Sports Illustrated* as the best sports movie of all time.

For all the success of Ron Shelton's film, it didn't much affect Steve Dalkowski. A few baseball fans did seek him out for interviews, including Robert Graziul writing for *Baseball Digest*. His December 1990 account was in line with stories over the previous two years from Jack Cullum and Bob Sudyk. Steve talked with him while sitting on the curb of the parking lot outside his apartment, idly kicking gravel on the pavement as he answered questions. He seemed to drift in and out of the interview, out of touch with the world around him. He said he thought maybe he'd seen Nolan Ryan pitch once on TV, but he wasn't sure.

Strikeouts, Steve told Graziul, were easy, "just like handing the catcher the ball. If I didn't strike out 18 in a game, it was a bad day." What was it, then, that made his control so unpredictable? "Sometimes I just lost my concentration," Dalko shrugged. "The truth is, I really don't know what it was."

Steve shared his versions of some of the stories that had grown up around him. He was playing with the Red Wings when a game was rained out. Catcher Andy Etchebarren "started betting a bunch of guys that I could throw a ball through this wall down at the end of the bullpen." The wall was made of split logs. Dalko told Andy he didn't know if he could do it or not, but "son-of-a-gun, my third pitch broke right through."

He also remembered a time in Stockton when catcher Frank Zupo bet him he couldn't throw a ball from where they were standing to the clubhouse 410 feet away. Without any warmup, he fired a ball that bounced off the roof. Steve told Graziul that after his injury in 1963, pitching "wasn't fun anymore. The arm was never the same."

Steve said in conclusion, "It still hurts when I think how close I was to making the big leagues. But if I had to do it all over again, I'd do it. I've made a lot of friends in the minor leagues. And it's nice to be remembered."

EIGHTEEN

Safe at Home

"We all thought he'd go far. It's just unfortunate that he didn't. But he's still a legend."
—Vin Cazzetta, Steve Dalkowski's junior high baseball coach, 2003

A decade of relative calm in the life of Steve Dalkowski came to an end in 1991. After ten years in their comfortable subsidized apartment on Douglas Street, he and Virginia moved into a small house nearby on Lincoln Avenue. It was one of a short row of identical rental properties—single-story ranch homes each with a picture window in the living room and a little patch of green lawn out front. Virginia still had her job at the bakery. Dalko evidently was not working when they moved, or afterward.

In August of that year, the Dalkowskis had a visit from two men on a mission trying once more to help Steve recover from alcoholism and also to claim his rightful place in baseball history. Frank Zupo was a former catcher who played with Dalko in Stockton in 1960 and appeared in a handful of major league games over three seasons. He had become an executive with the Major League Baseball Players Association, the players' collective bargaining operation. Tom Chiappetta was a former sportswriter, Fox Sports marketer, and PR consultant working on a documentary film about Dalkowski provisionally titled *Broken Wing.*

The first day the two came to talk with him, Steve was too impaired to carry on a conversation. Virginia told them to come back the next morning at eight o'clock, "before he hits the booze." On their second try, they found Dalko sitting on the couch with a quart of beer in his hand, watching a little twelve-inch television. "It was real sad," Zupo later recalled. The two visitors fought to hold Steve's attention despite his alcoholic confusion and the distraction of the TV. In a replay of Chuck Stevens and Ray Youngdahl's attempts to help him in the 1970s, Zupo and Chiappetta told Steve that if he didn't get help soon he was going to die.

Zupo had been one of the few players who thought Steve's drinking during his playing years was exaggerated. "So much has been distorted," he once said. "He was like every other ballplayer: You finish a game, you go have a sandwich and a couple of beers. No one was any different." Whether or not that accurately reflected Zupo's feeling at the time, the situation now was far different. "You've got to do something," Zupo told his old friend. Dalko replied, "Yeah, I think I better."

With help from the Baseball Assistance Team (BAT), formed in 1986 to quietly provide a temporary hand up to former players who need assistance and have nowhere else to turn, Steve Dalkowski was hospitalized in Los Angeles for three months beginning in October 1991. During that time he had a complete medical workup and physical diagnosis, went through alcohol detox, and had a special nutrition program to help restore his health. He might also have had reconstructive surgery on his nose, which had been caved in with a pool cue during a fight. In early 1992 Steve was transferred to the Rickman Center, an addiction treatment facility in Hawthorne that served as a halfway house during the next stage of his recovery.

Unfortunately, history repeated itself. In the seventies, when he was living with Ray Youngdahl after a stay in detox, Steve had asked to visit Virginia before starting a new job. But by the time his bus arrived in Oildale, he had disappeared into a bar en route. This time, on August 1, 1992, Steve walked out of the Rickman Center and never came back.

In September he disappeared completely. Virginia was by now a seasoned veteran of her husband's backsliding and powerlessness over his addiction. She had earned a living for the both of them throughout their time together, often working two jobs. He was unreliable and unpredictable. Even so, after he vanished, she became more worried every day that the worst had finally happened: Steve had drunk himself to death, his body lying in a gutter somewhere. After not hearing from him for months, Virginia left California in despair and moved back to her native Oklahoma to live with her family in Oklahoma City.

On December 18, 1992, she wrote a heartrending letter to Steve's old neighbor and teammate Andy Baylock, who in the thirty-five years since graduating from New Britain High had gone on to become the winningest college baseball head coach in Connecticut history. Virginia had never met Andy, but she knew how Steve admired him from the way he always talked about him. She wondered if Andy had any idea where Steve was.

"I know you don't know me," Virginia wrote, "but I have heard a lot about you. . . . As you know I guess, Steve is missing it will be three months the 22nd. I've really been on the edge worrying about him. I'm staying with my daughter and family now. Makes it a little easier for me. I make it through the day thinking that he will show up. I just hope and pray he's all right. I miss him so much."

Coach Baylock hadn't seen his old friend in years and had no idea where Steve might be either. He could offer sympathy and encouragement but no practical advice.

On Christmas Eve 1992, a woman and her family were doing their wash at a Laundromat in Glendale, a few miles north of Los Angeles.

A disheveled old man, drunk and disoriented, came stumbling in to escape the mid-forties temperature. He may have asked the family for spare change. Seeing his deteriorated state, the kind family didn't want this unfortunate stranger to spend Christmas Eve on the streets. They couldn't find out who he was at first; he wasn't able to carry on a conversation.

Some accounts report that the family was Hispanic and that they took him in for the night and to church with them on Christmas morning. They found a phone number on a slip of paper in the stranger's pocket. It was Frank Zupo's. When Frank got word that his troubled friend was found and safe, he picked him up and then called Virginia.

In January 1993 Steve and Virginia were reunited in Oklahoma City. Whatever time they had to rebuild their lives and their marriage was brutally short. A year later, in January 1994, Virginia died suddenly of a brain aneurysm. Steve was left in a strange city with debilitating alcohol-induced dementia and an uncertain future.

Frank Zupo and Steve's sister, Pat, formed a plan to bring Steve home to New Britain. The first step was for Steve to spend two months in an Oklahoma hospital updating his medical history and stabilizing his condition. This was a requirement for him to receive subsidized medical assistance in Connecticut. In March 1994 Steve flew home. His sister and others didn't know what to expect. Would he even realize what was happening? But when Steve got off the plane, Pat was relieved to see him recognize her right away and wrap her in a warm brotherly hug.

Tests in Oklahoma showed he had had internal bleeding at some point, though his liver was miraculously healthy. "He was in bad shape," Pat observed. "It was touch and go, and we didn't expect him to live very long. But he fooled us all."

Steve was moved into the Walnut Hill Convalescent Home in New Britain, his expenses covered by a state program for people who couldn't afford their own care. It was a homecoming on several levels. He was back in the town where he had first won fame as a baseball player. Unlike his professional career, his five years as a schoolboy star were an unqualified triumph. Everybody remembered the good-natured, hardworking player, who somehow managed to throw a baseball faster than anybody else. Many years and many miles later, he was still the hometown hero. Old friends such as his high school baseball coach Bill Huber and teammates Len Pare, Andy Baylock, and Jack Cullum loved and admired him as much as they ever had.

Walnut Hill was also across Grand Street from New Britain Hospital, where Steve and Pat were born. And it was on the edge of Walnut Hill Park, just down the hill from the baseball field where overflow crowds—including major league scouts—once gathered to watch Sizzling Steve in action. Steve settled into his new home, an upstairs semi-private room at the end of a hallway. The room had a big window at the far end looking out onto the trees. Its floor was bare linoleum, and the walls were painted concrete block. It was a simple and spare space, but polished and clean and flooded with sunlight. Steve and his roommate each had a hospital bed, a chair, a side table, a chest of drawers, and a small television. The area around each bed could be separated with a privacy curtain.

Steve was a few months shy of his fifty-fifth birthday when he entered Walnut Hill. He hadn't played an inning of professional baseball in twenty-eight years. Decades of heavy drinking had left him with severe alcohol-related dementia. His caregivers hoped that with proper diet, medication, and encouragement from friends and family he would be able to recover at least some of his faculties.

When Steve first arrived at Walnut Hill, he had almost no interaction with anyone. He didn't recognize his old teammate Len Pare, who came to visit. He couldn't remember the name of his late wife, Virginia. He often had a glassy-eyed look that made it seem he didn't know where he was or what was happening around him. What little conversation he had was typically one- or two-word answers to questions. He often lay for long periods on top of his bedcovers, one leg on the bed and the other dangling down the side, as if he wasn't sure if he was going to get out of bed or stay put.

Whatever his powers of perception, Steve loved having company to help pass the time.

None of the hometown crowd who knew him cared that he fell short of a major league career. Everyone was proud of him. "He's fine. He's comfortable," Pat told a *Hartford Courant* reporter in 1996. "He's happy. Right now, we just want to make sure that he's able to move on with life. Sometimes I think we've taken him to his limits here, but that's still great, because there were times when none of us even felt we'd be able to get Steve this far." That same year New Britain High inducted Steve into their Baseball Hall of Fame.

When his old coach Bill Huber learned that Steve was interested in going to church, Bill started bringing him along on Sundays. "Maybe he's interested in atonement," Huber said. "I don't know. That's not important." He remembered Steve during his high school days as "a very likable person. In the three years that I coached him, he never gave me one problem at all. Whatever I said, he did. Whatever I asked him to do, he did." Walking to and from church, the two stopped to chat with neighbors and for Steve to sign autographs. "I shoot questions at him and he fills in the blanks," Huber explained.

Huber also started driving him to high school baseball games and an occasional game at the University of Connecticut coached by Baylock. "What I remember are the happy days," Baylock recalled at the time. "I remember us as little kids over the Corbin Heights housing projects . . . running around, playing games, listening to records. Happy times."

In an earlier interview, Baylock recalled the time he was hosting Earl Weaver at a baseball clinic and wondered aloud if he could ask Weaver about an old friend who once played for him in Elmira. "I didn't even finish the name and Weaver said, 'Don't say any more! One time somebody in the press box in Elmira yelled down, 'Hey Dalkowski, you crazy Pollack!' Dalkowski turned around a threw a fastball right up through the window of the press box!'"

Home in New Britain, Dalkowski's alcohol-induced confusion gradually began to clear. Steve started talking more, interacting with other residents at Walnut Hill, playing gin rummy and bingo, seeming more alert and engaged with visitors. He played ping-pong and Wii with Pat's grandchildren. By 1998 he had improved enough to give interviews again. A caller saying he represented Joe Garagiola contacted Pat to ask if her brother was still alive.

One spring day Steve and Pat talked with Bill Madden of the *New York Daily News*. Thinking of the Walnut Hill baseball diamond just out of sight over the rise to the west, Dalko reflected on times past with the hint of a smile. "I know I could have won fifteen games a year if I'd have ever made it," he told the correspondent as the two sat in a conference room at the convalescent home. "I was that good. There were nights after when I'd curse the gods for what happened to me. But I didn't drink to forget. I just drank."

That acknowledgment, bittersweet as it was, marked a big improvement over Steve's condition when he'd first come home. "It's no wonder Dalkowski can't or doesn't want to remember the bad times," Madden wrote. "To all of those who loved him throughout them, though, it is at least heartening that he can still hear the cheers. Because it doesn't really matter if he never made it to the big leagues, or how hard he tried to drink the pain and frustration of it all away. Steve Dalkowski could never run away from his legend of being the fastest pitcher of them all." (Explaining his pitching prowess in *Vanity Fair* the year before, Dalkowski had said, "I pitched the same as everybody else. It just got there faster.")

Asked about the years since he had left baseball, Steve remembered only fragments of the past, including catching a bus at 3 a.m. for a long day working in the California fields and the legend of his face-off with

Ted Williams. In the version of the story Steve relayed to Madden, he wasn't trying to strike Williams out. "I just didn't want to hit him. I threw him more than one pitch, and when one of them kinda took off, he put up his hand and yelled, 'I'm getting' out.'" (Later that year he told another reporter that after ordering the batting cage removed, Williams "swung at thirty pitches and didn't hit one fair, but he fouled a bunch.") Steve also said the highlight of his career was striking out Mickey Mantle.

Madden mentioned others in Dalko's life who reflected on the times when alcohol took over. Sometimes, late at night and drunk, Steve had called old friends and carried on rambling conversations. His old manager Billy DeMars remembered getting his last call like that from Dalko about ten years before. "He said, 'I'm sorry for everything. I love you, Billy.'"

Now those years were past. For everyone "who shared his best of times and dreaded the worst," Madden concluded, "there is a happy ending after all. Steve Dalkowski is safe at home."

People were glad to know Dalko had made it home again. Fans remembered the phenomenal stories, and a new generation of baseball lovers began to recognize Steve's place in baseball history. In April 1999, *Baseball America* selected Dalkowski as one of the century's ten best minor-league legends.

On March 9, 2000, Steve Dalkowski was inducted into the New Britain Sports Hall of Fame. During the celebration banquet in the social hall of St. George's Greek Orthodox Cathedral in Hartford, he spoke to the room packed with old friends and new admirers. His appearance was a sign of how far he had come in continuing to recover from the lost years that had taken such a physical and mental toll. He posed for photos with old friends and teammates looking happy and relaxed, the old sparkle reappearing in his eyes after too long an absence.

Decades after his last professional appearance, Dalkowski's incredible skill and unique place in the lore of the game continued to work its way into the memories and stories of those who'd seen him. Writing a guest column for the *Hartford Courant* in the summer of 2000, former umpire and retired sportswriter Earl Yost reflected on his thirty-plus-year career. Writing about games in Hartford's Colt Park reminded him of a game he called between New Britain and Hartford High that was one of the famous pitching duels between Steve Dalkowski and Pete Sala. Dalko struck out 21 that day, while Sala fanned 20. New Britain won, 1–0, Yost remembered, thanks to a short backstop that kept Hartford base runners in check when Steve threw a wild pitch.

Later, during his years as a sportswriter, Yost covered Dalkowski's early rise through the ranks. Recalling one year in Miami during spring training, he wrote, "when I was covering the Grapefruit League for the *Manchester Herald*, . . . I saw Dalkowski strike out Roger Maris, Mickey Mantle, and Elston Howard on nine straight pitches. The next inning, he walked four straight batters."

The longer Steve led a sober and stable life, the more his health improved. Though memories of his middle years remained fuzzy to him, he recovered a lot of details about his friends and his playing days in New Britain. During the 2001 season, Coach Baylock invited Steve to give a talk to his team at the University of Connecticut. Steve rose to the occasion with advice he had given others even though he'd learned it too late himself: "Please don't be like me. Listen to your coach. Do what he says." When asked later what he would have done differently, Dalko answered, "Don't drink, and make curfew," admitting he had missed "two or three" curfews in his day. "You'd look up at the clock, see it's time to go and say, 'The hell with it; I'll worry about that tomorrow.' Whatever time you came in, you could always sleep until two o'clock the next day."

The world was remembering Steve Dalkowski. In early 2003 he was interviewed by ESPN for a video introduction of their broadcast of *Bull Durham*. On February 16 the *Baltimore Sun* ran a major feature on his life and career and his eventual return to New Britain. As reporter John Eisenberg framed the story, "His life careened through a succession of extremes before reaching this gentle autumn; he was a 100-mph phenom in the 1950s, a living legend in the 1960s and then a lost cause for more than a quarter century, drifting in and out of trouble. Unable to make a living from his gifted pitching arm, he was reduced to picking fruit. Yet many who crossed paths with him—from no-nonsense baseball lifers to the friends of his youth—to this day call Dalkowski the most unforgettable character they have known."

The *Sun* article covered Steve's early life in New Britain, his professional career, the sad years of decline, and his recent homecoming and recovery. Eisenberg allowed Dalko's junior high coach, Vin Cazzetta, to have the last word: "I wish he could have accomplished more. He was slated for big things in this world. We all thought he'd go far. It's just unfortunate that he didn't.

"But he's still a legend."

Later in the season Steve accepted an invitation to throw out the ceremonial first pitch before a homestand of the New Britain Rock Cats, a Double-A affiliate of the Minnesota Twins. That afternoon, June 11, Dalko sat in the office of manager Stan Cliburn as Stan and his twin brother, pitching coach Stu Cliburn, introduced him to members of the team. Asked if he had any advice for the young pitching staff Steve said softly, "Try to throw strikes."

More than four thousand cheering fans welcomed Dalkowski as he walked slowly out of the dugout and across the infield grass to the mound. The stadium announcer heralded him as "a New Britain legend." Andy Baylock was there to catch for him. As the two climbed the dugout steps Baylock turned to Dalko with a smile and said, "Don't throw the gas."

Steve smiled back and answered, "No gas today."

Baylock stood about fifteen feet in front of the plate. Steve managed a flat-footed windup of sorts and bounced the baseball halfway to Baylock's glove. No gas today. But the crowd roared anyway. After his pitch Steve watched the game from the stands with his family, visiting with his three-year-old grandniece Samantha and singing "God Bless America" during the seventh-inning stretch. But mostly he kept his eye on the ball, yelling for the pitcher to "let it all hang out" when he got two strikes on a batter.

Steve's mound appearance turned out to be the warm-up for a much bigger celebration honoring New Britain's legendary lefty. Audrey Turner read John Eisenberg's February feature about Dalkowski in the *Sun*. She and her husband were dedicated baseball fans who remembered Dalkowski and the stories of his antics on and off the field. Turner was also the marketing director at an assisted-living facility in nearby Pikesville specializing in dementia and Alzheimer's. Learning of Steve's return to the area and his encouraging improvement after years in assisted living, she came up with a plan to honor Dalko in Baltimore.

Over the next few weeks, Audrey organized a celebration like nothing Steve Dalkowski had ever experienced. On September 7, 2003, it started with a pregame luncheon in the Designated Hitter Lounge at Baltimore's Camden Yards catered by Steve's old teammate Boog Powell. Dozens of Steve's friends came up from New Britain for the day, and tickets were advertised to the public for $48.50. Powell spoke to the crowd at lunch, as did Steve's former manager Pat Gillick, who was in town as general manager for the opposing Seattle Mariners. "He was a great guy with a great heart," Gillick said. "He'd do anything for you." Steve himself said a few words of thanks. Maryland Governor Robert L. Ehrlich Jr. sent a proclamation. Tom Chiappetta also spoke, reaffirming Steve's place in baseball history and his own continuing work on a documentary about Dalko's life and career.

After lunch, a little before 1:30, Steve Dalkowski walked to the pitcher's mound in Camden Yards to a roar of approval from the stands. It had been forty-five long years since he last stood on a major league diamond. That day in 1958 during an exhibition game against Cincinnati—his only appearance in a major league park—he struck out the side on twelve pitches. Today there would only be one throw to make. He practiced ahead of time, telling his sister Pat, "My arm feels good." Now, with Orioles relief catcher Buddy Groom behind the plate, he threw the ball about halfway, and it rolled the rest of the way into Groom's glove.

"That was fun being out there," Steve said later.

Dalko's next honor was on a national scale. After ten years on the ballot, he was voted a member of the Shrine of the Eternals in 2009 by Baseball Reliquary, a nonprofit baseball educational association. The group was founded in 1996 to honor baseball players and others associated with the game who didn't meet the stringent requirements for consideration by the official Baseball Hall of Fame in Cooperstown, New York.

Baseball Reliquary curator Terry Cannon believed the delay between Dalko's first appearance on the ballot and his election might have been "a blessing. If this was five years ago, there's no way his health would have allowed him to come out. Eleven years ago, I'm not sure we'd even know where to find him." His winning year, Steve received 34 percent of the votes, the most of any eligible candidate. Other prospects that season included Casey Stengel and Dizzy Dean.

The organization covered expenses for Steve and Pat to fly to Los Angeles in mid-July to celebrate Steve's honor. On July 17 Steve threw out the ceremonial first pitch at Dodger Stadium before a game against the Houston Astros. This time he was pushed to the mound in a wheelchair. He stood briefly to make the throw, his bulky figure accented by the wide horizontal stripes on his shirt, then sat back down, raising both fists in triumph.

Two days later at the Pasadena Central Library, Steve was inducted into the eleventh class of Shrine of the Eternals honorees along with former outfielder Jim Eisenreich, who played fifteen years in the majors despite a long battle with Tourette syndrome, and the late Yankee slugger Roger Maris, then holder of the all-time record for single-season home runs with 61, whom Steve had struck out on three pitches minutes before injuring his elbow in 1963. Steve was introduced by screenwriter Ron Shelton. Even though Dalko was part of the inspiration for Shelton's hit film *Bull Durham,* the two former Oriole farmhands had never met.

That trip West was likely Steve's valedictory tour. Barring another unexpected turn in a life full of unexpected turns, Steve Dalkowski was back in New Britain to stay.

NINETEEN

The Legend Lives On

"He had one of those arms that come along once in a lifetime."
—Pat Gillick, Dalkowski teammate and Hall of Fame General Manager

Stephen Louis Dalkowski was born with a golden arm. No one taught him how to throw a fastball; it was, as he once described it, "a gift from God." His ability was an unequalled combination of natural athleticism, a fluid throwing motion, tireless commitment, and a perfectly timed delivery. In his pitching motion, he delayed releasing his throwing shoulder until the last instant, allowing each offering to be delivered with maximum torque. He also gave the ball a flick of the wrist upon release, which he claimed was a key to his unrivaled velocity.

Whatever the exact sequencing of Steve's pitching mechanics, Cal Ripken Sr., who had both caught and managed Dalkowski, insisted that his ball was "light as a feather, because he threw all with the wrist." At the same time, he believed it would come in at "somewhere in the neighborhood of 115 miles an hour" according to a modern radar gun. Also, according to Ripken Sr., the ball definitely rose: if Steve aimed at the plate, the ball would be at waist level; if he aimed at the waist it would be over the catcher's head.

From early accounts of high school games onward, many other eyewitnesses agree that Steve's ball rose on its way to the plate and that it made a buzzing or sizzling sound in flight. Physicists insist that a baseball *cannot* rise; they say the apparent motion is because players' eyes expect the ball to go to one place and it actually goes to another. Yet the reports of Dalko's rising fastball were frequent and consistent.

No one ever really knew what to do with the boy from New Britain and his superhuman skill. By today's standards, Steve was badly mismanaged throughout his professional career. Hundred-pitch appearances were commonplace, and two-hundred-pitch outings were not infrequent for him. On top of that, managers sometimes had Steve pitch for hours before a game in hopes of tiring him out and improving his control. He pitched way too much, far more than was healthy for him.

Steve's favorite coach, Earl Weaver, once warned him that he wouldn't live to be thirty-three years old. Too much drinking, too much wild living. So in 1972 when Steve turned thirty-three, he called Weaver to tell him, *"I'm still here!"* Meanwhile, Weaver went on to great success as a manager, leading the Baltimore Orioles to four American League pennants and a victory over the Cincinnati Reds in the 1970 World Series. The Orioles retired his number 4 in 1982, and he was elected to the Baseball Hall of Fame in 1996. He died in 2013 aboard a baseball fantasy cruise in the middle of the Caribbean.

The year Weaver died, against all odds, Steve Dalkowski was still visiting with fans and giving interviews. In his eightieth year, the living legend continued to be very much alive. His world was diminished and his awareness intermittent. But Sizzling Steve, the Connecticut Comet, remained as a unique and irreplaceable connection to a golden age of America's pastime. To his countless fans and admirers it was an amazing truth: *He's still here.*

There had been many disappointments. One that hit him hardest after his return to New Britain was the death in 2011 of his nineteen-year-old great-nephew, Pat's grandson, Ryan Thomas Lee. The young man was a student at Long Island University and a promising golfer. He was struck by a car while walking in Brooklyn and died the next day. Close friends say Steve never fully recovered from the loss.

The historical record has undergone revision as well. Sharp-eyed researchers discovered that Dalko's record of 24 strikeouts, a state high school record for fifty years, wasn't a record after all. A 2014 article in the *Hartford Courant* expanded on a report several years earlier that pitching ace Johnny Taylor had struck out 25 batters for Bulkely High before Steve Dalkowski was born.

The game was on June 2, 1933, a 13–4 win for Bulkely over New Britain in the last contest of the season. Taylor gave up one hit, walked nine, threw three wild pitches, hit one batter, and struck out 25 thanks largely to his "vicious" curve. The strikeout total might be a national record, but there are no nationwide records kept for nine-inning high school games. (Connecticut and numerous other states now play seven innings in high school.)

In a 1976 interview, Taylor said, "In 1933 a scout for the New York Yankees read clippings on me and came up to Hartford to see me pitch. He didn't know I was black. I've heard about and been asked many times about being born too soon. What can you do? You can't live in the past. I've always taken things as they come. . . . I like to think that what we did in the 1930s and 40s by barnstorming with white teams paved the way for the next generation."

Johnny Taylor went on to an eleven-year career in the Mexican, Cuban, and American Negro Leagues. Highlights included a 20-inning complete game victory with 22 strikeouts in 1937, and a 2–0 win for the Negro League All-Stars against the legendary Satchel Paige and his exhibition team in front of twenty thousand fans at the Polo Grounds later that same year. Taylor died in 1987 at the age of seventy-one.

In 2016, the baseball documentary *Fastball* was released and featured an entire segment on Dalkowski titled "The Fastest That Never Was." Steve sat for a long interview with the producers, demonstrated his grip and pitching motion, and answered questions. His face was drawn, his sentences short, and his speech sometimes indistinct. But when he talked about baseball, his face brightened.

Steve Dalkowski became a genuine baseball legend with all that entails. Many have been tempted to focus so much on the legend as to miss the man. Some of the stories about him are demonstrably true, others demonstrably untrue, and others demonstrably embellished in the endless retelling. For still other stories, we will never know. They hang suspended in a world where fact and fantasy intertwine. That uncertainty is part of the irresistible appeal of Steve Dalkowski's legend.

What towers above everything else, however, is the miracle of Steve's gift. Maybe it was too much. Maybe he never got comfortable with it. Maybe he needed other gifts to handle it. The way Ron Shelton described it, "Zeus quietly took back his thunderbolt." He compared Dalko to a Michelangelo who couldn't finish a painting. Too much, perhaps, but Steve Dalkowski's genius was absolutely real: flesh and bone and sinew that performed like none other, ever. Pat Gillick summed it up well: "As forty years go by a lot of stories get embellished. But this guy was legit. He had one of those arms that come once in a lifetime."

Decades after Steve Dalkowski played his last game for the Elmira Pioneers, one fan in particular remembers the impression the pitcher left on him. Marty Chalk is a former Elmira stadium announcer and the president of the Chemung County Sports Hall of Fame. Amidst all the tall tales and criticism, he wants to make sure history gets the story straight. "I hope you'll make two things clear," he says with conviction. "Steve was a good guy whose teammates loved him; and if he'd had the right coaching he would be a major league legend."

That leads us back to the Big Question: How fast did he throw? Was Steve Dalkowski the fastest pitcher ever to play the game? People in a position to know the facts answer with a resounding "Yes!" Earl Weaver had seen the legendary Bob Feller pitch and said Dalkowski was faster. Those who saw Sandy Koufax and Nolan Ryan say Dalkowski was not just faster but *a lot* faster.

The question can't be settled now with a radar gun, but these observers know what they know. Their life was baseball. Aroldis Chapman is officially the fastest pitcher in history at 105.1 mph from the point of release. Nolan Ryan is unofficially the fastest at 100.9 mph near the plate (this speed, if extrapolated back to the mound, as with Chapman, is calculated at 108.5 mph). But if those who saw Chapman and Ryan pitch nonetheless say Dalko was faster, it's reasonable to believe they're right.

Yet, this is the pitcher that Hall of Fame umpire Doug Harvey saw strike out nine batters in a row, then throw the next pitch forty feet over the catcher's head and never throw another strike before being relieved.

Steve Dalkowski had a gift with which he could never come to terms. His unequalled successes and abysmal failures haunted him and also haunt us. Yet they also inspire us to face squarely our demons and disappointments, overcoming them as best we can. This is perhaps Steve Dalkowski's greatest legacy to us all.

New Britain, Connecticut, is still a good place to grow up. It's still Hardware City, home today of the biggest hand-tool factory in the world. In Walnut Hill Park, boys still play baseball on fresh spring afternoons when the warm air stirs the new growth in the trees.

Until recently, Steve Dalkowski was still there, quietly passing the days in the same room he had lived in since 1994. A visitor would likely find him wearing a sweatsuit, shaven and combed. Conversation would be a challenge and limited to a few nods and two- or three-word answers that were indistinct. Yet, hearing praise for his achievements on the mound, Steve would perk up, a smile widening across his face, his eyes gleaming with the old sparkle.

Mantle, Maris, Weaver, so many others were gone. Steve Dalkowski had outlasted them all, living out his days quietly at the foot of the hill below the baseball diamond where boys still ran and pitched and fielded and dreamed of stardom.

Stephen Louis Dalkowski died on April 19, 2020, across the street from the retirement home, in the New Britain hospital where he was born. His death was hastened by the COVID-19 pandemic. According to his sister, Pat, he had "had a rough couple of months" at the end. His body was cremated. There was no public funeral or memorial service.

Dalko was eighty years old and had not played baseball in fifty-four years. Yet neither his long years in the twilight of dementia nor his passing in any way diminished his legend. On the contrary, his departure released that legend to the ages.

Dom Amore, who covered sports for the *Hartford Courant* for more than thirty years, met Dalko for the first time in the spring of 2019, just before the pitcher's eightieth birthday. "I couldn't consider a long career writing about baseball truly complete if I never met this man," Amore wrote of the visit.

As so many have mused before him, Amore wondered how fast the Connecticut Comet really threw, and wished there had been some accurate way to measure the speed of that legendary fastball. But, "it happened when it happened, in the wrong decades, and we are left with the mystique, to last as long as people talk baseball."

In an interview with *Sports Illustrated* shortly after Steve's death, Emma Baccellieri echoed Amore. "We'll never really know" how fast the ball flew from his hand. "But," she added, "I think it's fine to let him take that place in history."

History bestows its honors where it will. It becomes more than the sum of all the stories and myths and wild tales about a supremely gifted but troubled young pitcher who, literally hours away from the Show, had his lifelong dream torn from his grasp by an injury that in another era might never have happened. Or if it had, it could have been quickly diagnosed and treated by a serious yet routine surgical procedure. In a different world, at a different time, he could have been the best of the best. But God—or Zeus, or fate—had other plans.

Steve Dalkowski was the fastest baseball pitcher who ever played the game. Rewind the video of his life, stop it anywhere, and ask anyone who saw him in action on the mound. Nobody claims otherwise. We don't have to allow him a place in history. He's there. He earned it.

Authors' Note

Steve Dalkowski's unlikely story as told in these pages has itself an unlikely story. In 2016, Bill Dembski, intrigued by the many converging lines of evidence pointing to Dalko as the fastest pitcher of all time, was hunting for some Dalko memorabilia on eBay. There, Brian Vikander, a pitching coach and photographer, offered a signed photo by Dalko. Bill bought it from Brian, and an instant simpatico developed between the two. Their love of baseball, their love of pitching, and their love of Dalkowski's legend quickly cemented a friendship.

As Brian and Bill compared notes on Dalkowski, it became clear that Dalko's story had never been adequately told. Further investigation revealed that any of the promised biographies and documentaries about Dalko were unlikely to see the light of day any time soon. Brian and Bill were therefore "all in" for doing the definitive biography of Dalko. But they needed help. Bill, as an entrepreneur focused on educational technologies, had worked closely with Alex Thomas on a biography of the famed East LA high school math teacher Jaime Escalante, immortalized by Edward James Olmos in the 1988 film *Stand and Deliver*.

Alex, a seasoned "old school" writer who knows his way around newspaper archives, thus seemed like the ideal third musketeer for this project. Dalko's pitching career spanned the 1950s and '60s, well before digital technologies were available to record Dalko's feats on the mound in real time. Somebody like Alex who could perform fundamental archival work and interview key people was therefore necessary.

Indeed, Alex ended up crisscrossing the US for this book and even took a "vacation" in Mexico to check out one of the winter leagues (the Venados of Mazatlán) where Dalko had played in the 1960s.

Alex did much of the heavy lifting on this book, writing four separate drafts with seemingly unending input from Brian and Bill. Yet all three authors were indispensable to this project. Brian, with his vast experience as a pitching coach and with his contacts in that world, to say nothing of his voluminous reading and large personal library of baseball books (two thousand plus), was crucial to our biography's "street cred." Bill, besides his skills as a writer, editor, and project manager, also applied his expertise in mathematics to the biomechanics of accelerating a baseball to 110 miles per hour, which is the speed Dalko must have achieved if his claim to being the fastest ever is to stand.

This has been an exhilarating and exhausting book to complete. Yet as close as we have been to this subject for four years now, we continue to be captivated by it. In the thousands of sports biographies out there (and not just in baseball), there is none quite like it:

- Dalko's freakish, unmatched ability to accelerate a baseball.
- His very average look, physique, and stature.
- The universal reverence for his speed (though not control) of those who witnessed Dalko pitch.
- The divine gift that promised greatness around every corner.
- The demonic conspiracy that caused greatness continually to elude him.
- The absence of any reliable measurements of his pitching speed.
- The disappearance of any video showing him pitch.

The disappearance of video showing Dalko pitch needs a word. All the fireballers of the past have video. This is true even of Walter Johnson, who was born fifty years before Dalko! Yet try as we might (and we were hardly alone in our quest), we could not lay hands on any such video. The trip to Mexico by Alex mentioned above was in part to see if any video might exist there of Dalko pitching. Its elusiveness has caused us to call video of Dalko pitching "the holy grail."

Given the overwhelming testimony of eyewitnesses that Dalko's pitching speed was the fastest ever, the absence of reliable measurements of Dalko's pitching speed and of any video of his pitching motion was not a deal killer for this book. Still, we didn't want our entire case for Dalko being the fastest ever to rest on testimony. We wanted in addition to understand *how* Dalko could have pitched in the 110 mph and above range. What must his body have been doing? What sorts of stresses would it have felt? How could those stresses have been biomechanically minimized? And what sort of training and techniques could potentially take a pitcher of Dalko's stature and raise his speed to Dalko's level?

We intended to address these questions at length in two appendices to this book, one titled "Accelerating a Fastball to 110 MPH" and the other "The Gods Build the Perfect Pitcher." These were in effect technical articles to try to make plausible that Dalko, or someone like him, could have equaled or exceeded the 110-mph speed barrier that he must have attained if he was indeed as fast as everyone said he was. On further reflection, however, we thought these articles simply didn't fit in the book, which is at its heart a story and not a technical analysis. We therefore moved these articles/appendices to a website for this book: DalkoBook.com. Look for those articles there as well as other information that will emerge with the book's publication.

Speaking of geopolitics in 1939, Winston Churchill referred to "a riddle, wrapped in a mystery, inside an enigma." Dalko is such a riddle, mystery, enigma, and more. He combines mortality and myth. He is Icarus, granted an ability that takes him too high and then sends him hurtling down. He is Sisyphus, repeatedly laboring his way up to the very precipice of glory, only to tumble back again and again. He is Tantalus, with the best that baseball had to offer and the best that he had to offer baseball always just out of reach. His story has it all: zenith, nadir, and everything in between.

Bill Dembski
Alex Thomas
Brian Vikander

Acknowledgments

The true story of Steve Dalkowski—as opposed to the legend—is out there, but it took some doing to find it. The three of us have spent a sizable part of the last four years running down sources, following leads, and digging through the forgotten corners of sports history in small-town America. Our objective was to uncover the facts about a remarkable man who was the fastest baseball pitcher of all time. While a cluster of legends and rumors have been endlessly repeated about him for decades, reliable, firsthand information has been in short supply. We were determined to separate fact from fiction.

Along the way we've had help, encouragement, and support from a small army of current and retired baseball players, sports professionals, and fans whose contributions have added priceless insights to the saga, setting the record straight based on their own experience. These collaborators, most of them now ranging in age from mid-seventies to nearly one hundred, are eyewitnesses to history. A number of them have never told their stories before, simply because they've never been asked. To all of them we extend our heartfelt thanks. Steve's story is their story, too.

Andy Baylock, Dalkowski's childhood friend, neighbor, and teammate, took the time to sit for hours answering questions in the athletic complex at the University of Connecticut, where he holds the all-time state record for most wins by a college baseball head coach. In the spring of 2017, he was as busy as ever as director of football alumni and community affairs. In his spare time he pitched batting practice to the Red Sox.

All the way across the country in California, Linda Moore graciously answered a stranger's knock at the door and opened her home for an afternoon of conversation and reminiscences. Her undiminished love of adventure makes it easy to imagine her as an enthusiastic partner with Steve in a previously unknown chapter of his life.

Pete Sala generously shared his time, memories, and recollections about confrontations with Steve from high school through the minor leagues. Bob Beavers kindly supplied key historic information about one of the most enduring of the Dalkowski legends, officially setting the record straight. "Sudden" Sam McDowell brought the excitement of 1960s baseball to the narrative, along with stories of Dalko's legendary arm and recollections of Dalko on the hill.

In some ways, the biggest surprise of all in running the Dalkowski legend to ground has been the story of Dalko's career in Mazatlán, Mexico. Our first conversations about the possibility of a research trip there were mostly in jest. But the more we discussed it, the more we figured it was worth the trouble. What we found there completely reoriented our thinking about Steve's later career and especially his final season. Seemingly on his last legs in the minor leagues, he was a star with the Venados and had the statistics to back up his reputation.

The first person we met at the ballpark in Mazatlán turned out to be one of the most indispensable and generous people of our Mexican sojourn. Omar Garzon was at the security gate we happened to approach. Once we explained our mission, he became our self-appointed guide to the entire Venados organization. He introduced us to "Señor Beisbol," Ramón Flores, the team's play-by-play radio broadcaster who is a walking encyclopedia of baseball history. He announced our project on the air and invited anyone who had seen Dalkowski play ball to call in. Within days we were interviewing Sr. Eduardo Jimenez, whose eyewitness account of a near-perfect game pitched by Dalko in 1960 remains a highlight of the entire project. One night we were guests of Venados marketing director Alejandro Donadieu, who graciously hosted us in a private box.

Thanks also to Venados team members Mitch Lively and Nick Struck, two friendly, ambitious, and successful young American pitchers who love baseball south of the border. They helped us get a real feel of what Mexican baseball is like for American players. (And thanks to the whole team for signing a ball.)

We're indebted to the writers who have gone before us, especially Pat Jordan for his superb work over the years in keeping the Dalko legend alive.

We owe a special word of gratitude to a class of sportswriters that has all but disappeared: seasoned local newspapermen who took local sports seriously and lavished their craft on it. In places like New Britain and Hartford, Connecticut; Elmira, New York; Aberdeen, South Dakota; and Stockton, California, writers covered high school and minor league baseball with skill, wit, and professionalism. Jimmy Cunavelis, Frank Cline, Larry Desautels, Bill Lee, Al Mallette, and Larry Press are a few who represent the many. Their legacy—often awaiting us in dusty boxes of microfilm read with creaky machines that few people seem to know how to keep running—is in danger, and is an irreplaceable foundation stone of twentieth-century Americana. Without their stories this book would not have been possible.

On the technical side, Glenn Fleisig, PhD, and the entire staff at American Sports Medicine Institute lent their unwavering support to our project in assessing how Dalko might have done it. As described in the Authors' Note, this material has been moved to the book's website: DalkoBook.com.

We're grateful to the Society for American Baseball Research (SABR) for *always* being there with their six-thousand-plus members who love and care about the game. Also to Harvey Meiselman and Sports Address Lists for tremendous effort over three years in locating former minor-league players. We received valuable assistance as well from Dick Beverage and Jen Madison with the Association of Professional Ball Players of America (APBPA); and from Terry Cannon and Baseball Reliquary.

Other contributors who provided interviews or additional valuable information include:

Dom Amore
Chip Atkison
Bruce Babcock
Dan Berlind
Henry Berman
Alfonso Aronjo Bojorquez
Marty Butterick
Roy Carter
Marty Chalk
Stu Cliburn
Angel Colon
Warren Corbett
Angie Dickinson
Jim Dickson
Andy Etchebarren
Doak Ewing
Jack Fisher
Jack Fitzpatrick
Lloyd "The King of New Orleans" Fourroux
Pat Gillick
Dick Hall
Bill Hickman
Tom House, Ph.D.
Bill Huber
Davey Johnson
Jay Johnstone

King of the Hill Pitching
Darold Knowles
Frank Kostro
Jeff Lantz
Leonte Landino
Gordon Lund
Nick Lyons
Mark Manders
Gary "Pops" O'Maxfield
Barry Mednick
Gene Michael
Dan Moushon
Rod Nelson
Keith Olberman
Frank Peters
Tom Petranoff
George Plimpton
John Pregenzer
Gil Reyes
Eddie Robinson
Bruce Slutsky
Ron Stone
Dan Taylor
Fred Valentine
John Van Ornum
Jerry Walker
Walnut Hill Care Center (later Grandview Rehabilitation and
     Healthcare Center)
Carl Warwick
Eddie Watt

Of course, when we began this project nearly four years ago, we
had no way of knowing that, just as we were readying the manuscript

for the typesetter, Steve Dalkowski would pass away. We had hoped to release our book while Dalko was still with us. His loss will no doubt produce a flurry of writing about him. While some results will be responsible, and some will be sloppy and opportunistic, none of them will surpass this effort in degree of respect for a flawed, heroic man with a gift that comes along once in a lifetime. And whose legacy lives on.

Notes

CHAPTER 1

1   **Epigraph**—"Baltimore To Call Up Hurler Steve Dalkowski," *Hartford Courant*, August 31, 1957, 15.

1   **Diamond No. 1 at Walnut Hill Park**—Andy Baylock, interview by Alex Thomas, May 8, 2017, Storrs, CT.

1   **Several of the cars had out-of-state plates**—Pat Jordan, "Going Nowhere Fast," *Inside Sports*, July 1982, 72–80.

1   **Fans knew they had to arrive two hours before game time**—Bill Madden, "Safe at Home," *New York Daily News*, May 17, 1998.

2   **During the summer they played on one of the industrial leagues (industrial league background)**—John Eisenberg, "Lost Phenom Finds His Way," *Baltimore Sun*, February 16, 2003; Linda Moore, interview by Alex Thomas, September 30, 2017, Stockton, CA.

3   **With a smooth, seemingly effortless (windup technique)**—Madden, "Safe At Home"; Eisenberg, "Lost Phenom"; John Altavilla, "What Might Have Been," *Hartford Courant*, September 1, 1996, A1.

3   **The ball sizzled as it split the air**—John Eisenberg, *From 33rd Street to Camden Yards* (New York: McGraw-Hill, 2001), 111; Madden, "Safe at Home"; Eisenberg, "Lost Phenom"; Pat Hruby, "The Legend of Steve Dalkowski," *Washington Times*, June 4, 2000.

4   **"A lot of pitchers have a fastball . . ."**—Paul Dickson, *Baseball's Greatest Quotations* (New York: HarperCollins, 2008), 342.

4   **"It's easy, man . . ."**—Vida Blue and Bill Libby, *Vida: His Own Story* (Upper Saddle River, NJ: Prentice Hall, 1972), 2.

4   **Had to develop a technique**—Baylock, interview.

4   **In his first start that spring**—"Dalkowski Pitches No-Hit Shutout,"
      Hartford Courant, April 19, 1957, 29A; "Dalkowski Hurls No-Hitter
      against Hornets," *New Britain Herald*, April 19, 1957, 21.

5   **Dalkowski had hurled back-to-back no-hitters**—Frank Cline,
      "Steve Dalkowski Pitches Second Straight No-Hit Game," *Hartford
      Courant*, April 25, 1957, 20; "New Britain's Dalkowski Does It Again,"
      New Britain Herald, April 25, 1957.

5   **Dalkowski again struck out 20**—"Hornets Finally Hit Dalkowski
      But Lose, 13–4," *Hartford Courant*, May 23, 1957, 21A.

5   **Dalkowski settled down to strike out 24**—"Steve Dalkowski Fans
      24 As New Britain Wins 5–0," *Hartford Courant*, May 26, 1957, 6D.

5   **He ended his senior year**—"Oriole Squad Game Tonight," *Kingsport
      Times-News*, June 22, 1957, 8.

5   **The big league scouts were paying attention**—Gerald Crean, "NBHS
      Nine to Play Tomorrow, Injuries Force Lineup Changes," *New Britain
      Herald,* April 17, 1957, 30; "New Britain's Dalkowski"; "Scouts Set To
      Stalk Southpaw Dalkowski," *Hartford Courant*, June 18, 1957, 17A;
      Madden, "Safe at Home."

CHAPTER 2

9   **Epigraph**—"New Britain High Baseball Team Has Several Newcom-
      ers in Lineup," *Hartford Courant*, April 20, 1956, 30F.

10   **Adele worked in a ball bearing factory**—Richard Goldstein, "Steve
      Dalkowski, Model for Erratic Pitcher in 'Bull Durham,' Dies at 80,"
      New York Times, April 26, 2020.

10   **He called it a "buzzing"**—John Eisenberg, "Lost Phenom Finds His
      Way," *Baltimore Sun*, February 16, 2003.

10   **A trip to Fenway on August 6, 1953**—Bob Elliott, "Dunlop Awards,"
      Toronto Sun, August 2, 1998.

11   **Lou Boudreau told Williams**—Clif Keane, "Williams Pops Up in
      Pinch-Hit Role as Sox Lose, 8–7," *Boston Daily Globe*, August 7, 1953,
      4.

11   **The Sox tied the game**—"St. Louis Browns at Boston Red Sox Box
      Score, August 6, 1953," Baseball Reference, Sports Reference, https://
      www.baseball-reference.com/boxes/BOS/BOS195308060.shtml.

11   **Back home in Corbin Heights**—Frank Cline, "Squads Chosen
      For Courant-Jaycee Baseball League All-Stars," *Hartford Courant*,
      August 9, 1953, C5; Frank Cline, "Five Teams Fight for Two Posts As

Jaycee-Courant Playoffs Loom," *Hartford Courant*, August 16, 1953, C3; "Caval Tool Nine Blanks American Phils For No. 14," *Hartford Courant*, August 18, 1953, 17; Frank Cline, "Courant-Jaycee All-Stars Triumph Over CYO Rivals By 12–9 Margin," *Hartford Courant*, August 29, 1954, C6.

12   **Bill Huber told his catcher**—Eisenberg, "Lost Phenom."

12   **"Like most southpaws"**—"New Britain High Baseball."

13   **"Whoosh! Whoosh! Whoosh!"**—John Eisenberg, *From 33rd Street to Camden Yards* (New York: McGraw-Hill, 2001), 111; Pat Hruby, "The Legend of Steve Dalkowski," *Washington Times*, June 4, 2000; Eisenberg, "Lost Phenom."

13   **On his second start**—Eisenberg, "Lost Phenom."

13   **For Steve's junior year baseball season**—"New Britain High Baseball."

13   **This was when he developed**—Baylock, interview.

14   **Although Steve was throwing smoke**—Baylock, interview; Eisenberg, "Lost Phenom"; Hruby, "Legend of Steve Dalkowski."

14   **Lenny Pare, Steve's catcher**—John Altavilla, "What Might Have Been," *Hartford Courant*, September 1, 1996, A1; Eisenberg, "Lost Phenom."

15   **As Sandy Koufax stated**—David Plaut, *Speaking of Baseball* (Philadelphia: Running Press Books, 1993), 126.

16   **His father was warming him up**—Bob Sudyk, "A Matter of Control," *Hartford Courant*, March 5, 1989, E11A.

16   **Steve played the first game of his junior season**—"New Britain Host to Hartford and Sala in Big Test," *Hartford Courant*, April 25, 1956, 22; Jimmy Cunavelis, "New Britain Clips Hartford 3–2 As Dalkowski Bests Sala," *Hartford Courant*, April 26, 1956, 19.

16   **Steve couldn't find the strike zone**—"New Britain Bows to New London," *Hartford Courant*, May 2, 1956, 18A.

17   **May 8 brought the two best pitchers**—"Sala, Dalkowski to Renew Rivalry as Owls Entertain New Britain Nine," *Hartford Courant*, May 8, 1956, 18A; Jimmy Cunavelis, "Sala Throws One Hitter, Owls Nip New Britain In 10th 1–0," *Hartford Courant*, May 9, 1956, 22A.

17   **Again striking out 20**—"Steve Dalkowski Strikes Out 20 As New Britain Beats Hornets," *Hartford Courant*, May 16, 1956, 20.

17   **5–3 loss to Bulkeley High**—Jimmy Cunavelis, "Bulkeley Sinks New Britain 5–3 On Big Rally," *Hartford Courant*, May 18, 1956, 28.

17   **Steve once again played**—"St. Lawrence Scores Fifth Victory: Graduate Loop in a Three Way Tie," *Hartford Courant*, July 20, 1956, 18A; "St. Lawrence Nine Still Unbeaten As Jaycees Start Second Round," *Hartford Courant*, August 1, 1956, 18; "Dalkowski No-Hits Phils In Jaycee-Courant Loop," *Hartford Courant*, August 10, 1956, 19A.

18   **As the high school baseball season began**—Jimmy Cunavelis, "New Britain Nine Also Needs Batting Help," *Hartford Courant*, April 17, 1957, 20; Gerald Crean, "NBHS Nine to Play Tomorrow, Injuries Force Lineup Changes," *New Britain Herald*, April 17, 1957, 30; Baylock, interview.

18   **Coach Huber was pleased**—Altavilla, "What Might Have Been."

18   **Steve joined a social club at school**—Eisenberg, "Lost Phenom."

CHAPTER 3

21   **Epigraph**—"Orioles Acquire Steve Dalkowski, New Britain Ace," *Hartford Courant*, June 22, 1957, 14B.

21   **A new head coach in the fall of 1954**—"New Britain Bows to Mount Pleasant Eleven 26–19," *Hartford Courant*, September 26, 1954, C3.

21   **Improve their prospects for 1955**—Jimmy Cunavelis, "Toner Cheerful at New Britain Despite Ill Luck," *Hartford Courant*, September 22, 1955, 23.

22   **Steve tipped the scale**—Frank Cline, "Bulkeley Favored to Defeat New Britain Eleven Today," *Hartford Courant*, November 25, 1954, 55.

22   **With Dalkowski and Barrows alternating**—"Rising New Britain Eleven Home to Weaver High," *Hartford Courant*, October 8, 1955, 15; "New Britain Eleven Trounces Norwich Free Academy 36 To 6," *Hartford Courant*, October 18, 1955, 25.

22   **Undefeated New Britain High**—Jimmy Cunavelis, "Undefeated New Britain High Whacks East Hartford 33–6," *Hartford Courant*, October 23, 1955, C4A.

22   **New Britain's next game**—Cunavelis, "Undefeated New Britain."

24   **"We have more than enough money"**—John C. Wentworth, "NBHS Trip to Miami Fund Success Sure with $12,500 Available from All Sources," *New Britain Herald*, December 2, 1955, 1; "NBHS Fund Drive Over Top, Collections Exceed $9,000: Fafnir Folk Donate $1,117," *New Britain Herald*, December 3, 1955, 1; "Amount on Hand Soars Past $20,300 Already, More Due: Citizens Praised for Effort," *New Britain Herald*, December 5, 1955, 1.

24 **The school's chartered Pan American DC-6B**—Henry M. Keezing, "NBHS Football Team Emplanes for Miami Battle Amid Cheers of Students, Kin and Friends," *New Britain Herald*, December 6, 1955, 1.

24 **Once in Miami the team took time for swimming and sightseeing**— Leonard C. Joyce, "NBHS Football Team Works Out in Sunshine after Plane Flight and Gala Welcome To Florida," *New Britain Herald*, December 7, 1955, 1; Leonard C. Joyce, "NBHS Football Players Cool Off in Hotel Pool between Practice Stints," *New Britain Herald*, December 8, 1955, 1.

24 **By the time of the 8:15 p.m. kickoff**—Leonard C. Joyce, "500 from City among 20,000 Due at Orange Tilt Tonight with Cool, Fair Weather in Sight," *New Britain Herald*, December 9, 1955, 1; John Wentworth, "NBHS Football Team Loses, 20–12, When Miami Comes from Behind in Second Half in Orange Bowl," *New Britain Herald*, December 10, 1955, 1; Jimmy Cunavelis, "Miami Favored Over New Britain High," *Hartford Courant*, December 9, 1955, 25; Jimmy Cunavelis, "Miami Whips New Britain With Last Period Rally,"*Hartford Courant*, December 10, 1955, 1.

26 **The mayor, Principal Sala**—Pete Sala, interviewed by Brian Vikander, July 6, 2017, Palm Desert, CA.

26 **The boys were happy to be home**—Jimmy Cunavelis, "New Britain Grid Squad Given Big Welcome Home," *Hartford Courant*, December 14, 1955, 19.

26 **For the 1956 season, Steve Dalkowski to right halfback**—Jimmy Cunavelis, "Zisk, Dalkowski Give New Britain Fine Halfbacks," *Hartford Courant*, September 20, 1956, 16B.

27 **The team's opening game**—Mike Caruso, "Mt. Pleasant Checks New Britain To Take Thrilling 19–13 Victory," *Hartford Courant*, September 23, 1956, 3D.

27 **Hurricanes shellacked Hartford**—Jimmy Cunavelis, "New Britain High Eleven Crushes Rival Hartford, 42 to 0: Dalkowski, Zisk Run Wild—'Canes Lead 35–0 At Half," *Hartford Courant*, November 11, 1956, 3D.

27 **The traditional Thanksgiving Day football game**—Jimmy Cunavelis, "Zisk, Dalkowski Bag Seven Touchdowns in Display Before 11,000," *Hartford Courant*, November 23, 1956, 15.

28 **Steve Dalkowski was the winner of the James M. Conley Memorial Award**—"Steve Dalkowski Gets Grid Award," *Hartford Courant*, June 6, 1957, 21.

28   **He was also an honorable-mention high school All-American—** Joe Posnanski, "How Do You Solve a Problem like Dalkowski?" *Sportsworld*, NBC Sports, https://sportsworld.nbcsports.com/fixing -steve-dalkowski/.

28   **He was offered a scholarship to Notre Dame—**Linda Moore, interview by Alex Thomas, September 30, 2017, Stockton, CA.

29   **Frank McGowan had secretly watched Dalkowski—**Eisenberg, *From 33rd Street*, 110.

CHAPTER 4

31   **Epigraph—**Pat Jordan, "The Wildest Fastball Ever," *Sports Illustrated*, October 12, 1970, S5–S7.

31   **His big weakness, wildness—**Gerald Crean, "NBHS Nine to Play Tomorrow, Injuries Force Lineup Changes," *New Britain Herald*, April 17, 1957, 30.

31   **Coach Bill Huber fielded calls—**John Eisenberg, "Lost Phenom Finds His Way," *Baltimore Sun*, February 16, 2003.

32   **Came down with colds—**Crean, "NBHS Nine."

32   **Dalkowski had opened his senior year—**"Dalkowski Hurls No-Hitter against Hornets," *New Britain Herald*, April 19, 1957; "Dalkowski Pitches No-Hit Shutout," *Hartford Courant*, April 19, 1957.

33   **"Could hardly have improved"—**"Dalkowski Pitches No-Hit Shutout."

34   **Steve Dalkowski had done it: back-to-back no-hitters—**Frank Cline, "Steve Dalkowski Pitches Second Straight No-Hit Game," *Hartford Courant*, April 25, 1957.

34   **Steve's performance also riveted the attention of major league scouts—**John Wentworth, "New Britain's Dalkowski Does It Again," *New Britain Herald*, April 25, 1957, 16.

34   **According to former Yankees scout Roy Carter—**Roy Carter, interview by Alex Thomas, April 16, 2018, Nashville, TN.

35   **What Casey Stengel said—**Ryne Duren with Robert Drury, *The Comeback: The Ryne Duren Story* (Dayton, OH: Lorenz Press, 1978), 69.

36   **Steve gave a pitching exhibition at a fair—***Berlin Fair Tab*, September 28, 1993.

37   **His sister, Pat, repeatedly said—**Eisenberg, "Lost Phenom."

38   **Ken Cullum recalled—**Pat Jordan, "Going Nowhere Fast," *Inside Sports*, July 1982, 72–80.

38   **Steve's friend and neighbor Andy Baylock**—Andy Baylock, interview by Alex Thomas, May 8, 2017, Storrs, CT.

39   **Hurricanes lose their next game**—"New London Routs 'Canes, Dalkowski to Romp. 18–5," *Hartford Courant*, May 1, 1957, 22.

39   **The Hartford Owls won 5–0**—"Owls, New Britain Twilight Contest Features Schoolboy Baseball Slate," *Hartford Courant*, May 7, 1957, 18; Frank Cline, "Mike Heneghan Hurls Owls to 5–0 Victory Over New Britain," *Hartford Courant*, May 8, 1957, 23.

39   **The 5–4 victory**—"Dalkowski Hurls, Bats New Britain to 5–4 Triumph," *Hartford Courant*, May 17, 1957, 26A.

39   **13–4 win over the East Hartford Hornets**—"Hornets Finally Hit Dalkowski But Lose, 13–4," *Hartford Courant*, May 23, 1957, 21A.

39   **Dalkowski magic was on full display**—"Steve Dalkowski Fans 24 as New Britain Wins 5–0," *Hartford Courant*, May 26, 1957, 6D.

40   **Away game against Weaver High**—"Dalkowski Whiffs 16 in Six-Inning Stint," *Hartford Courant*, May 30, 1957, 19A.

40   **Henry Berman provides some amusing insights**—Henry Berman, telephone interview by Brian Vikander, June 17, 2018, Palm Desert, CA.

41   **He might have a shot at Seattle University**—"Scouts Set to Stalk Southpaw Dalkowski," *Hartford Courant*, June 18, 1957, 17A.

41   **They were wonderful fellows**—Jordan, "Wildest Fastball Ever."

42   **As McGowan later recalled**—Jordan, "Wildest Fastball Ever."

43   **Orioles signed right-hander Jerry Walker**—Rich Marazzi and Len Fiorito, *Baseball Players of the 1950s: A Biographical Dictionary of All 1560 Major League Players* (Jefferson, NC: McFarland & Company, 2004), 415.

43   **Sandy Koufax, signed for $24,000**—Brent Kelley, *Baseball's Bonus Babies: Conversations with 24 High-Priced Ballplayers Signed from 1953 to 1957* (Jefferson, NC: McFarland & Company, 2015), 55.

43   **Several versions of the offer Steve Dalkowski accepted**—Eisenberg, "Lost Phenom"; Bob Sudyk, "A Matter of Control," *Hartford Courant*, March 5, 1989, E11A.

44   **Baltimore Orioles issued a press release**—"Orioles Acquire Steve Dalkowski, New Britain Ace," *Hartford Courant*, June 22, 1957, 14B.

45   **The Open League was set up because of the possibility**—John Cronin, "Truth in the Minor League Class Structure: The Case for the Reclassification of the Minors," *Spring 2013 Baseball Research Journal*,

https://sabr.org/research/truth-minor-league-class-structure-case
-reclassification-minors.

CHAPTER 5

47 **Epigraph**—"Bluefield Slaughters Kingsport Orioles, 18–8: Blue-Grays Hand Locals 4th Loss," *Kingsport Times-News*, June 30, 1957, 1C.

47 **The Kingsport Orioles revived professional baseball**—Frank Creasy, "Spikes, Cleats 'n Sneakers," *Kingsport Times-News*, July 28, 1957, 2C.

48 **The Kingsport team's first public appearance**—"Oriole Squad Game Tonight," *Kingsport Times-News*, June 22, 1957.

48 **"Left-hander Steve Dalkowski's first professional start"**—"Bluefield Slaughters Kingsport."

49 **Bob Beavers remembered the moment vividly**—Bob Beavers, telephone interviews by Brian Vikander, August 29, 2017 and November 21, 2017, Palm Desert, CA.

50 **"Beavers was reported in 'fair' condition"**—"Kingsport Orioles Edge Bluefield 16 to 14 in Wild Scoring Melee," *Bluefield Daily Telegraph*, July 1, 1957, 14.

50 **He had indeed torn an ear off with a baseball**—Linda Moore, interview by Alex Thomas, September 30, 2017, Stockton, CA.

51 **Approaching eighty years of age**—Beavers, telephone interviews.

51 **Pitching great Hal Newhouser**—Joe Posnanski, "How Do You Solve a Problem like Dalkowski?" Sportsworld, NBC Sports, https://sportsworld.nbcsports.com/fixing-steve-dalkowski/.

51 **The 17–4 drubbing**—"Bluefield Baseball Nine Tramples Kingsport Orioles by 17 to 4 Tally: Leading Teams Also Cop Wins," *Bluefield Daily Telegraph*, July 11, 1957, 19.

51 **That didn't stop his coaches and the press**—Gerald P. Crean, "Speaking of Sports," *New Britain Herald*, August 21, 1957, 42; Creasy, "Spikes, Cleats 'n Sneakers."

52 **Summoned Dalkowski to Baltimore**—Creasy, "Spikes, Cleats 'n Sneakers."

52 **Steve struck out 19**—Frank Creasy, "Steve Dalkowski Whiffs 19, but Bucs Bump Birds, 5–4," *Kingsport News*, August 3, 1957, 6.

52 **As sportswriter Frank Creasy wrote**—Creasy, "Steve Dalkowski Whiffs 19."

52 **A 15–5 loss**—"Birds to Play Benefit Tonight," *Kingsport News*, August 23, 1957, 6.

52   **Walked 21 batters**—"Orioles Win 7–6 Over Pulaski Cubs," *Kingsport News*, August 26, 1957, 5.

53   **Dalkowski surpassed the major league record for wild pitches**—"Orioles Win 7–6," 5; "Orioles Home after 9–0 Lose," *Kingsport News*, August 28, 1957, 7.

53   **Through the steel mesh of the backstop**—John Eisenberg, *From 33rd Street to Camden Yards* (New York: McGraw-Hill, 2001).

53   **Ripken went to see if the hole was still there**—Ken Nigro, "Steve Dalkowski—DTs Dead but Legend Lives," *Sporting News*, June 30, 1979, 11; Danny Peary, *Cult Baseball Players: The Greats, the Flakes, the Weird, and the Wonderful* (New York: Simon & Schuster, 1990), 2.

53   **"That ought to teach you"**—Eisenberg, *From 33rd Street*.

54   **Steve struck out 24 batters**—"24 Strike Out As Birds Win," *Kingsport Times-News*, September 1, 1957, 10.

54   **Youse moved him to right field**—Eisenberg, *From 33rd Street*.

54   **"Lefty gonna pitch tonight?"**—Eisenberg, *From 33rd Street*.

54   **Dalkowski's final record for his first season**—Creasy, "Spikes, Cleats 'n Sneakers," 1C.

54   **Steve called his parents in New Britain**—"Baltimore to Call Up Hurler Steve Dalkowski," *Hartford Courant*, August 31, 1957, 15.

54   **Second intensive coaching session**—Creasy, "Spikes, Cleats 'n Sneakers," 1C.

55   **Oriole scout Jim Russo later admitted**—Jim Russo with Bob Hammel, *Super Scout: Thirty-five Years of Major League Scouting* (Chicago: Bonus Books, 1992), 168.

55   **Christmas Day column**—Frank Cline, "Grist from the Sports Mill," *Hartford Courant*, December 25, 1957, 25.

56   **"Big league speed right now"**—Bill Lee, "Malice Toward None," *Hartford Courant*, March 11, 1958, 17A.

57   **"We saw the fastest ever"**—Fred Valentine, telephone interview by Brian Vikander, January 6, 2019, Palm Desert, CA.

58   **Robinson remembers Steve**—Eddie Robinson, telephone interview by Brian Vikander, December 15, 2017 and January 17, 2018, Palm Desert, CA.

58   **Orioles first baseman Bob Boyd**—John Eisenberg, "Lost Phenom Finds His Way," *Baltimore Sun*, February 16, 2003.

58   **"The No. 1 pitching prospect"**—Hugh Trader, "Rookie Dalkowski Rates Raves as a 'Billy Pierce' in Potential," *Baltimore News-Post*, February 27, 1958, 25.

59   **An exhibition game against Cincinnati**—John F. Steadman, "Dalkowski Blinds Reds with Speed," *Baltimore News-Post*, April 14, 1958, 23; "The Wildest Pitcher," *Time*, July 18, 1960, 51; Eisenberg, "Lost Phenom"; Posnanski, "Solve a Problem."

59   **"The most effective pitch the southpaw speedster threw"**—Steadman, "Dalkowski Blinds Reds with Speed."

59   **You could hear it, but you couldn't see it**—"'Radio Pitch' by Steve Dalkowski Is Heard, Not Seen Says Tebbetts," *Hartford Courant*, May 7, 1958.

60   **"He still needs work"**—Steadman, "Dalkowski Blinds Reds."

CHAPTER 6

61   **Epigraph**—Frank Cline, "Spikes, Cleats 'n Sneakers," *Kingsport News-Times*, July 28, 1957, 29.

61   **Steve couldn't get outs when the pressure was on**—Eddie Robinson, telephone interviews by Brian Vikander, December 15, 2017 and January 17, 2018, Palm Desert, CA.

62   **Dalkowski found himself on another Tennessee team**—Cline, "Spikes, Cleats 'n Sneakers," 29.

62   **Set up a wooden target**—Untitled article, *New Britain Herald*, September 10, 1974, 24.

62   **Sandy Koufax pegged the secret to successful pitching**—Leonard Koppett, *A Thinking Man's Guide to Baseball*, (New York: E. P. Dutton & Co., 1967), 38.

63   **Richards told reporters**—John Eisenberg, "Lost Phenom Finds His Way," *Baltimore Sun*, February 16, 2003.

63   **A firsthand account of facing Steve Dalkowski**—Frank Kostro, telephone interview by Brian Vikander, November 3, 2018, Palm Desert, CA.

65   **Tim Sommer gives Dalkowski credit for an expanded version of the story**—Tim Sommer, *Beating About the Bushes: Minor League Baseball in the 60's*, (Pennsylvania: Infinity Publishing, 2008), 239.

66   **We do know the details about the test itself from an article**—Frank Cashen, "Dalkowski's Speed: Ball Goes 85.8 MPH," *Baltimore American*, June 6, 1958, 35; photo caption, *Baltimore American*, June 8, 1958, 3C.

68   **Pitching speed recorded in Maryland at the Aberdeen Proving Ground**—Cashen, "Dalkowski's Speed"; "Steve Dalkowski Throws Pitches at 85.8 M.P.H.," *Hartford Courant*, June 7, 1958, 14A.

68 **To transfer, and thereby demote, Steve from Knoxville**—"Steve Dalkowski Sent to Carolina League," *Hartford Courant*, June 19, 1958, 17; "CL Has It's Share of Bonus Players," *High Point Enterprise*, June 18, 1958, 14.

68 **His debut in a 4–3 win over the Durham Bulls**—Bernard West, "Freddie's Double Wins It in Ninth," *Wilson Daily Times*, June 17, 1958, 6.

69 **His second start on June 20**—Bernard West, "Sportlite," *Wilson Daily Times*, June 21, 1958.

69 **Pitching in relief the next night**—Bernard West, "Raleigh, Danover Win Over Wilson," *Wilson Daily Times*, June 23, 1958.

69 **On June 24 Steve recorded his first loss with the Tobs**—"Wilson Tumbles 4th Time In Row," *Wilson Daily Times*, June 25, 1958, 9.

69 **He walked in three runs in an 8–4 loss**—"Fisher, Warren Expected to Hurl," *Wilson Daily Times*, June 26, 1958, 13.

69 **On June 30 he struck out seven batters**—"Al Barth Shines as Relief Hurler," *Wilson Daily Times*, July 1, 1958, 11.

69 **Jack Fisher, signed by the Orioles**—Jack Fisher, telephone interview by Brian Vikander, February 28, 2018, Palm Desert, CA.

70 **1958 All-Star Game lineup**—Bill Hunter, "Highlightin' Sports," *Burlington Daily Times-News*, July 3, 1958, 6.

70 **Headed to Aberdeen, North Dakota**—"Dalkowski, Dunlap Sent to Aberdeen," *Wilson Daily Times*, July 16, 1958, 7.

70 **DeMars himself stepped into the batting cage**—Pat Hruby, "The Legend of Steve Dalkowski," *Washington Times*, June 4, 2000.

71 **Made his debut in the fourth inning**—Larry Desautels, "Guckert Loses," *Aberdeen Daily News*, July 19, 1958, 6.

71 **Appearance in a forfeited game on July 11**—Bernard West, "Tobs Get Charged with Forfeit Loss to Greensboro Team," *Wilson Daily Times*, July 12, 1958, 6.

71 **Belcher refused to face it again**—Larry Desautels, "Batting Around," *Aberdeen Daily News*, July 20, 1958, 11.

71 **DeMars was amazed at Dalkowski's spare, no-windup windup**—"The Wildest Pitcher," *Time*, July 18, 1960, 51.

72 **The young pitcher threw his glove**—Hruby, "Legend of Steve Dalkowski."

73 **He struck out 12 and walked 17**—"Belinksy Hurls Neat Two-Hitter," *Aberdeen Daily News*, July 23, 1958, 8.

73   **Struck out the first 10 batters he faced**—Associated Press, "Dalkowski Whiffs 14 and Walks 12 in 9–8 Defeat," *Aberdeen Daily News*, July 28, 1958, 7.

73   **His first win of the year**—"Dalkowski Whiffs 17 in 6–3 Victory," *Aberdeen Daily News*, August 1, 1958, 7.

73   **Dalkowski's start on August 5**—"St. Cloud Takes Both Games from Pheasants," *Aberdeen Daily News*, August 6, 1958, 8.

73   **Steve's ball rose as it traveled toward the plate**—John Eisenberg, *From 33rd Street* (New York: McGraw-Hill, 2001), 110–111; Eisenberg, "Lost Phenom"; Andy Baylock, interview by Alex Thomas, May 8, 2017, Storrs, CT.

73   **Hall of Fame manager Walter Alston**—Walter Alston and Don Weiskopf, *The Complete Baseball Handbook: Strategies and Techniques for Winning*, (Boston: Allyn and Bacon), 1972, 100 and 104.

73   **Physics experts insist that a baseball cannot rise**—Robert K. Adair, *The Physics of Baseball* (New York: HarperCollins, 2002), 57–59, 70.

74   **Steve pitched wearing glasses for the first time**—Brian A. Bennett, *On a Silver Diamond* (Scottsville, NY: Triphammer Publishing, 1997), 60–62; Jordan, "Wildest Fastball Ever," S5–S7.

74   **He struck out 20 batters**—Larry Desautels, "Dalkowski Whiffs 20 in 2–1 Victory," *Aberdeen Daily News*, August 21, 1958, 14.

74   **He struck out 17 to great applause**—Sporting News, "Glasses Aida Him; Dalkowski Fans 20," *Wilson Daily Times*, August 27, 1958, 13.

75   **The last game of the season**—"Hub Fans See Big Drama," *Aberdeen Daily News*, September 2, 1958, 8.

75   **Pheasants earned a profit**—"Rox Top Pheasants; Phillies Come Here," *Aberdeen Daily News*, July 16, 1958, 8; Desautels, "Batting Around."

CHAPTER 7

77   **Epigraph**—Luther Evans, "Dalkowski: Fast Man, Fast (But Wild)," *Miami Herald*, March 1, 1959, 79.

78   **Richards took Dalkowski aside**—Evans, "Dalkowski," 79; John Eisenberg, "Lost Phenom Finds His Way," *Baltimore Sun*, February 16, 2003.

78   **Pat Gillick would say the ball rose like a rocket**—Tim Wendel, *High Heat* (Boston: Da Capo Press, 2010), 162.

78   **Another future teammate, Frank Zupo, would observe**—Pat Hruby, "The Legend of Steve Dalkowski," *Washington Times*, June 4, 2000.

78 **Carl Warwick emphatically stated**—Carl Warwick, telephone interview by Brian Vikander, October 22, 2018, Palm Desert, CA.

79 **Hit a fan in the stands in line to buy a hot dog**—Bill Madden, "Safe at Home," *New York Daily News*, May 17, 1998.

79 **Jack Fisher saw him throw wild pitches**—Jack Fisher, telephone interview by Brian Vikander, February 28, 2018, Palm Desert, CA.

79 **Determined to calm him down, manager Paul Richards**—Evans, "Dalkowski"; Eisenberg, "Lost Phenom."

79 **"My philosophy is simple," Gibson explained**—Bob Gibson and Phil Pepe, *Ghetto to Glory: The Story of Bob Gibson* (Upper Saddle River, NJ: Prentice Hall, 1968).

79 **Orioles coach Ray Miller preached to all pitchers**—Thomas Boswell, *How Life Imitates the World Series* (New York: Doubleday & Company, 1982), 66.

80 **Sportswriter Luther Evans spoke for many**—Evans, "Dalkowski,"

80 **Orioles road secretary John Lancaster**—Bill Lee, "Steve Dalkowski Learning Control Report of Orioles," *Hartford Courant*, March 24, 1959, 17.

80 **Orioles decided to send Steve back**—"Pheasants' Lineup Has Familiar Names," *Aberdeen Daily News*, April 8, 1959, 19.

80 **Weaver saw a lot of himself in Dalkowski**—Joe Posnanski, "How Do You Solve a Problem like Dalkowski?" Sportsworld, NBC Sports, https://sportsworld.nbcsports.com/fixing-steve-dalkowski/.

82 **According to the great Jim Palmer**—Jim Palmer and Jim Dale, *Palmer and Weaver: Together We Were Eleven Foot Nine* (Kansas City: Andrews and McMeel, 1996), 91.

82 **"Strikeout sensation of the 1958 Northern League"**—"Dalkowski Whiffs 7 In First Start," *Aberdeen Daily News*, April 12, 1959, 12.

82 **Seventeen consecutive scoreless innings**—"Phil Bows to Dons 7–4," *Aberdeen Daily News*, April 21, 1959, 9.

82 **1959 season debut on May 4**—"Pheasants In Lead After 15–7 Victory," *Aberdeen Daily News*, May 5, 1959, 8.

83 **Chiefs pitcher John Pregenzer**—John Pregenzer, telephone interview by Brian Vikander, October 15, 2017, Palm Desert, CA.

83 **Jim Dickson remembered**—Jim Dickson, telephone interview by Brian Vikander, September 15, 2017, Palm Desert, CA.

84 **Steve's old high school crosstown rival Pete Sala**—Pete Sala, telephone interview by Brian Vikander, July 6, 2017 and December 9, 2017, Palm Desert, CA.

84 **Gene "Stick" Michael was also in the lineup**—Gene Michael, telephone interview by Brian Vikander, April 2017, Palm Desert, CA.

85 **It was the first no-hitter of Steve's professional career**—Larry Desautels, "Dalkowski Whiffs 21 In No-Hit Triumph," *Aberdeen Daily News*, May 18, 1959, 7; "Steve Dalkowski Hurls No-Hitter, Whiffs 21 Strictly on Fastballs," *Hartford Courant*, May 19, 1959, 18.

86 **Branch Rickey, Jr., vice president and farm system director**—Gene Michael, telephone interview by Brian Vikander, April 2017, Palm Desert, CA.

CHAPTER 8

87 **Epigraph**—John Eisenberg, *From 33rd Street to Camden Yards* (New York: McGraw-Hill, 2001), 114.

87 **On May 28, Dalkowski had another shutout going**—"Rozich, Dalkowski Lead 12–2 Triumph," *Aberdeen Daily News*, May 29, 1959, 8.

87 **June was a mixed bag. On the third of the month**—"Minot Wins 7–6 in 9th," *Aberdeen Daily News*, June 4, 1959, 9.

87 **On June 9 he retired the first six batters in a row**—Associated Press, "Dalkowski Gets 4th Win," *Aberdeen Daily News*, June 10, 1959, 23.

88 **June 14, after winning four games without a loss**—"Pheasants Drop Twin Bill," *Aberdeen Daily News*, June 15, 1959, 9.

88 **Former Baltimore pitching coach Ray Miller points out**—Thomas Boswell, *How Life Imitates the World Series* (New York: Doubleday & Company, 1982), 60.

88 **Steve's next game was his second loss in a row**—Randall Fisher, "Philbert Loses 8–3 Despite 11 Hits," *Aberdeen Daily News*, June 20, 1959, 6.

88 **A complete disaster unfolded on June 30**—Larry Desautels, "Losing Streak Hits 7: Minot Wins 15–7," *Aberdeen Daily News*, July 2, 1959, 40.

88 **Steve Dalkowski was optioned to the Pensacola Dons**—"Dalkowski Traded for Pitcher," *Aberdeen Daily News*, July 5, 1959, 11.

88 **The Dons responded to Steve's arrival by losing 13 games in a row**—Joe Posnanski, "How Do You Solve a Problem like Dalkowski?" Sportsworld, NBC Sports, https://sportsworld.nbcsports.com/fixing -steve-dalkowski/.

89 **Pat Jordan credits Dalkowski with observations about Belinksy's wild night life**—Pat Jordan, "Going Nowhere Fast," *Inside Sports*, July 1982, 72–80.

89 **Dalkowski pitch hit the umpire and knocked him out**—Cal Ripken, Sr., *The Ripken Way: A Manual for Baseball and Life*, (New York: Pocket Books), 1999, 62–63.

90 **The two young hurlers first met on a train**—Linda Moore, interview by Alex Thomas, September 30, 2017, Stockton, CA.

90 **"Steve's hero was Bo Belinsky"**—Lloyd Fourroux, telephone interview by Brian Vikander and author correspondence, December 2018 through January 2019, Palm Desert, CA.

91 **According to fellow pitcher Herm Starrette**—Eisenberg, *From 33rd Street*. This quotation is also attributed to Joe Altobelli.

91 **As Steve's wife Linda said**—Moore, interview.

91 **Barber pulled back the historical curtain to reveal a glimpse of Dalkowski**—Eisenberg, *From 33rd Street*.

93 **In Linda Moore's words**—Moore, interview.

93 **Continuing his story, Dalkowski told Sommer**—Tim Sommer, *Beating About the Bushes: Minor League Baseball in the 60's* (Pennsylvania: Infinity Publishing, 2008).

CHAPTER 9

95 **Epigraph**—Greg Gallo, "Wild Steve. . . . The One That Got Away," 1973.

96 **Yogi Berra, who said, "Baseball is 90 percent mental. The other half is physical."**—Yogi Berra with Tom Horton, *Yogi: It Ain't Over . . .* (New York: McGraw-Hill, 1989), 7.

96 **Former scout and MLB executive Harry Dalton**—John Eisenberg, *From 33rd Street to Camden Yards* (New York: McGraw-Hill, 2001).

96 **Cal Ripken said they were easy to catch**—Eisenberg, *From 33rd Street*.

96 **"The ball was light, not heavy like some pitchers"**—Andy Etchebarren, telephone interview by Brian Vikander, January 22, 2018, Palm Desert, CA.

97 **Dunlop heard a player yell, "Get that clown outta there before he kills somebody!"**—Gallo, "Wild Steve."

97 **John "Boog" Powell**—Eisenberg, *From 33rd Street*.

97   **He made his debut with the Ports on April 22, 1960**—"Ports Triumph 9–2 Behind Dalkowski: Fans 13 in Two-Hitter," *Stockton Record*, April 23, 1960, 23; Larry Press, "Bears Play Twin Bill Tomorrow," *Bakersfield Californian*, April 23, 1960, 5.

98   **Planned to start him every fourth game**—John Peri, "Peri-Graphs," *Stockton Record*, April 28, 1960, 31.

98   **Start him pitching fifteen feet from the plate then gradually increase the distance**—"The Wildest Pitcher," *Time*, July 18, 1960, 51.

98   **Another idea was to position a wooden target over the plate**—"Wildest Pitcher," 51.

98   **"This kid has the arm of a Bobby Feller, Rex Barney or a Ryne Duren when it comes to speed," DeMars said**—Peri, "Peri-Graphs,"

98   **Victory over the Fresno Giants on May 6**—Jim Price, "Dalkowski Gets Ports Back to Winning, 8–2," *Stockton Record*, May 7, 1960.

98   **Ports were trampled 11–3**—Associated Press, "Race Tightens in Cal Loop: Ports Lose", *Stockton Record*, May 11, 1960, 37.

99   **The number of pitches he sometimes threw**—Sean Holtz, "Fastest Pitcher in Baseball," *Baseball Almanac*, February 2003; Eisenberg, *From 33rd Street.*

99   **The night of May 20, 1960, was a highlight of the season**—Al Goldfarb, "'Dal' Hurls Ports to 4–0 Win: Dalkowski Snaps Losing Streak," *Stockton Record*, May 21, 1960, 23.

100   **Ports catcher Ralph Larimore**—Goldfarb, "'Dal' Hurls Ports."

100   **Stockton sportswriter Al Goldfarb**—Goldfarb, "'Dal' Hurls Ports."

100   **The game went downhill from there to a 4–1 loss for the Ports**—Al Goldfarb, "Fresno Rallies to Overcome Dalkowski: Ports Beaten, 4–1, by Late Wildness," *Stockton Record*, May 27, 1960, 25.

100   **Dalkowski celebrated his twenty-first birthday on June 3 with a 7–5 win**—Jim Price, "Improving Ports Capture Doubleheader from A's," *Stockton Record*, June 4, 1960, 27.

101   **A reporter's account of a game later that month in Bakersfield**—Jim Price, "Ports Hit Road after 3–1 Loss to Bears," *Stockton Record*, June 18, 1960, 20.

101   **Tying a league record for strikeouts with 19**—"Dalkowski Ties Record with 19 Whiffs, Loses 8–3: Grand Slam Beats Him," *Stockton Record*, June 22, 1960, 17; "Dalkowski Matches Whiff Mark, Eyes Big Time as Control Improves," *Hartford Courant*, June 23, 1960, 22.

101 **The Associated Press story of his loss in Reno**—quoted in *San Rafael Daily Independent Journal*, June 22, 1960, 19.

102 **Sizzling Steve Dalkowski, hotter'n a Fourth of July firecracker**— Al Goldfarb, "One-Hit Win for Steve as Ports Sweep Set," *Stockton Record*, July 5, 1960, 22; "Dalkowski Pitches One-Hit, 3–2 Win," *Hartford Courant*, July 6, 1960, 17A; *Bakersfield Californian*, July 5, 1960, 31.

102 **Time magazine, which didn't typically provide**—"Wildest Pitcher."

103 **He shattered the league record for walks in a season with 262 (the old record was 202) and also chalked up a record 262 strikeouts**— Al Goldfarb, "Ports Explode to Scuttle Fresno: Dalkowski Sets Team Record," *Stockton Record*, August 22, 1960, 20.

104 **In Mazatlán that fall**—Linda Moore, interview by Alex Thomas, September 30, 2017, Stockton, CA.

105 **Sounded like the buzzing of a bee**—Eduardo Jimenez, interview by Alex Thomas, December 15, 2017, Mazatlán, Mexico.

105 **Years later Powell remembered a night in Phoenix**—Eisenberg, *From 33rd Street*.

106 **Herm Starette remembered**—Eisenberg, *From 33rd Street*.

106 **During a typical game in Phoenix**—Larry Desautels, "Batting Around," *Aberdeen Daily News*, July 20, 1958.

106 **Larry Desautels summed up the situation**—Desautels, "Batting Around."

106 **As a non-roster minor-league player**—"Expansion of 1961," Baseball Reference, Sports Reference, https://www.baseball-reference.com /bullpen/Expansion of 1961.

106 **Other Baltimore pitchers in the pool were**—Associated Press, "Woodling, Bauer Top AL 'Available' List," *Democrat and Chronicle*, November 19, 1960, 22; John Eisenberg, "Lost Phenom Finds His Way," *Baltimore Sun*, February 16, 2003.

107 **Orioles announced that Dalkowski had signed his contract**— "Dalkowski, Dropo Sign with Orioles," *Hartford Courant*, February 16, 1961, 21.

CHAPTER 10

109 **Epigraph**—"Tri-City Early Favorite for Northwest Loop Flag," *Daily Chronicle*, April 19, 1961, 10.

109 **McDowell watched Steve throw batting practice**—Sam McDowell, email correspondence and telephone interview by Brian Vikander, October 5, 2018, July 2019, Palm Desert, CA.

110 **Described by a reporter watching the Pirates game**—Bill Lee, "Nutmeg Rookies Impress Baltimore Brass," *Hartford Courant*, March 12, 1961, 1C.

111 **Dalko felt his confidence level rising**—Lee, "Nutmeg Rookies."

111 **"You've got to stay with anybody who has Dalkowski's kind of speed"**—Lee, "Nutmeg Rookies."

111 **The annual Miss Universe competition**—Maury Allen, *Bo: Pitching and Wooing* (New York: The Dial Press, 1973), 42–45; David Lamb, *Stolen Season: A Journey Through America and Baseball's Minor Leagues* (New York: Random House, 1991), 194. Lamb and others claim Miss Ecuador was the contestant. This seems more likely since the Colombian entrant that year, Patricia Whitman Owen, looked as American as her name sounded. Owen was actually a runner-up, but the winner of the Miss Colombia title that year, Sonia de la Candelaria Heidman Gómez, was too old to compete for Miss Universe. Lamb writes that the incident took place in 1963, which is highly unlikely since Belinski was in spring training that year with the Los Angeles Angels in Palm Springs, California. Lamb also mistakenly identifies Miss Ecuador as Tania Valle Moreno, who was Ecuador's 1963 entry in the Miss International competition in California.

112 **Cut from the Orioles roster on April 7**—"Dalkowski Optioned to Thomasville, Ga.," *Hartford Courant*, April 7, 1961, 18.

112 **"White Lightning . . . a Baltimore farmhand"**—"Tri-City Early Favorite."

112 **"Fantastic young fireball pitcher"**—Sherm Mitchell, Jr., "Side-Lines," *Union-Bulletin*, April 23, 1961, 9.

112 **Screen behind home plate had been doubled**—"Baltimore Bolstered Braves Appear Sunday," *Union-Bulletin*, May 9, 1961, 13.

113 **A profile of the new celebrity**—Sherm Mitchell, Jr., "Sidelines: Fireball Finger," *Union-Bulletin*, April 23, 1961, 11.

113 **Steve got off to a slow start**—"Braves Get Catcher as Part of Oriole Package," *Union-Bulletin*, May 12, 1961, 11.

113 **The first regular season professional baseball game . . . the possibility that Dalkowski might pitch**—Mitchell, "Side-Lines."

113 **A 3–12 record and an ERA of 8.39**—Associated Press, "Morhardt Is Bat Winner," *Union-Bulletin,* September 10, 1961, 11.

114 **Dalkowski might be drafted by the expansion Houston Colt .45s**— Milton Richman, "Draft Pickings Slim for Major Loop Teams," *Daily Independent,* November 13, 1961.

114 **"Assigned outright to the Rochester Red Wings"**—"Rochester Gets Steve Dalkowski from Baltimore," *Hartford Courant,* October 13, 1961, 21A.

114 **"Special spring project"**—"Liggett, Christian Home for 'Sislers'," *Democrat and Chronicle,* March 25, 1962, 32.

114 **"Throwing more breaking balls"**—Pat Gillick, telephone interview by Brian Vikander, October 30, 2018, Palm Desert, CA.

114 **"No, that's enough," King said**—"King Uses Psychology: Dalkowski Needs Only Control, Wing Skipper Says," *Democrat and Chronicle,* April 2, 1962, 15.

115 **"The wild ones never learn"**—"Good Reason for Bad Year: The Roof Fell In," *Democrat and Chronicle,* April 1, 1962, 23.

115 **"Dalkowski feels the change has helped him immeasurably already"**—"Good Reason."

115 **As Chief Bender once said**—Chief Bender, "Baseball's Ten Commandments," Baseball Almanac, https://www.baseball-almanac.com /legendary/libend.shtml.

116 **"I think I'm in the groove"**—"King Uses Psychology."

116 **"There are dozens of pitchers"**—"King Uses Psychology."

116 **"Watch this now," King said**—"King Uses Psychology."

116 **"See, it's mental"**—"King Uses Psychology."

116 **Sandy Koufax once said**—Thomas Boswell, *How Life Imitates the World Series* (New York: Doubleday & Company, 1982), 53.

116 **Hitting legend Rod Carew observed**—Boswell, *Life Imitates.*

116 **"Certain managers can get to certain players"**—"King Uses Psychology."

117 **Steve pitched in relief on April 5**—Bill Vanderschmidt, "Wings Breeze Past Portland, 5–1, As 'Regulars' Join Ballclub," *Democrat and Chronicle,* April 6, 1962, 14.

117 **On April 12 Steve relieved starter Pat Gillick**—Bill Vanderschmidt, "Wing Pitchers Continue to Start in 10–2 Win Over Columbus," *Democrat and Chronicle,* April 13, 1962, 31.

117 **When Dalkowski went to the mound on April 19**—Bill Vanerschmidt, "Wings Acquire Vet Catcher, Lose to Leafs," *Democrat and Chronicle*, April 20, 1962, 26.

117 **On Easter Sunday, April 22, 1962, Dalkowski and catcher Frank Zupo were sent back to the Orioles for reassignment**—Bill Vanderschmidt, "Wings Cut Dalkowski, Zupo as They Wait IL Opener," *Democrat and Chronicle*, April 23, 1962, 24.

CHAPTER 11

119 **Epigraph**—Joe Posnanski, "How Do You Solve a Problem like Dalkowski?" Sportsworld, NBC Sports, https://sportsworld.nbcsports.com/fixing-steve-dalkowski/.

119 **Elmira had a long and distinguished baseball history**—speech by Arthur W. Wellington, "One Hundred Years of Baseball in Elmira," Elmira Rotary Club, November 17, 1987.

120 **Sports editor Bill Lee spoke for many when he suggested that Dalkowski "would be with Baltimore right now if he had the remotest idea where home plate is located"**—Bill Lee, "With Malice toward None," *Hartford Courant*, June 11, 1962, 17.

120 **Darold Knowles, a teammate in 1962**—Darold Knowles, interview by Brian Vikander, January 23, 2018, Palm Desert, CA.

121 **Weaver believed that by the time Steve joined the team**—Terry Pluto, *The Earl of Baltimore* (New Jersey: New Century Publishers, 1982), 39–40.

121 **Weaver strongly believed that Steve should vary his pitch selection**—Earl Weaver with Terry Pluto, *Weaver on Strategy* (New York: Simon & Schuster, 1984), 68.

122 **"Earl wanted every pitch to be a slider"**—Palmer and Dale, *Palmer and Weaver*, 98–105.

122 **Knowles recalled, "I saw George Bamberger once very briefly"**—Darold Knowles, interview by Brian Vikander, January 23, 2018, Palm Desert, CA.

122 **"The only thing Earl Weaver knew about the slider was that he couldn't hit one"**—Palmer and Dale, *Palmer and Weaver*.

122 **"Anxious to watch Steve burn that famed (and feared) fastball"**—Al Mallette, "Change of Pace," *Elmira Star-Gazette*, April 28, 1962, 9.

123 **Dalkowski's first start on May 7**—Jack Wheeland, "Dalkowski Whiffs 15—But Pioneers Lose," *Elmira Star-Gazette*, May 8, 1962, 14.

123 **He started a game on May 20**—"Pioneers Home to Battle York," *Elmira Star-Gazette,* May 21, 1962, 12.

123 **He was lifted after two-thirds of an inning**—"Pioneers Bow at York, 5–2; Youngdale Blasts 2nd Homer," *Elmira Star-Gazette,* May 27, 1962, 11.

124 **Dalko pitched six shutout innings**—"Pioneers Open Series with EL-Leading Grays," *Elmira Star-Gazette,* May 29, 1962, 11.

124 **Elmira was pummeled 15–4**—Jack Wheeland, "Ex-Pioneers Return to Haunt Elmira in 15–4 Bombardment," *Elmira Star-Gazette,* May 30, 1962, 22.

124 **Dalkowski was the player in the spotlight**—"Meet Pioneers," *Elmira Star-Gazette,* June 12, 1962, 14.

124 **On June 18 the Pioneers played the Williamsport Grays**—"Pioneers End Grays' Streak 4–3: 21 Inning Elmira Marathon Ties EL Record," *Elmira Star-Gazette,* June 19, 1962, 15; Al Mallette, "A Game to Remember," *Elmira Star-Gazette,* June 20, 1962, 25.

124 **"June 18, 1962, was the day that Steve became a pitcher"**—Lloyd Fourroux, telephone interview by Brian Vikander and author correspondence, December 2018 through January 2019, Palm Desert, CA.

125 **Instead he "appeared to be working smoothly, just trying to get his good pitches over"**—Mallette, "Game to Remember," 25.

125 **Andy remembers that Steve was throwing "only" 95–97 mph that season**—Andy Etchebarren, interview by Brian Vikander, January 22, 2018, Palm Desert, CA.

125 **Darold Knowles confirms the observation**—Darold Knowles, interview by Brian Vikander, January 23, 2018, Palm Desert, CA.

125 **On June 26, Dalko won his first game of the season**—Mallette, "Change of Pace."

125 **"Steve was easy and fluid that day"**—Etchebarren, interview.

125 **June 30 doubleheader against the Binghamton Triplets**—"Pioneers Divide Pair with Trips," *Elmira Star-Gazette,* July 1, 1962, 8.

126 **On July 4 he shut out the York White Roses**—Posnanski, "Problem like Dalkowski."

126 **"Steve had a good slider working"**—Etchebarren, interview.

126 **His win over Springfield on July 9**—Jack Wheeland, "Dalkowski Makes It 4 in Row," *Elmira Star-Gazette,* July 10, 1962, 14.

126 **"A winning pitcher and the hottest one"**—Al Mallette, "Dalkowski's Changed—He's Not Sure How," *Elmira Star-Gazette,* July 10, 1962, 14.

126 **Weaver was beside himself**—Posnanski, "Problem like Dalkowski."

127 **Weaver considered Dalkowski one of the top players on the team**—Al Mallette, "Weaver Lauds Pitching, Defense of Pioneers," *Elmira Star-Gazette,* July 18, 1962, 24.

127 **On July 25 Steve pitched a three-hit, 6–0 shutout**—"'Steve the Stopper' Blanks York, 6–0: Dalkowski Halts Elmira Skid," *Elmira Star-Gazette,* July 26, 1962, 29.

127 **He walked one in 3⅓ innings**—Bill Burbaum, "Gilbert Show on Rainy Day," *Elmira Star-Gazette,* July 30, 1962, 13.

127 **On the 16th he shut out the Binghamton Triplets**—"Doubleheader Here Tonight: Dalkowski's 2-Hit, 4–0 Win Tigthens Elmira's Grip on 2nd," *Elmira Star-Gazette,* August 17, 1962, 15.

127 **Steve started against Binghamton again on August 20**—"Winging Pioneers Ready for Tailspinning Grays: Dalkowski, Youngdalh Spark 6–0 Win over Trips," *Elmira Star-Gazette,* August 21, 1962, 11.

127 **First game of the league playoffs at York on September 10**—"Dalkowski to Pitch Playoff Opener Tonight," *Elmira Star-Gazette,* September 10, 1962, 13; "Pioneers Hope McNally Can End Semis Tonight," *Elmira Star-Gazette,* September 11, 1962, 13.

127 **Their second playoff victory came on the 14th**—Hank Newlin, "Rollin' Pioneers Whip Grays Again, 2–0," *Elmira Star-Gazette,* September 15, 1962, 8.

127 **Elmira went on to win the playoff title**—Al Mallette, "Pioneers Bring Elmira 1st Playoff Title Since 1943," *Elmira Star-Gazette,* September 17, 1962, 10.

128 **"He's always had the stuff"**—Al Mallette, "Weaver Called Shot on Playoff Title in June," *Elmira Star-Gazette,* September 18, 1962, 10.

128 **"Earl never pitched, never caught, and wasn't much of a hitter"**—Palmer and Dale, *Palmer and Weaver.*

129 **"While Earl couldn't coach pitchers, he could find them"**—Palmer and Dale, *Palmer and Weaver.*

130 **"That friggin' midget"**—Tim Sommer, *Beating About the Bushes: Minor League Baseball in the 60's* (Pennsylvania: Infinity Publishing, 2008), 238.

130 **Orioles scout Jim Russo considered Dalko "dumb"**—Jim Russo with Bob Hammel, *Super Scout: Thirty-five Years of Major League Scouting* (Chicago: Bonus Books, 1992), 167.

130 **Steve signed a contract to play winter ball for the Orioles in Puerto Rico**—Mallette, "Change of Pace,"; "Dalkowski to Hurl in Puerto Rico Loop," *Hartford Courant*, October 22, 1962, 19; John Eisenberg, *From 33rd Street to Camden Yards* (New York: McGraw-Hill, 2001), 116.

131 **"I hadn't seen Steve since I faced him in the Sally League in 1958"**—Frank Kostro, telephone interview by Brian Vikander, November 3, 2018, Palm Desert, CA.

131 **Harry Dalton figured that Dalkowski and other top players had "earned a boost" to Baltimore**—Al Mallette, "Orioles' Dalton Sees Stronger Eastern Loop," *Elmira Star-Gazette*, January 24, 1963, 25.

131 **Dave McNally, John Miller, and Dalkowski had the best chance of making the Orioles**—Mallette, "Orioles' Dalton"; Larry Desautels, "Batting Around," *Aberdeen Daily News*, July 20, 1958.

131 **Dalkowski had signed his contract for the coming season**—Associated Press, "Sidelights: Dalkowski Signs," *Elmira Star-Gazette*, February 21, 1963, 39.

131 **Headed for the Orioles spring training camp in Miami**—Associated Press, "Dalkowski Shines for Birds; Zimmer, Mays Blast Homers," *Elmira Star-Gazette*, March 8, 1963, 11.

CHAPTER 12

133 **Epigraph**—TOPPS, Baltimore Orioles Rookie Stars baseball card #496, 1963.

133 **Dalkowski would also collect pointers this spring from manager Clyde King**—"Living Legend Released, Dalkowski Eyes New Life," *Sporting News*, May 7, 1966, 39.

134 **"The new strike zone is good for a pitcher with a hard, high fast ball"**—Gene Levy, "Leading Off: Colecchi Real Big League Name," *Elmira Star-Gazette*, February 7, 1963, 23; Associated Press, "Don't Judge Hitters on Spring Hitting—Cronin," *Elmira Star-Gazette*, April 2, 1963, 13.

134 **"A gangbuster of a new pitcher in Steve Dalkowski"**—George Beahon, "In This Corner," *Democrat and Chronicle*, March 5, 1963, 26.

134 **Billy Hitchcock believed he had "a good chance of making the staff"**—Billy Hitchcock, "Orioles Stronger In '63," *Kingsport News,* January 28, 1963, 4.

134 **"Steve was coming off a very good year in Elmira"**—Eddie Watt, telephone interview by Brian Vikander, January 17 and 18, 2019, Palm Desert, CA.

134 **Pitching batting practice at the beginning of spring training**—Rich Ashburn, "All-Time Fastest Pitcher Never Made the Majors," *Baseball Digest,* November 1980, 62–63.

135 **In an intrasquad game on March 7**—Associated Press, "Sidelights: Dalkowski Shines," *Elmira Star-Gazette,* February 21, 1963, 39.

135 **Dalkowski was "out with a severe sore arm"**—George Beahon, *Rochester Democrat and Chronicle,* March 15, 1963, 22.

135 **Watt doesn't remember throwing the errant pitch**—Watt, telephone interview.

135 **Hitchcock believed Dalkowski had earned a place on the roster**—"Orioles," *Hartford Courant,* March 9, 1963, 13.

135 **Dalko pitched three innings in an exhibition game against the Detroit Tigers**—"Dalkowski Tough," *Elmira Star-Gazette,* March 13, 1963, 23; "Dalkowski's Hitless Relief Paces Birds," *Hartford Courant,* March 13, 1963, 18.

135 **On March 17 he pitched three more hitless innings**—Associated Press, "Dalkowski, Brandt Pace Orioles to 8th Straight," *Elmira Star-Gazette,* March 18, 1963, 13; "Unbeaten Orioles Nudge L.A. in 9th," *Oneonta Star,* March 18, 1963, 10.

136 **Fans in Miami loved him**—Gene Levy, "Leading Off: Court Hoop-La Not Over Yet," *Elmira Star-Gazette,* March 21, 1963, 28.

136 **Topps baseball card titled "1963 Rookie Stars"**—TOPPS, Baltimore Orioles Rookie Stars baseball card #496, 1963.

136 **Bill Lee asked Billy Hitchcock about Dalkowski's chances**—Bill Lee, "With Malice toward None," *Hartford Courant,* March 23, 1963, 13.

136 **"Pitching winter ball helped a lot"**—Lee, "With Malice toward None."

137 **Measure Dalkowski for a Baltimore uniform**—John Eisenberg, "Lost Phenom Finds His Way," *Baltimore Sun,* February 16, 2003; John Steadman, "The Saga of Steve Dalkowski," *News American,* August 28, 1981, 1D.

137 **Steve Barber, watching Dalkowski from the sidelines, remarked, "This kid is faster than I am"**—Beahon, "In This Corner."

137 **"A pinched nerve in his pitching arm"**—AP Newswire, "Dalkowski Injures Arm as Orioles Edge Yanks 7–6," *Elmira Star-Gazette*, March 23, 1963, 9.

137 **Dalkowski's injury was "not serious"**—Harry Grayson, "The Scoreboard," *Gastonia Gazette*, April 12, 1963.

137 **"It isn't believed to be serious"**—Posnanski, "How Do You Solve a Problem like Dalkowski?" Sportsworld, NBC Sports, https://sports world.nbcsports.com/fixing-steve-dalkowski/.

137 **Some reports said he had strained a tendon**—Lou Pavlovich, Jr., "Fastest Pitcher Ever," *Collegiate Baseball*, October 3, 2003, 1, 3.

138 **"Was theoretically standing near home plate in Miami, but his fanny was more or less in the Bahamas"**—George Vecsey, "A Hall of Fame for a Legendary Fastball Pitcher," *New York Times*, July 18, 2009, SP3.

138 **"He was throwing great," Starrette said**—John Eisenberg, *From 33rd Street to Camden Yards* (New York: McGraw-Hill, 2001), 116–117.

138 **"Steve was throwing real well"**—Dick Hall, telephone interview by Brian Vikander, August 29, 2017, Palm Desert, CA.

138 **Eddie Watt added that the team trainer went with Brecheen to the mound**—Watt, telephone interview.

139 **Retelling the story himself five years or so after the fact**—Linda Moore, interview by Alex Thomas, September 30, 2017, Stockton, CA.

139 **In another retelling, he said his hand went numb after the pitch**—Eisenberg, "Lost Phenom."

139 **According to teammate Boog Powell, Steve had "hurt his arm a little"**—Eisenberg, *From 33rd Street.*

139 **He was also hit on the wrist during a plate appearance March 7 in Miami**—Associated Press, "Dalkowski Shines," *Elmira Star-Gazette*, March 8, 1963, 11.

139 **Steve later said he had never had arm problems in his life**—Pat Jordan, "Going Nowhere Fast," *Inside Sports*, July 1982, 78.

139 **Dalkowski "fielded a bunt and threw off-balance to first base"**—Pat Jordan, "The Wildest Fastball Ever," *Sports Illustrated*, October 12, 1970.

139 **The injury happened when Steve was fielding a bunt from Jim Bou-ton**—Ron Shelton, "Steve Dalkowski Had the Stuff of Legends," *Los Angeles Times*, July 19, 2009.

139 **Yet another version claims the batter was Bobby Richardson**—Tim Wendel, "Steve Dalkowski: The Fastest Ever?" The National Pastime Museum, January 25, 2013, https://www.thenationalpastimemuseum .com/article/steve-dalkowski-fastest-ever/.

139 **Believed well-intentioned coaching was part of Dalkowski's prob-lem**—Fred Valentine, telephone interview by Brian Vikander, January 6, 2019, Palm Desert, CA.

140 **Three players were shipped back to the minors on March 28, but the team held on to Dalko**—Associated Press, "Sidelights: Herm to Rochester," *Elmira Star-Gazette*, March 29, 1963, 13.

140 **On April 5, the last day to cut players**—Associated Press, "Dalkowski, Miller Sent to Rochester by Orioles," *Elmira Star-Gazette*, April 6, 1963, 9.

140 **Dalkowski appeared in the bullpen for the first time since his injury**—"Luke's 3-Run Homer Wasted as Wings Bow to Jets, 7–6," *Democrat and Chronicle*, April 8, 1963, 25.

140 **On April 15, Dalkowski went on the disabled list**—Bill Vander-schmidt, "Wings, Lose, Smith Hurt in Grapefruit Finale," *Democrat and Chronicle*, April 15, 1963, 24.

140 **"Fifty years ago 'rest' was the treatment for everything"**—Pat Gil-lick, correspondence and telephone interview by Brian Vikander, Octo-ber 30, 2018, Palm Desert, CA.

140 **In his syndicated column "The Scoreboard," . . . essentially a mem-ber of the Orioles squad**—Grayson, "Scoreboard."

141 **On April 20 Steve's former teammate Dave McNally**—"McNally Tames Tribe, 8–1; Whiffs 9," *Elmira Star-Gazette*, April 21, 1963, 9.

141 **Dalkowski remained on the disabled list**—Bill Vanderschmidt, "Club Opposed Travelers after Downtown Parade," *Democrat and Chronicle*, April 24, 1963, 30.

141 **Restored to the lineup on April 30**—Bill Vanderschmidt, "Wing Game Postponed: Moford Gets Release," *Democrat and Chronicle*, May 1, 1963, 14.

141 **Game was called on account of snow**—Vanderschmidt, "Wing Game Postponed."

141 **"Dalkowski is a valuable property"**—Beahon, "In This Corner."

142 **"He had big plans for the young left-hander"**—Beahon, "In This Corner."

142 **"With his fire-power, three-quarters speed is more than plenty"**— Beahon, "In This Corner."

142 **Steve pitched the bottom of the tenth inning in relief for Rochester**—"Richmond Defeats Red Wings by 5–4," *Democrat and Chronicle*, May 3, 1963, 45.

142 **By May 12 Dalkowski was back in Baltimore for more treatment on his elbow**—Bill Vanderschmidt, "Red Wings' Miller Shackles Leafs," *Democrat and Chronicle*, May 12, 1963, 59; Al Mallette, "Change of Pace," *Elmira Star-Gazette*, April 28, 1962.

142 **His manager decided against putting him on the mound because of game time temperatures in the thirties**—Bill Vanderschmidt, "Bouchee Pinch Homer Beats Wings," *Democrat and Chronicle*, May 25, 1963, 24.

142 **Back on to the active roster May 27**—Bill Vanderschmidt, "Short and Bowens Click as Wings Humble Jets, 3–1," *Democrat and Chronicle*, May 28, 1963, 41.

142 **First appearance for the Red Wings at home**—Bill Vanderschmidt, "Ackley's One-Hit Job Shaves Wings, 2–0," *Democrat and Chronicle*, May 30, 1963, 45.

142 **On June 3 Dalkowski registered his second loss**—"Red Wings Lose Twin Bill to Crackers, 1–0, 6–3," *Democrat and Chronicle*, June 4, 1963, 41.

143 **On the road against Toronto**—Canadian Press, "Red Wings Edge Leafs for 10th Straight Win," *Democrat and Chronicle*, June 20, 1963, 75.

143 **Dalko was "solidly unhappy about the switch"**—Bill Vanderschmidt, "Wings Outslug Chiefs! Just Came Back; They're Here Tonight," *Democrat and Chronicle*, July 3, 1963, 25.

143 **"If Steve can get enough work to get his control in shape, he's a major league pitcher"**—Vanderschmidt, "Wings Outslug Chiefs!"

143 **"I always felt that they should have turned him into an outfielder"**—Valentine, telephone interview.

143 **They cheered him as the "hero returning"**—"Pioneers Get Dalkowski in Return," *Elmira Star-Gazette*, July 2, 1963, 17.

144 **3–1 loss to York on July 12**—Gene Levy, "York's Hughes Hews Pioneers, 3–1," *Elmira Star-Gazette,* July 13, 1963, 9.

144 **On July 24 he came on in relief in the sixth**—Tom Page, "Stormin' Norman Silences Pioneers," *Elmira Star-Gazette,* July 25, 1963, 21.

144 **Dalkowski made his first start since returning to Elmira on July 28**—Tom Page, "Pioneers Continue Skid," *Elmira Star-Gazette,* July 29, 1963, 7.

144 **Dalkowski could throw a ball through a split log wall**—Robert Graziul, "The Greatest Prospect Never to Make It to the Majors," *Baseball Digest,* December 1990, 40.

144 **He returned to the disabled list August 21**—Tom Page, "Knowles' 15th Win Gives Elmira Splits," *Elmira Star-Gazette,* August 21, 1963, 33.

144 **Johnson spoke of how the team missed Fred Valentine's "infectious spirit" and hitting ability along with Herm Starrette's pitching skills**—Bill Vanderschmidt, "'Attitude' Beat Wings: Team Seen Lacking Needed Spirit," *Rochester Democrat and Chronicle,* September 4, 1963, 27.

144 **October 12, Dalko was sent back up to Rochester**—"Williamsport in EL," *Elmira Star-Gazette,* October 13, 1963, 29; "Viney Birds, Bilko Released," *Democrat and Chronicle,* October 13, 1963, 56.

145 **"The hardest part is trying to consider the value of these players"**—"Houston Colt .45s: Too Much Too Soon in Houston," *Sports Illustrated,* April 8, 1963, https://www.si.com/vault/1963/04/08/593568/houston-colt-45s-too-much-too-soon-in-houston.

145 **Orioles evidently didn't think Dalkowski's future was promising**—Al Mallette, "Grid Rhubarb," *Elmira Star-Gazette,* November 19, 1963, 15.

CHAPTER 13

147 **Epigraph**—Gene Levy, "Dalkowski Returns to Pioneers Again," *Elmira Star-Gazette,* April 21, 1964, 14.

147 **Earl Weaver arrived in Elmira near the end of February, 1964**—Gene Levy, "Weaver Visits Elmira, Stokes Hot Stove," *Elmira Star-Gazette,* February 23, 1964, 33.

147 **"He is the greatest unharnessed pitching talent ever to set foot on the mound"**—Al Mallette, "Won't Need Scorecard to Recognize '64 Pioneers," *Elmira Star-Gazette,* March 29, 1964, 10; Associated Press, "Pioneers Not Yet Organized," *Elmira Star-Gazette,* March 31, 1964, 13.

148 **Opened their spring training camp in Daytona Beach on March 19**—"Wings' Johnson Satsified," *Democrat and Chronicle*, March 22, 1964, 75.

148 **His first outing, pitching in relief against Seattle**—"Red Wings Win On 2 Hits in 1964 'Opener'," *Democrat and Chronicle*, March 27, 1964, 29.

149 **Rochester sustained its first loss of the training season against the Dallas Rangers on March 31**—George Beahon, "Wings Beaten, 7–5, By Dallas And Rookies' Wildness," *Democrat and Chronicle*, April 1, 1964, 34.

149 **Bill Vanderschmidt gave a measured yet frank assessment of Dalkowski**—Bill Vanderschmidt, "Crackers Stop Wings: Dalkowski Blows Up," *Democrat and Chronicle*, April 9, 1964, 69.

150 **Steve was sent to the Orioles' Thomasville, Georgia camp**—Bill Vanderschmidt, "Wings' 12 Hits Not Enough In 5–2 Setback," *Democrat and Chronicle*, April 10, 1964, 55.

150 **The Orioles fined him $20 a day, $100 in all, for failure to report to Thomasville**—Tom Page, "Pioners Set for EL Grind," *Elmira Star-Gazette*, April 19, 1964, 42; Gene Levy, *Elmira Star-Gazette*, April 21, 1964, 14.

150 **Tim Sommer, a second-year player who recalled meeting Dalkowski that day**—Tim Sommer, *Beating About the Bushes: Minor League Baseball in the 60's* (Pennsylvania: Infinity Publishing, 2008), 251–255; Ken Nigro, "Steve Dalkowski—DTs Dead but Legend Lives," *Sporting News*, June 30, 1979, 11.

151 **Eddie Watt . . . clearly remembered Steve's arrival**—Eddie Watt, telephone interview by Brian Vikander, January 17 and 18, 2019, Palm Desert, CA.

151 **Weaver announced on April 20 that Steve Dalkowski would be suiting up with the Elmira Pioneers**—Levy, "Dalkowski Returns to Pioneers Again."

151 **Weaver assigned first baseman Joe Altobelli as his roommate**—Bob Sudyk, "A Matter of Control," *Hartford Courant*, March 5, 1989, E13.

152 **"Can you throw the ball through the fence?"**—Kevin Kernan, "Legendary Flameout Steve Dalkowski and His 110 MPH Fastball," *New York Post*, July 6, 2013, http://sabr.org/latest/kernan-legendary -flameout-steve-dalkowski-and-his-110-mph-fastball.

152 **Steve threw the ball from the center-field fence over a 40-foot-high backstop**—Ron Shelton, "Steve Dalkowski the Hardest Throwing Pitcher Who Ever Lived?" *Seattle Times*, July 23, 2009.

152 **Dalkowski vs. traffic cop story**—John Eisenberg, *From 33rd Street to Camden Yards* (New York: McGraw-Hill, 2001), 115.

153 **Rooming with Steve Dalkowski was like rooming with a suitcase**—Eisenberg, *From 33rd Street*.

153 **His first start of the regular season for Elmira on May 25**—Tom Page, "Youngdahl Hit in 9th Pulls It Out," *Elmira Star-Gazette*, May 26, 1964, 14.

153 **On June 4 Dalkowski started the second game of a doubleheader**—"Pioneers Get Split at York," *Elmira Star-Gazette*, June 5, 1964, 14.

153 **The last straw for Weaver and the Pioneers came on June 8, 1964**—Gene Levy, "Pioneer Starters Get Nobody Out," *Elmira Star-Gazette*, June 9, 1964, 15.

153 **Weaver told the press Steve was cut**—Gene Levy, "Pioneer Pennant Push Has Made a Beliver of Weaver," *Elmira Star-Gazette*, August 30, 1964, 35.

153 **Harry Dalton asked Stockton skipper Harry Dunlap if he wanted the troubled lefty**—Greg Gallo, "Wild Steve. . . . The One That Got Away," 1973.

154 **"One of the most promising careers in Oriole baseball history has apparently ended"**—Gene Levy, "Bertaina Blanks York: Stymies Roses on 4 Hits; Pioneers Ship Dalkowski," *Elmira Star-Gazette*, June 12, 1964; Larry Desautels, "Batting Around," *Aberdeen American-News*, June 23, 1964.

154 **On June 13, 1964, the Stockton Ports announced Dalkowski was rejoining the team**—"Dalkowski Joins Ports," *Stockton Record*, June 13, 1964, 25; "Krall Handcuffs Ports on Two-Hit Effort," *Stockton Record*, June 15, 1964, 49.

154 **The manager corrected Steve**—Frank Peters, telephone interview by Brian Vikander, January 23, 2018, Palm Desert, CA.

154 **His first appearance was three days later against the Fresno Giants**—Dick Kranz, "Fresno Giants Clip Ports by 7 to 4," *Stockton Record*, June 17, 1964, 67.

154 **On June 18 he did better against the Bakersfield Bears**—Larry Press, "Bears' Rookie Hard Luck Guy," *Bakersfield Californian*, June 19, 1964, 13.

154 **He threw a ball from the bullpen to the top of the backstop behind the plate 420 feet away**—Danny Peary, "Steve Dalkowski," *Cult Baseball Players: The Greats, the Flakes, the Weird, and the Wonderful* (New York: Simon & Schuster, 1990), 2.

155 **"Steve was pitching against the Santa Barbara Dodgers at Laguna Park"**—Bruce Babbock, correspondence and telephone interview by Brian Vikander, October 18, 2017, Palm Desert, CA.

155 **"Dazzling Dalkowski" was in top form on Independence Day 1964**—Dick Kranz, "Ports Divide Two with San Jose over Weekend: Dalkowski Fans 14 in Victory," *Stockton Record*, July 6, 1964, 25.

155 **"The whole team was amazed but excited about being part of the Dalkowski legend"**—Peters, telephone interview.

155 **Steve had long since developed a reputation as a ladies' man**—Linda Moore, interview by Alex Thomas, September 30, 2017, Stockton, CA; Sommer, *Beating About the Bushes.*

156 **Another resident at the Pershing Apartments was Linda Moore**—Moore, interview.

157 **Dalko told Herm he was going to throw his first warmup pitch over the press box**—Eisenberg, *From 33rd Street.*

157 **Christened the Ports' Pitching Poles**—Kranz, "Ports Divide Two."

157 **Turned in a solid performance on August 14**—"Dalkowksi Flips Win for Ports," *Stockton Record*, August 15, 1964, 25.

157 **"Steve Dalkowski, is back with the Stockton Ports and seems to be sharper than ever"**—"Dalkowski Hurls Stockton to Win over Bakersfield in Cal League," *Humboldt Standard*, August 15, 1964, 9.

157 **5–0 shutout against Modesto on August 19**—"Ports Sweep Doubleheader; Dalkowski Hurls Shutout," *Stockton Record*, August 20, 1964, 31.

157 **Ports lost to Bakersfield 6–1 on August 28**—Hugh Donnelly, "Bears Score 6–1 Victory over Ports; Dalkowski Has 18 Strikeouts," *Stockton Record*, August 29, 1964, 23.

158 **Sounded like they were being thrown "nine hundred miles an hour!"**—Jay Johnstone, telephone interview by Brian Vikander, June 26, 2017, Palm Desert, CA.

158 **The last home game of the season for the Ports**—United Press International, "Salinas Gains Ground on California League Leaders," *Humboldt Standard*, September 2, 1964, 16; Dick Kranz, "Ports Drop Reno Twice by 1–0, 2–1," *Stockton Record*, September 2, 1964, 65.

158 **"Everybody loved him. He was just easily led astray and couldn't stop drinking"**—Madden, "Safe at Home."

158 **Orioles announced they had traded Steve Dalkowski to the Pittsburgh Pirates' Triple-A Columbus Jets**—"Dalkowski Claimed by Columbus," *Elmira Star-Gazette,* September 2, 1964, 31.

159 **He was moving to Ohio**—Moore, interview; Gallo, "Wild Steve."

159 **Arrested for breach of the peace**—"Man Fined $30 for Violation of Traffic Light," *Hartford Courant,* January 16, 1965, 10D.

159 **Jets announced that he would go back to Baltimore**—United Press International, "Jets Reduce Roster Down to 24," *Defiance Crescent-News,* March 31, 1965, 15.

159 **Back with Elmira in April and May**—"Pioneers Shaping Up: Watt to Start," *Elmira Star-Gazette,* April 6, 1965, 10; Tom Page, "Pioneers Have 3 WHIZ Kids: Barnowski, Caria, Darwin Take Aim with Flame," *Elmira Star-Gazette,* May 16, 1965, 46.

160 **In May he was once more on the Tri-City team**—Associated Press, "Cold Night, Cold Hopes at Yakima," *Union-Bulletin,* May 17, 1965, 6.

CHAPTER 14

161 **Epigraph**—"Living Legend Released, Dalkowski Eyes New Life," *Sporting News,* May 7, 1966, 39.

161 **When Steve moved back to Kennewick, Washington**—Tim Sommer, *Beating About the Bushes: Minor League Baseball in the 60's* (Pennsylvania: Infinity Publishing, 2008), 230–255.

166 **Landed a spot on the roster of the Class-A San Jose Bees**—Wes Mathis, "Bees Blanked By Salinas," *San Jose Mercury,* July 28, 1965, 19.

166 **First start for the Bees against the Salinas Indians on July 29**—Wes Mathis, "Dalkowski Wild: Salinas Posts Sweep," *San Jose Mercury,* July 30, 1965, 51.

167 **Game against Santa Barbara on August 5**—"Bees Smash Santa Barbara," *San Jose Mercury,* August 6, 1965, 50.

167 **After chalking up his second win for the Bees on August 12, Steve was in good form on the mound August 19**—"Bees Down Fresno By 6–1," *San Jose Mercury,* August 13, 1965, 59; Bob Kohn, "Grand Slam Home Deals Bees 7–4 Loss," *San Jose Mercury,* August 20, 1965, 65.

167 **"I got to first with a big smile on my face and was happy to have survived"**—Frank Peters, telephone interview by Brian Vikander, January 23, 2018, Palm Desert, CA.

168 **Steve went south again to play in Mexico**—*El Regional,* December 8, 1965.

168 **Billed as "el lanzador más veloz de todos los tiempos" (the fastest pitcher of all time), Steve reportedly hurled the baseball at 108 miles per hour**—Roberto Riveros, "Mi Columna," August 3, 2017; Alfonso Araujo, "Lanzando Para Home," September 9, 2013.

169 **Game in Hermosillo on December 8, 1965**—*El Regional.*

169 **Young American players still play in Mazatlán**—Mitch Lively and Nick Struck, interview by Alex Thomas, December 14, 2017, Mazatlán, Mexico.

170 **Steve appeared in 20 games for Mazatlán**—Mexican Pacific League statistics courtesy of Sr. Ramon Flores.

171 **The Angels then gave Steve Dalkowski his unconditional release**—Larry Desautels, "Batting Around," *Aberdeen Daily News,* July 20, 1958; Mark Fleisher, "Dalkowski—the Fastest Ever," *Elmira Star-Gazette,* June 17, 1979, 1C.

171 **"A baseball legend in his own time, apparently has thrown his last professional pitch"**—"Living Legend Released."

CHAPTER 15

173 **Epigraph**—Linda Moore, interview by Alex Thomas, September 30, 2017, Stockton, CA.

173 **By the spring of 1966 Steve was back in Stockton**—Tim Sommer, *Beating About the Bushes: Minor League Baseball in the 60's* (Pennsylvania: Infinity Publishing, 2008).

174 **One night Steve was at a bowling alley**—Linda Moore, interview by Alex Thomas, September 30, 2017, Stockton, CA.

183 **Steve Dalkowski was in town with hopes of returning to baseball**—Larry Press, "In the Press Box," *Bakersfield Californian,* January 27, 1970, 15.

185 **Steve was settled in Oildale, California**—*Oildale City Directory* (Oildale, CA), 1970.

CHAPTER 16

187 **Epigraph**—Mark Fleisher, "Dalkowski—The Fastest Ever," *Elmira Star-Gazette,* June 17, 1979, 23.

187 **Ted Williams taking batting practice against Dalko**—Pat Jordan, "The Wildest Fastball Ever," *Sports Illustrated,* October 12, 1970, S5–S7.

188 **A credible variation of the story comes from Orioles scout Walter Youse**—John Eisenberg, *From 33rd Street to Camden Yards* (New York: McGraw-Hill, 2001), 111.

188 **Bob Beavers, who isn't named by McGowan**—Bob Beavers, interview by Brian Vikander, August 29, 2017 and November 21, 2017, Palm Desert, CA.

189 **Attended a union-sponsored landscaping school**—Fleisher, "Dalkowski—The Fastest Ever," 23; "Steve Dalkowski" memo released by Supervisor of Physical Education, New Britain Public Schools, January 18, 1979.

190 **For the next five years he spent most of his time picking crops up and down the central valley of California**—John Steadman, "Fastest with a Ball and a Bottle, Dalkowski Threw Away Career," *Baltimore Sun*, August 11, 1996; John Altavilla, "What Might Have Been," *Hartford Courant*, September 1, 1996, A1; Bill Madden, "Safe at Home," *New York Daily News*, May 17, 1998; John Eisenberg, "Lost Phenom Finds His Way," *Baltimore Sun*, February 16, 2003; Ken Nigro, "Steve Dalkowski—DTs Dead but Legend Lives," *Sporting News*, June 30, 1979, 10.

191 **He was arrested repeatedly**—Eisenberg, "Lost Phenom"; Nigro, "Steve Dalkowski."

191 **Sometimes he would go to Sam Lynn Field in Bakersfield**—Ron Shelton, "Steve Dalkowski the Hardest Throwing Pitcher Who Ever Lived?" *Seattle Times*, July 23, 2009.

192 **Late in the 1974 season**—Ron Fimrite, "Speed Trap for an Angel," Vault, Sports Illustrated, https://vault.si.com/vault/1974/09/16/speed-trap-for-an-angel; Ryan was already recognized as one of the fastest pitchers of all time—AP, "New Britain's Dalkowski among Swiftest Pitchers," *New Britain Herald*, August 22, 1974; staff, "Remembering the Ryan Express," *Baseball Almanac*, September 14, 2006.

193 **"Last known address"**—Loel Schrader, "Ryan Fast, but How about Dalkowski?" *Long Beach Press-Telegram*, September 6, 1974, 29.

193 **"Not only does he not look like a fireballing pitcher"**—Larry Press, "Ex-Fireballer Steve Dalkowski Battles Tough Times Here," *Bakersfield Californian*, September 16, 1974, 18.

193 **Dalko a chapter all his own: "The Living Legend"**—George Smith, "Sportswriter Chronicles Former Athletes' 'Good Old Days,'" *Hartford Courant*, December 4, 1977, 11H.

194 **Steve met Virginia Greenwood**—Bob Sudyk, "A Matter of Control," *Hartford Courant*, March 5, 1989, E11A.

194 **Steve and Virginia became a couple and then evidently married in 1975**—Bart Fisher, "Dalkowski Has Things under Control," *Hartford Courant*, August 17, 1988, 13.

194 **"The saddest experience of all, however"**—Smith, "Sportswriter Chronicles Former Athletes."

195 **Remembered seeing him at Candlestick Park**—Eisenberg, *From 33rd Street.*

195 **Youngdahl and Stevens**—Fleisher, "Dalkowski—The Fastest Ever,"; Pat Jordan, "Going Nowhere Fast," *Inside Sports*, July 1982, 72–80; John Altavilla, "What Might Have Been," *Hartford Courant*, September 1, 1996, A1; Nigro, "Steve Dalkowski."

196 **Steve Jacobson wrote a feature for Newsday about the Dalkowski legend**—Steve Jacobson, "Though Long Gone, Dalkowski's Legend Blazes On," *Hartford Courant*, April 12, 1979.

197 **The story was a mixture of old statistics and Steve's current life**—Fleisher, "Dalkowski—The Fastest Ever."

197 **Quoted Chuck Stevens as saying Steve had gotten rehab help**—Nigro, "Steve Dalkowski."

198 **An apartment on Douglas Street**—Bakersfield, CA city directory, 1981.

CHAPTER 17

199 **Epigraph**—Al Mallette, "Change of Pace," *Elmira Star-Gazette*, July 7, 1981, 22.

200 **The fastest he ever saw**—Mallette, "Change of Pace."

200 **Story about Steve on the front of the sports section on August 28, 1981**—John Steadman, "The Saga of Steve Dalkowski," *News American*, August 28, 1981.

201 **"A very, very nervous kid"**—Pat Hruby, "The Legend of Steve Dalkowski," *Washington Times*, June 4, 2000.

201 **A long feature about Dalkowski**—Pat Jordan, "Going Nowhere Fast," *Inside Sports*, July 1982, 72–80.

202 **Earl Weaver was reminiscing about his first season coaching in Elmira**—Al Mallette, "Game That Turned Around '62 Season," *Elmira Star-Gazette*, July 3, 1983, 29.

202   **Players swapped stories of seeing him once in a while**—John Eisenberg, *From 33rd Street to Camden Yards* (New York: McGraw-Hill, 2001), 117.

203   **Boog Powell would get a call now and then**—Eisenberg, *From 33rd Street.*

205   **The story of his 1988 visit is an encouraging one**—Bart Fisher, "Dalkowski Has Things under Control," *New Britain Herald*, August 17, 1988, 13.

206   **"Tell 'em he's doin' OK"**—Bob Sudyk, "A Matter of Control," *Hartford Courant*, May 5, 1989, E11A.

206   **Steve was part of the inspiration for the character Nuke Laloosh**—Ron Shelton, "Steve Dalkowski the Hardest Throwing Pitcher Who Ever Lived?" *Seattle Times*, July 23, 2009.

209   **"It's nice to be remembered"**—Robert Graziul, "The Greatest Prospect Never to Make It to the Majors," *Baseball Digest*, December 1990, 43.

CHAPTER 18

211   **Epigraph**—John Eisenberg, "Lost Phenom Finds His Way," *Baltimore Sun*, February 16, 2003.

211   **Moved into a small house nearby on Lincoln Avenue**—Bakersfield, CA city directory, 1991.

212   **Zupo and Chiappetta told Steve that if he didn't get help soon he was going to die**—Eisenberg, "Lost Phenom."

212   **Zupo had been one of the few players who thought Steve's drinking during his playing years was exaggerated**—Pat Hruby, "The Legend of Steve Dalkowski," *Washington Times*, June 4, 2000.

212   **Dalkowski was hospitalized in Los Angeles for three months beginning in October 1991**—Tom Hoffarth, "A Post Script on Steve Dalkowski, and His L.A. Connection in Beginning His Road to Recovery," *Los Angeles Daily News*, July 18, 2009.

213   **On December 18, 1992, she wrote a heartrending letter**—Andy Baylock, interview by Alex Thomas, May 8, 2017, Storrs, CT.

213   **On Christmas Eve 1992**—John Altavilla, "What Might Have Been," *Hartford Courant*, September 1, 1996, A1.

214   **Steve to spend two months in an Oklahoma hospital**—Eisenberg, "Lost Phenom."

214 **Steve was moved into the Walnut Hill Convalescent Home**—John Steadman, "Fastest with a Ball, and a Bottle, Dalkowski Threw Away Career," *Baltimore Sun*, August 11, 1996.

216 **"He's fine. He's comfortable"**—Altavilla, "What Might Have Been."

216 **Bill Huber learned that Steve was interested in going to church**—Altavilla, "What Might Have Been."

216 **Baylock recalled at the time. "I remember us as little kids"**—Altavilla, "What Might Have Been."

216 **Baylock recalled the time he was hosting Earl Weaver**—Pete Zanardi, *Baseball in Connecticut*, 1990.

217 **A caller saying he represented Joe Garagiola contacted Pat to ask if her brother was still alive**—Bob Elliott, "The Dunlop Awards: The Untouchable," *Toronto Sun*, August 2, 1998.

217 **Steve and Pat talked with Bill Madden**—Bill Madden, "Safe at Home," *New York Daily News*, May 17, 1998.

217 **"I pitched the same as everybody else. It just got there faster"**—David Margolick, "The Boys of Spring," *Vanity Fair*, May 1997, 92.

218 **Steve Dalkowski was inducted into the New Britain Sports Hall of Fame**—Bill Bernardi, "NB Honors Its Own," *New Britain Herald*, March 13, 2000.

219 **Earl Yost reflected on his thirty-plus year career**—Earl Yost, "Foul Balls Were a Hit as Game Souvenirs," *Hartford Courant*, August 17, 2000, 7.

219 **Steve to give a talk to his team at the University of Connecticut**—Eisenberg, "Lost Phenom."

219 **Interviewed by ESPN for a video introduction of their broadcast of Bull Durham**—Eisenberg, "Lost Phenom."

220 **Throw out the ceremonial first pitch before a homestand of the New Britain Rock Cats**—Pete McEntegart, "The Wild One," *Sports Illustrated*, June 30, 2003, 84–88.

221 **Steve Dalkowski walked to the pitcher's mound in Camden Yards**—Bart Fisher, "Dalkowski to Finally Throw a Pitch in Baltimore," *New Britain Herald*, August 11, 2003, B1; John Eisenberg, "With a Single Pitch, Dalkowski to Earn Long-Elusive Victory," *Baltimore Sun*, September 6, 2003; John Eisenberg, "Minors Legend Has Major Moment," *Baltimore Sun*, September 8, 2003.

222 **Voted a member of the Shrine of the Eternals in 2009 by Baseball Reliquary**—Ron Shelton, "Steve Dalkowski Had the Stuff of Legends,"

Los Angeles Times, July 19, 2009; George Vecsey, "A Hall of Fame for a Legendary Fastball Pitcher," *New York Times*, July 18, 2009.

CHAPTER 19

225 **Epigraph**—Pete McEntegart, "Steve Dalkowski: The Wild One," *Sports Illustrated*, June 30, 2003.

225 **"Somewhere in the neighborhood of 115 miles an hour"**—Cal Ripken, Sr. and Larry Burke, *The Ripken Way: A Manual for Baseball and Life* (New York: Atria, 1999), 60–63.

226 **He called Weaver to tell him, "I'm still here!"**—John Eisenberg, "Lost Phenom Finds His Way," *Baltimore Sun*, February 16, 2003.

227 **The death in 2011 of his nineteen-year-old great-nephew**—Obituary of Ryan Thomas Lee, *Hartford Courant*, May 1, 2011, B6.

227 **Dalko's record of 24 strikeouts, a state high school record for fifty years, wasn't a record after all**—Tom Yantz, "Johnny Be Good: Hartford's 'Schoolboy' Taylor Was Negro League Star; 250 Years, Moments in History," *Hartford Courant*, March 8, 2014, A1.

228 **Documentary Fastball was released and featured an entire segment on Dalkowski**—Jonathon Hock, *Fastball: The Game Is Played in the Blink of an Eye*, Hock Films Production, 2015.

228 **The way Ron Shelton described it**—Danny Peary, *Cult Baseball Players: The Greats, the Flakes, the Weird, and the Wonderful*, 4.

228 **Pat Gillick summed it up well**—McEntegart, "Steve Dalkowski."

228 **Marty Chalk is a former Elmira stadium announcer**—Marty Chalk, interview by Alex Thomas, May 9, 2017, Elmira, NY.

229 **Chapman is officially the fastest pitcher in history**—"Fastest Baseball Pitch (Male)," Guiness World Records, https://www.guinnessworld records.com/world-records/fastest-baseball-pitch-(male)/.

229 **Ryan is unofficially the fastest**—Mark Rivard, "Nolan Ryan's 108 MPH Fastball," Game Haus, August 19, 2018, https://thegamehaus .com/mlb/nolan-ryans-record-108-mph-fastball/2018/08/19.

230 **Dalkowski died on April 19, 2020**—Dom Amore, "Steve Dalkowski, Flame-Throwing Figure of Baseball Lore, Dies of Coronavirus in New Britain," *Hartford Courant*, April 24, 2020, https://www.courant.com /sports/hc-sp-baseball-steve-dalkowski-obit-20200425-20200424 -wwoynutxgjen5mq4d7sibmnfai-story.html.

230 **His body was cremated. There was public funeral or memorial service**—Amore, "Steve Dalkowski, Flame-Throwing Figure."

230 **Dom Amore, who covered sports**—"Dom Amore: Face to Face with Steve Dalkowski, and Baseball's Timeless Tale," *Hartford Courant*, May 6, 2019, https://www.courant.com/sports/hc-sp-amore-column-baseball -steve-dallkowski-20190507-20190506-qyu6gqievglijk7q5qhnsr4msu -story.html.

230 **As so many have mused before him, Amore wondered**—Amore, "Dom Amore: Face to Face."

230 **Emma Baccellieri echoed Amore**—"No One Will Ever Throw Harder Than Steve Dalkowski," *Sports Illustrated*, April 27, 2020 (see video interview), https://www.si.com/mlb/2020/04/27/steve-dalkowski -death-baseball-history.

Bibliography

NEWSPAPERS

Aberdeen American-News, Aberdeen, South Dakota
Bakersfield Californian, Bakersfield, California
Baltimore American, Baltimore, Maryland
Baltimore News-Post, Baltimore, Maryland
Baltimore Sun, Baltimore, Maryland
Bluefield Daily Telegraph, Bluefield, West Virginia
Burlington Daily Times-News, Burlington, North Carolina
Christianity Today, Carol Stream, Illinois
Citizen-Advertiser, Auburn, New York
Daily Chronicle, Centralia, Washington
Daily Independent, Kannapolis, North Carolina
Daily News, Los Angeles, California
Defiance Crescent-News, Defiance, Ohio
Democrat and Chronicle, Rochester, New York
Dunkirk Evening Observer, Dunkirk-Fredonia, New York
Elmira Advertiser, Elmira, New York
Elmira Star-Gazette, Elmira, New York
El Regional, Hermosillo, Mexico
Evening Telegram, Herkimer, New York
Gastonia Gazette, Gastonia, North Carolina
Hayward Daily Review, Hayward, California
Hartford Courant, Hartford, Connecticut
High Point Enterprise, High Point, North Carolina
Houston Chronicle, Houston, Texas
Humbolt Standard, Humbolt, California
Humbolt Times, Humbolt, California

283

Kingsport News, Kingsport, Tennessee
Kingsport News-Times, Kingsport, Tennessee
Kingston Daily Freeman, Kingston, New York
Lima News, Lima, Ohio
Long Beach Press-Telegram, Long Beach, California
Los Angeles Times, Los Angeles, California
Mercury News, San Jose, California
Miami Herald, Miami, Florida
Middletown Daily Record, Middletown, New York
New Britain Herald, New Britain, Connecticut
New York Daily News, New York, New York
New York Post, New York, New York
New York Times, New York, New York
News American, Baltimore, Maryland
Oneonta Star, Oneonta, New York
Orange County Register, Anaheim, California
Panama City Herald, Panama City, Florida
Post-Standard, Syracuse, New York
Republican Courier, Findlay, Ohio
San Mateo Times, San Mateo, California
San Rafael Daily Independent Journal, San Rafael, California
Seattle Times, Seattle, Washington
Stockton Record, Stockton, California
Times Record, Troy, New York
Toronto Sun, Toronto, Canada
Union-Bulletin, Walla-Walla, Washington
USA Today, McLean, Virginia
Washington Times, Washington, DC
Wilson Daily Times, Wilson, North Carolina

ARTICLES, BOOKS, INTERVIEWS

Allen, M. *Bo: Pitching and Wooing.* New York: Dial Press, 1973.
Alston, W., and D. Weiskopf. *The Complete Baseball Handbook: Strategies and Techniques for Winning.* Boston: Allyn and Bacon, 1972.
Altavilla, J. "What Might Have Been." *Hartford Courant*, September 1, 1996, p. A1.
Armchair GM Wiki. "Article: Players from the Past: Steve Dalkowski." April 21, 2008. https://armchairgm.fandom.com/wiki/Article:Players_From_the_Past:_Steve_Dalkowski.

Ashburn, R. "All-Time Fastest Pitcher Never Made the Majors." *Baseball Digest*, November, 1980, pp. 62–63.

Babbock, B. Interview by B. Vikander, October 18, 2017.

Baseball Almanac. "Remembering the Ryan Express." September 14, 2006.

Batter's Box. "There Goes the Fastest Man Who Ever Pitched . . ." September 8, 2003. https://www.battersbox.ca/article.php?story=20030908093020999.

Baylock, A. Interview by A. Thomas, May 8, 2017.

Beavers, B. Interview by B. Vikander, August 29 and November 21, 2017.

Bennett, B. A. *On a Silver Diamond*. Scottsville, NY: Triphammer Publishing, 1997.

Berlin Fair Tab. September 28, 1993

Berman, H. Interview by B. Vikander, June 17, 2018.

Berra, Y., and T. Horton. *Yogi: It Ain't Over . . .* New York: McGraw-Hill, 1989.

Blue, V., and B. Libby. *Vida: His Own Story*. Upper Saddle River, NJ: Prentice Hall, 1972.

Boswell, T. *How Life Imitates the World Series*. New York: Doubleday & Company, 1982.

Carter, R. Interview by A. Thomas, April 16, 2018.

Chalk, M. Interview by A. Thomas, May 9, 2017.

Connecticut Life. "The Rise, Fall, and Resurgence of Steve Dalkowski." August, 2005, p. 16.

Corso, J. "Steve Dalkowski: Baseball's Ultimate Flamethrower." Bleacher Report, May 28, 2009, https://bleacherreport.com/articles/186672 -baseballs-ultimate-flamethrower-steve-dalkowski.

Curran, W. *Strikeout: A Celebration of the Art of Pitching*. New York: Crown, 1995.

Dickson, J. Interview by B. Vikander, September 15, 2017.

Dickson, P. *Baseball's Greatest Quotations*. New York: HarperCollins, 2008.

Duren, R., and R. Drury. *The Comeback: The Ryne Duren Story*. Dayton, OH: Lorenze Press, 1978.

Eisenberg, J. *From 33rd Street to Camden Yards: An Oral History of the Baltimore Orioles*. New York: McGraw-Hill, 2001.

Eisenberg, J. "Lost Phenom Finds His Way." *Baltimore Sun*, February 16, 2003. https://www.baltimoresun.com/news/bs-xpm-2003-02-16-0302 160411-story.html.

Elliott, B. "The Dunlop Awards: The Untouchable." Toronto Sun, October 2, 1998.

Etchebarren, A. Interview by B. Vikander, January 22, 2018.

Fisher, J. Interview by B. Vikander, February 28, 2018.

Fleisher, M. "Dalkowski—The Fastest Ever." *Elmira Star-Gazette*, June 17, 1979, p. 23.

Fourroux, L. Interview by B. Vikander, December 2018–January 2019.

Gibson, B., and P. Pepe. *Ghetto to Glory: The Story of Bob Gibson.* Upper Saddle River, NJ: Prentice Hall, 1968.

Gillick, P. Interview by B. Vikander, October 30, 2018.

Graziul, R. "The Greatest Prospect Never To Make It to the Majors." *Baseball Digest*, p. 40.

Hall, D. Interview by B. Vikander, August 29, 2017.

Harwell, E. *Stories from My Life in Baseball.* Detroit: Detroit Free Press, 2001.

Henneman, J., and J. Palmer. *Baltimore Orioles: 60 Years of Orioles Magic.* San Rafael: Insights Editions, 2015.

Hock, J., dir. *Fastball.* Legendary Entertainment, 2016.

Holtz, S. "Fastest Pitcher in Baseball." Baseball Almanac, February 2003. https://www.baseball-almanac.com/articles/fastest-pitcher-in-baseball .shtml.

Hruby, P. "The Legend of Steve Dalkowski." *Washington Times*, June 4, 2000.

Jacobson, S. "Though Long Gone, Dalkowski's Legend Blazes On." *Hartford Courant*, April 12, 1979.

James, B., and R. Neyer. *The Neyer/James Guide to Pitchers.* New York: Touch-stone, 2004.

Jimenez, E. Interview by A. Thomas, December 15, 2017.

Jordan, P. *A False Spring.* New York: Dodd, Mead & Company, 1975.

Jordan, P. "Going Nowhere Fast." *Inside Sports*, July 1982, pp. 72–80.

Jordan, P. *The Suitors of Spring.* New York: Dodd, Mead & Company, 1973.

Jordan, P. "The Wildest Fastball Ever." *Sports Illustrated*, October 12, 1970, pp. S5–S7.

Kelley, B. *Baseball's Bonus Babies: Conversations with 24 High-Priced Ballplay-ers Signed from 1953 to 1957.* Jefferson, NC: McFarland & Company, 2015.

Kerlegand, E. "Éxito día dedicado a Héctor Espino." Puro Beisbol, Octo-ber 23, 2016. https://www.albat.com/lmp/Exito-dia-dedicado-a-Hector -Espino-20161023-0015.html.

Kernan, K. "Kernan: Legendary Flameout Steve Dalkowski and His 110 MPH Fastball." Society for American Baseball Research, July 6, 2013. https://sabr.org/latest/kernan-legendary-flameout-steve-dalkowski-and -his-110-mph-fastball.

Kerrane, K. *The Hurlers: Pitching Power and Precision*. Alexandria: Redefinition, Inc., 1989.

Knowles, D. Interview by B. Vikander, January 23, 2018.

Koppett, L. *A Thinking Man's Guide to Baseball*. New York: E. P. Dutton & Co., 1967.

Kostro, F. Interview by B. Vikander, November 3, 2018.

Lamb, D. *Stolen Season: A Journey through America and Baseball's Minor Leagues*. New York: Random House, 1991.

Littlefield, B. "Littlefield: A Baseball Story (or Two) for the All-Star Break." WBUR Boston, July 8, 2016. https://www.wbur.org/only agame/2016/07/08/ted-williams-dalkowski-baseball.

Lively, M. Interview by A. Thomas, December 14, 2017.

Madden, B. "Safe at Home." *New York Daily News*, May 17, 1998.

Marazzi, R., and L. Fiorito. *Baseball Players of the 1950s: A Biographical Dictionary of All 1560 Major League Players*. Jefferson, NC: McFarland & Company, 2004.

McDowell, S. Interview by B. Vikander, October 5, 2018.

McEntegart, P. "The Wild One." Vault, Sports Illustrated, June 30, 2003. https://vault.si.com/vault/2003/06/30/the-wild-one-he-became-a-legend-throughout-baseball-by-throwing-the-fastest-fastball-everand-rarely-getting-it-over-the-plate-then-he-flamed-out-on-and-off-the-field.

Michael, G. Interview by B. Vikander, April 2017.

Moore, L. Interview by A. Thomas, September 30, 2017.

Nelson, K. *The Greatest Stories Ever Told About Baseball*. New York: Perigree, 1986.

Neyer, R. *Big Book of Baseball Legends*. New York: Touchstone, 2008.

Nigro, K. "Steve Dalkowski—DTs Dead but Legend Lives." *Sporting News*, June 30, 1979, p. 11.

Owens, T. "Steve Dalkowski Expert John-William Greenbaum, TTM Minor League Detective." Baseball by the Letters, July 2, 2012. https://www.baseballbytheletters.com/2012/07/02/stev-dalkowski-expert-john-william-greenbaum-ttm-minor-league-detective/.

Palmer, J., and J. Dale. *Together We Were Eleven Foot Nine*. Kansas City: Andrews McMeel Publishing, 1996.

Pavlovich, L. "Fastest Pitcher Ever." *Collegiate Baseball*, October 3, 2003, pp. 1, 3.

Peary, D. *Cult Baseball Players: The Greats, the Flakes, the Weird, and the Wonderful*. New York: Simon & Schuster, 1990.

Peters, F. Interview by B. Vikander, January 23, 2018.

Plaut, D. *Speaking of Baseball*. Philadelphia: Running Press Books, 1993.

Plimpton, G. *The Curious Case of Sidd Finch*. New York: Macmillan, 1987.

Pluto, T. *The Earl of Baltimore*. New Jersey: New Century Publishers, 1982.

Posnanski, J. "How Do You Solve a Problem Like Dalkowski?" NBCSports, NBC SportsWorld, n.d. https://sportsworld.nbcsports.com/fixing-steve-dalkowski/.

Pregenzer, J. Interview by B. Vikander, October 15, 2017.

Ripken Sr., C., and L. Burke. *The Ripken Way*. New York: Atria Books, 1999.

Robinson, E. Interview by B. Vikander, December 15, 2017, and January 17, 2018.

Rowan, R. *Throwing Bullets*. Lanham: Taylor Trade Publishing, 2006.

Russo, J., and B. Hammel. *Super Scout: Thirty-five Years of Major League Scouting*. Chicago: Bonus Books, 1992.

Ryan, N., and M. Herskowitz. *Kings of the Hill*. New York: HarperCollins, 1992.

Sala, P. Interview by B. Vikander, July 6, 2017.

Sanzone, Z. "The Prospect That Scared Ted Williams." Yawkey Way Report, July 15, 2016. http://yawkeywayreport.com/prospect-scared-ted-williams/.

Shelton, R. "Steve Dalkowski Had the Stuff of Legends." *Los Angeles Times*, July 19, 2009.

Shelton, R. "Steve Dalkowski, the Hardest Throwing Pitcher Who Ever Lived?" *Seattle Times*, July 23, 2009.

Smith, G. "Sportswriter Chronicles Former Athletes' 'Good Old Days'." *Hartford Courant*, December 4, 1977, p. 11H.

Sommer, T. *Beating about the Bushes*. Conshoshocken: Infinity Publishing, 2008.

Sporting News. "Living Legend Released, Dalkowski Eyes New Life." May 7, 1966, p. 39.

Sports Illustrated. "Houston Colt .45s: Too Much and Too Soon in Houston." Vault, April 8, 1963. https://vault.si.com/vault/1963/04/08/houston-colt-45s-too-much-and-too-soon-in-houston.

Sports Reference. "St. Louis Browns at Boston Red Sox Box Score, August 6, 1953." Baseball Reference. Retrieved May 2020. https://www.baseball-reference.com/boxes/BOS/BOS195308060.shtml.

Stewart, W. *Pitching Secrets of the Pros*. New York: McGraw-Hill, 2004.

Struck, N. Interview by A. Thomas, December 14, 2017.

Sudyk, B. "A Matter of Control." *Hartford Courant*, March 5, 1989, p. E11A.

Thorn, J., and J. Holway. *The Pitcher*. Des Moines: Prentice Hall Direct, 1987.

Time. "The Wildest Pitcher." July 18, 1960, p. 51.

Tomsick, T. A. *Strike Three! My Years in the 'Pen.* Cincinnati: Cincinnati Book Publishers, 2010.

Topps. TOPPS Baseball Card #496. 1963 Rookie Stars, 1963.

Treder, S. "Delving into the Dalkowski Depths." Hardball Times, Fangraphs, May 29, 2007. https://tht.fangraphs.com/delving-into-the-dalkowski-depths/.

TV Guide. "Who's Baseball's Fastest Pitcher?" October 4, 1986, pp. 18–19.

Valentine, F. Interview by B. Vikander, January 6, 2019.

Vecsey, G. "A Hall of Fame for Legendary Fastball Pitcher." *New York Times,* July 18, 2009, p. SP3.

Warwick, C. Interview by B. Vikander, October 22, 2018.

Watt, E. Interview by B. Vikander, January 17–18, 2019.

Weaver, E., and T. Pluto. *Weaver on Strategy.* New York: Collier Books, 1984.

Weaver, E., and B. Stainback. *It's What You Learn after You Know It All That Counts.* New York: Doubleday, 1982.

Wellington, A. W. *One Hundred Years of Baseball in Elmira.* Elmira Rotary Club, Elmira, NY., November 17, 1987.

Wendel, T. *High Heat.* Boston: Da Capo Press, 2010.

Wendel, T. "Steve Dalkowski." *Cloud 9,* Winter 2015. http://www.omag digital.com/article/STEVE+DALKOWSKI/1893014/0/article.html.

Wendel, T. "Steve Dalkowski: The Fastest Ever?" National Pastime Museum, January 25, 2013. https://www.thenationalpastimemuseum.com/article /steve-dalkowski-fastest-ever/.

Will, G. F. *Men at Work: The Craft of Baseball.* Norwalk: Easton, 1990.

Wimmer, D. *The Sandlot Game.* Dallas: Masters Press, 1997.

Zanardi, P. *Baseball in Connecticut.* N.p., 1990.

Index